WHAT IS THE USE OF
JEWISH
HISTORY?

WHAT IS THE USE OF

JEWISH

HISTORY?

Essays by

LUCY S. DAWIDOWICZ

Edited and with an Introduction by
Neal Kozodoy

Schocken Books • New York

Grateful acknowledgment is made to the following for permission to reprint previously published material by Lucy S. Dawidowicz:

CLAL: "Visualizing the Warsaw Ghetto," originally published in *Shoah,* September 1978. Reprinted by permission of CLAL—The National Jewish Center for Learning and Leadership. · *Commentary:* "Lies About the Holocaust," December 1980; "Indicting American Jews," June 1983; "The Politics of Americans Jews" (under the title "Politics, the Jews, and the '84 Election"), February 1985; "In Berlin Again," August 1986; "Poles, Jews, and History" (under the title "The Curious Case of Marek Edelman"), March 1987; "History as Ideology" (under the title "Perversions of the Holocaust"), October 1989; "How They Teach the Holocaust," December 1990; originally published in *Commentary.* Reprinted by permission. All rights reserved. · *The New York Times:* "The True History of Babi Yar," originally published in *The New York Times Magazine,* September 27, 1981 (under the title "Babi Yar's Legacy"). Copyright © 1981 by The New York Times Company. Reprinted by permission. · *Pantheon Books:* Excerpts from the poem "Babi Yar" by Yevgeny Yevtushenko (pp. 112–13) translated by Max Hayward, originally published in *The New York Times Magazine.* From *Dissonant Voices in Soviet Literature,* edited by Patricia Blake and Max Hayward. Copyright © 1962 by Patricia Blake and Max Hayward. Reprinted by permission of Pantheon Books, a division of Random House, Inc. · *The Rockford Institute:* "Could America Have Rescued Europe's Jews?" originally published in *This World,* Fall 1985 (under the title "Could the United States Have Rescued the European Jews from Hitler?"). Copyright © 1985 by The Rockford Institute. Reprinted by permission.

Library of Congress Cataloging-in-Publication Data

Dawidowicz, Lucy S.
   What is the use of Jewish history? : essays / by Lucy S.
Dawidowicz ; edited by Neal Kozodoy.
     p.   cm.
   Includes index.
   ISBN 0-8052-1010-5
   1. Jews—Historiography. 2. Jews—History—Philosophy.
3. Holocaust, Jewish (1939–1945)—Influence. 4. Holocaust, Jewish
(1939–1945)—Errors, inventions, etc. I. Kozodoy, Neal.
II. Title.
DS115.5.D38 1992
909'.04924—dc20   92-6576

CONTENTS

CONTENTS

EDITOR'S NOTE

In late November 1990, just before she died, Lucy S. Dawidowicz set aside a folder containing the major essays she had published in the 1980s; these, she told me, she would like to have brought out in a posthumous book (adding, severely, "if they're worthy"). In drawing up and organizing the present volume I have been guided largely but not entirely by her own selection. A couple of pieces have been omitted as being somewhat too specialized in their focus. More importantly, I have included five manuscripts found among her unpublished papers; all of them, in one form or another, had been delivered as public lectures, and together they seem to me to help round out this portrait of the historian at her work.

Chapter 1, "What Is the Use of Jewish History?" Unpublished manuscript, last delivered as a lecture in October 1990.

Chapter 2, "History as Autobiography: Telling a Life." Unpublished manuscript, last delivered as a lecture in October 1990.

Chapter 3, "In Berlin Again." *Commentary*, August 1986.

Chapter 4, "How They Teach the Holocaust." *Commentary*, December 1990.

Chapter 5, "Lies About the Holocaust." *Commentary*, December 1980.

Chapter 6, "The True History of Babi Yar." *New York Times Magazine*, September 27, 1981 (under the title "Babi Yar's Legacy").

Chapter 7, "History as Ideology." *Commentary*, October 1989 (under the title "Perversions of the Holocaust").

vii

Chapter 8, "Poles, Jews, and History." *Commentary*, March 1987 (under the title "The Curious Case of Marek Edelman").

Chapter 9, "Visualizing the Warsaw Ghetto." *Shoah*, September 1978.

Chapter 10, "Could America Have Rescued Europe's Jews?" *This World*, Fall 1985 (under the title "Could the United States Have Rescued the European Jews from Hitler?").

Chapter 11, "Indicting American Jews," *Commentary*, June 1983.

Chapter 12, "On Equal Terms: Jewish Identity in America." Unpublished manuscript, delivered as a lecture in 1984.

Chapter 13, "East European Jewry and Us." Unpublished manuscript, last delivered as a lecture in December 1989.

Chapter 14, "The Business of American Jews (Notes on Work in Progress)." Unpublished manuscript, delivered as a lecture in 1982, reworked in October 1990.

Chapter 15, "The Politics of American Jews." The 1984 State of World Jewry Address, delivered at the 92nd Street Y in December 1984 and published under the title "Politics, the Jews, and the '84 Election" in *Commentary*, February 1985.

INTRODUCTION

by Neal Kozodoy

"Being an American was itself enough to give anyone a bushelful of courage."

Thus, the historian Lucy S. Dawidowicz contemplating at a remove of five decades the inner impulse which in 1938 had led her, a girl of twenty-three, on a year's flight out from the freedom and safety of America into the heart of East European Jewry, a human civilization already then being readied for the rack and soon by human will to be smashed from the earth, obliterated in blood and soot. To be an American in those days was to feel sheltered, impervious, consequently full of defiance and bravado. In this condition there was, as she would later acknowledge, much danger, the danger of falling victim to the very dangers (societal evil, frenzy, corruption) of which Americans in their impetuousness tended to be dismissive, or simply ignorant; but there was true, heavenly favor as well, and purity and fortune and strength, energetic gifts out of the political and social constitution of the United States which in her later adult life Mrs. Dawidowicz would never forget, or fail to act upon in gratitude.

In particular she would not fail to repay with courage the legacy of courage which being an American had freely conferred upon her. That courage was hers, it was her distinguishing and sometimes lonely mark, plain in the path she chose as a student of the darkened past, and also in the role she would play, irreplaceably, as a public intellectual, speaking with a historian's consciousness and a polemicist's heat to controversies of the moment. In the realm of thought and judgment

Lucy Dawidowicz was a tough woman, and in her bold American and in her stubborn Jewish way, the more faithfully she performed the duties of thought and judgment, the more indomitable she grew.

The essays and lectures in this volume, illustrative of her driving preoccupations, are drawn from the final ten years of Mrs. Dawidowicz's life and thus supplement an earlier collection, *The Jewish Presence* (1977). Thematically they are grouped around: personal statements, which are also in the nature of a historian's credos; considerations of recent understandings and misunderstandings of the Holocaust, its use, misuse, and abuse; and thoughts of the past and present configuration of American Jewry, the subject on which, at the time of her death at the age of seventy-five on December 5, 1990, she was preparing to write a major historical study. Taken together, they reflect and may thus help to clarify some of the deep issues of history and identity—and of history as the shaper of identity—which all her life impelled and absorbed her.

2

"The terrible finality of the murder of the European Jews and their disappearance from history darken our memories and cloud our vision of the past."

Lucy Dawidowicz's magnum opus, *The War Against the Jews 1933–1945* (1975, tenth anniversary edition 1985), and its companion volume, *A Holocaust Reader* (1976), were products of an overriding sense of obligation and compulsion—obligation to her murdered kin, the Jews of Europe; compulsion to set down a record already seen by her as slipping away in forgetfulness and selective distortion. Probably nothing less than obligation and compulsion, sparkers of courage, would have sufficed to bring someone of her sensibility—someone, that is, who took Jewish history personally—through the endless nausea of research which the writing of these books inescapably required. Sickening, she would report in despair to friends, was the ordeal of immersing herself in, of vicariously experiencing, the facts themselves, the foul implacable detail of legislation and enactment, of roundup, sequestration, plunder, and pogrom, of transport, enslavement, denudation, torture, beating, shooting, starvation, gas. Sickening, too, was the burden of confronting and then of explicating the vertiginous Fact itself, a human assault without recourse and without letup, and bearing, for the assailants, an urgency beyond any calculation of expedience, reason, or opportunity. Sickening and soul-crushing, finally, was the already-to-be-glimpsed prospect, hatefully realized in due course, of having for the rest of her life and with ceaseless grim vigilance to "defend" both facts and Fact against a succession of ingenious efforts, by the disreputable and even by the reputable, to deny, revise, or suborn them.

Then there was, and still is, something else again, something prior, and something interior: the sickening awareness, never to be blinked, of "terrible finality," of everything which with the *success* of Hitler's war against the European Jews, and with their "disappearance from history," had become, for Mrs. Dawidowicz as for the Jewish people itself, irreparable and irretrievable, and, full in the face of the most desperate need for some kind of inward and eventually even outward reconciliation, irreconcilable.

Before she set herself to record the death of the European Jews, Mrs. Dawidowicz had, in fact, retrieved a part of the irretrievable. Her book *The Golden Tradition* (1967), a large anthology of individual memoirs and personal documents, introduced by a historical essay of ninety closely printed pages, is a teeming capsule of Jewish *life* in Eastern Europe, from the end of the eighteenth century until the edge of destruction in 1939. "Something to conjure with, what this small people has done!" marvels an excited native of Vitebsk named Marc Chagall in a passage reprinted in this entrancing, heartbreaking volume. Heartbreaking, for the contemporary reader, is of course the inevitable awareness of encroaching cataclysmic destruction; but heartbreaking as well is the recognition, gradually borne in by these subtle, humane, combative writings, of how much of what "this small people" had done was, long before the hour of physical extinction, already being undone, from within and from without.

As to the undoing from within, a very long and many-sided story, that was never Mrs. Dawidowicz's proper subject, although she touched on at least one central aspect of it both in her books and in essays on the historically enfeebled nature of Jewish political reflexes. In any case, traces of its workings are everywhere evident in *The Golden Tradition*. The marveling Chagall supplies a hint of some of the elements at play in this process of internal debilitation as, immediately following his eager apostrophe—"Something to conjure with, what this small people has done!"—he explains without irony what he means: "When it wished, it brought forth Christ and Christianity. When it wanted, it produced Marx and socialism." What, one may wonder, has happened, here, to the antique, unconceding pride of the Jews in themselves, in the abundant sufficiencies of their own creed? What has happened to that powerful assurance and reserve which, whatever else may be said of or even against it, had for so long dignified their historical existence, spurred their genius, helped to inure them to the blandishments of hostile, variant, or supersessive faiths? It has been corroded by the salts of modernity—the very same salts now pungently flavoring the meats which many like Chagall, and many more who lacked Chagall's saving affections, were hungering, too understandably, to feed upon.

To Mrs. Dawidowicz, nevertheless, it was always an error, if not indeed a species of moral dereliction, to focus overmuch on the appetites, or the manners, of the would-be banqueters when the doors of the great hall were being slammed and locked upon them even as they were preparing to sit down to table. It was the slammers she was after. By the same token, she had no use for the ranks of second-guessers who grew up in the decades after the successful completion of the war against the Jews, latter-day critics who with greater or lesser subtlety, and only sometimes with honorable intent, effectively pinned upon the murdered Jews and their contemporaries and forebears an indictment of historical blindness, cowardice, even complicity. Whether the ostensible occasion was an inquiry into the (allegedly irresponsible) communal organization of Jewry in pre-Hitler Europe, or into the (allegedly collaborative) behavior of ghetto leaders during the war itself, or into the (allegedly pusillanimous) response of Jews in America to the news of the Holocaust, she for her part categorically repudiated the charge of passivity, let alone of collusion. The irrefutable point, she demonstrated again and again, was that just as the trapped and encircled European Jews had been innocent of provoking, so they were powerless to repeal, the total, unrelenting fury loosed upon them. During the war the point, for someone like her, had been to commit every moral and spiritual resource to the Allied effort to defeat the fury by dint of countervailing arms. After the war, the point (for her) was not only to understand the fury but to render upon it a definitive historical judgment—and in this way, for the victims, to raise up a memorial.

The judgment rendered by *The War Against the Jews* rests on a fully argued thesis: namely, that the Nazi enterprise as a whole was not just furthered, it was *defined,* by the war against the Jews, that for Hitler racial ideology, that is, the intention to destroy every last Jew, was an end in itself, on a par with his more "conventional" aims, over which, indeed, in the latter stages of World War II it came to assume a terrifying, metaphysical priority. The thesis was consciously framed as a counter to a then more customary view of Hitler's anti-Semitism as an instrumental rather than an essential element of Nazi doctrine and deed; and this alone guaranteed that, even as many would be persuaded by her argument and embrace it, others would find reason to resist it. There would also emerge a second point of contention, having to do with the emphasis which Mrs. Dawidowicz, in common now with other traditional historians of the period, placed on the role of human agency and personal will, as opposed to impersonal historical or institutional "forces," in the execution of Nazi ideas.

The ensuing debate over these (inevitably) twinned matters was partly a debate among professional historians, and as such a debate—between "intentionalists," of whom Mrs. Dawidowicz is spectacularly one, versus "functionalists" of various stripes and allegiances—it continues to this day. In one way or another, it forms the subject of Mrs. Dawidowicz's analysis in each of the essays gathered here under the heading "In Pursuit of Truth," just as it did of her scrupulous and indispensable book, *The Holocaust and the Historians* (1981). But as the reader of these works quickly grasps, the debate, touching as it does on the issue of human responsibility for human history, carries with it a charge of the profoundest political and moral import.

She was, truly, obsessed with the memory of the dead—or rather, with the memory of the living who had disappeared, not only from the earth but from the history books, our designated preservers of memory. "For if," she wrote wrenchingly, "they are not recorded in history, the events of the past vanish into memorylessness, irretrievably lost to the present and the future." And to the prospect of vanishment by which she confessed herself haunted was added the even more outrageous specter of banishment: of a past not so much ignored as twisted and falsified by "revisionists," of a people not overlooked but perjured and once again cast out. Through the project of establishing a true and faithful record of the living and the dead, through the project of guarding that record from distortion and defilement, Lucy Dawidowicz meant to assume her own, activist share of responsibility for Jewish history.

Being activist, this responsibility could not halt at the borders of a correct understanding of the past alone. Times changed, and in the course of things old enemies gave way to new, while old alliances proved to be founded on illusion on one side, bad faith on the other; the Jewish disposition required, even if it did not always welcome, an understanding of the present in which the past's dark lessons might guide without paralyzing, might serve as a warning without acting as a stumbling-block. Uniquely placed to provide that sometimes unwelcome understanding, Lucy Dawidowicz in the last ten years of her life added the role of political to that of historical conscience.

If in that role she never shrank from the task of rethinking old affinities in the light of present political reality, perhaps unexpectedly she also did not shrink from the task, emotionally even more costly, of rethinking old enmities, including the one which for many contemporary Jews has been the most sustaining enmity of all.

In his mournful and magisterial essay, "Jews and Germans" (1966), the great scholar Gershom Scholem undertook retrospectively to locate and diagnose the "false start," the canker, which from the moment of its birth had infected the modern German-Jewish civic arrangement, a fabled "symbiosis" of which Scholem himself was, gloriously, a late product but whose deadly fruits he had repudiated personally as early as the 1920s in the name of Jewish national self-respect and regeneration (that is, in the name of Zionism). His sorrowing, pitiless analysis, sparing neither Gentile nor Jew, concludes on a guardedly wistful note: "Only by remembering a past that we will never completely master can we generate new hope in the resumption of communication between Germans and Jews, and in the reconciliation of those who have been separated."

For her own part, Lucy Dawidowicz was not German-born but American-born, and as a Jew she was a child of Eastern, not Western, Europe. Anyway, even though memory was her business, mourning was not her style. Where enemies were concerned, her style was to curse. After her return home from Eastern Europe in 1939, what had seen her through the war years in New York was guilt, rage, and a thirst for personal vengeance—already in 1940 she was confiding to her best friend a fantasy of getting back over to the European theater to find the beloved companions she had left behind ("If I get killed, OK. If not, I shall probably never come home and just wander Europe looking for [Zelig] Kalmanovitch and Chaim Grade")—and fifty years later these emotions remained vivid enough in memory to keep many pages of her 1989 memoir, *From That Place and Time*, at a boil of execration. In 1986 she wrote her own magisterial essay of retrospective meditation, "In Berlin Again," and it opens, typically, by recalling the vindictive pleasure she took when, in Berlin right after the end of the war, she beheld the "felicific vistas of burned-out hulks of buildings, tottering skeletons of houses, the shards and rubble to which the Third Reich had been reduced." "I liked," she reports with satisfaction of the Germans she encountered then, "to watch them scrounge and scramble for cast-off American cigarette butts."

Yet "In Berlin Again," occasioned by another return visit forty years later to the Nazi capital, turns out, perhaps surprisingly, to be itself an essay of reconciliation, and in Scholem's complicated sense if not by his route. Informing it is a deep if unspoken acknowledgment: that the curse wherewith any Jew was entitled, and more than entitled, to curse the German nation to eternal hell was finally, wholly, inadequate, and in any case a puny thing next to the savage, annihilating curse which the German nation had preemptively laid upon the Jews of Europe, when it met their desire for acceptance with a thundering rescission and then marked them out as *worthy* candidates for extinction. This shattering judgment, which even after the war thoroughly blighted the spirit of many who yet remained in life, was what lingered on from the "terrible finality" of the Holocaust. It had seeped into the Jewish marrow, withering confidence and the possibility of contentment, instilling doubt, anxiety, skepticism, exhaustion, dread— even in that mighty enterprise of liberation and self-assertion that was the state of Israel. It had become a form of ineradicable knowledge; it made up the forces that "darken our memories and cloud our vision of the past," retroactively casting a pall over whatever had been green and generous in that past itself, engulfing every bygone moment of hope and enthusiasm in the black aura of certain betrayal and doom.

Only time, much time, would dispel some of the effects—on Jews, but also on Germans—of this long-acting poison, itself injected in the twinkling of an eye; time, and the courage to look straight not only into the unmastered past (Scholem) but into the present. The duty was incumbent upon all, although not everyone was willing to perform it. In *The Golden Tradition* and *The War Against the Jews* Lucy Dawidowicz had undertaken to master the past by recalling it with painstaking honesty. She wrote those books in service to historical truth, and as tributes to the memory of the murdered European Jews; in the event, they proved of service to Germans as well.

There was no denying that after the war Germans at times seemed merely embarrassed, to the point of tedium, by their unmastered past; at other times they appeared almost swaggeringly stricken by it, regaling with their shame and guilt a world they had formerly stunned with their viciousness; at still other times, among some few of them, they seemed positively nostalgic. Yet all the while, Mrs. Dawidowicz reports in "In Berlin Again," deep changes were taking place in German politics and in German society that required acknowledgment, especially by one whose own decades-long rage against "the Germany that had turned Europe into a vast Jewish necropolis" had been unremitting. "In Berlin Again," a work of transcendent Jewish selflessness and objectivity, documents those changes.

General and preeminent were the establishment and institutionalization in West Germany of a stable political democracy which—despite recrudescences of extremist nationalism, militarism, racism, and anti-Semitism—had by the mid-1980s become *the* German reality. But equally significant was the evident and specific determination of Germans no longer to dodge but rather to come to grips with their historical relation to the Jews, to learn and openly to teach not only the history of the Holocaust—now being presented, Mrs. Dawidowicz was gratified to learn at an exhibit she attended in the old Reichstag, as a German "war against the Jews"—but also the history of the Jewish people and of Jewish civilization. Through the promise held out by this self-imposed program of moral reparation, in which her own intellectual contribution had been formative, Mrs. Dawidowicz glimpsed the possibility, never of putting aside or of surmounting the murder of the European Jews, for that was an event that existed forever in the "timeless present," an event "forever lodged in history's throat," but rather of relinquishing at long last the disabling torture that was the accursed memory of Nazi Germany, an entire edifice of institutions, deeds, and attitudes which, except for the murder of the European Jews, and notwithstanding contemporary instances in Germany itself of unregenerate hatred, had left, she now permitted herself to say, "no lasting heritage." This is what she had come to Berlin to see, and, having seen it, found the courage to say she was reconciled.

Fidelity, then, to the life and death of the European Jews was one thing, a national and religious duty. Obsession with their Nazi murderers was another. It threatened to turn into a fascination; worse, it threatened to become a political investment, requiring, and justifying, ever fresher infusions of capital in the form of discovered Nazi-like perils to the Jews of today; worse yet, it encouraged a search for those perils in politically ambiguous or even innocuous places (like, in America, among Christian fundamentalists), while truly perilous growths elsewhere went scanted or ignored. Among contemporary Jews afflicted with this species of misplaced zeal, Mrs. Dawidowicz discerned the workings of a merely self-protective fixation with the past; there was also a desire not to confront present reality, a will to deny, by-products (in part) of the fact that most Jews, most American Jews, being on and of the liberal Left—and how much more so, Jewish professors and Jewish intellectuals and spokesmen for the organized Jewish community—were constitutionally all but incapable of acknowledging danger from any direction but the Right, or of registering new opportunity anywhere but on the Left. For Lucy Dawidowicz, whose own voyage away from the Left can be documented in a number of essays stemming from the 1970s and 1980s, all this represented blindness and unaffordable luxury.

As part of her responsibility to history she aimed to be alert, and to alert others, to the assault upon the Jewish people emanating in these particular decades from the international Left, its proprietors and its paid and unpaid agents in the Soviet Union, in Europe, at the United Nations, among the Arabs, in precincts dominated or influenced by black and Third World radicals in the United States. She had an integrated agenda here, since frequently the same sources involved in constructing and disseminating lies about the dead Jews of yesterday were among the major defamers of the living Jews of today; by the weird logic of politics, the interests of the two parties had coalesced grotesquely in 1975 when the United Nations, in its "Zionism-Racism" resolution, erased the memory of the Jews as victims of Nazism and recast them indelibly as Nazis themselves. Less theatrical but more insidious was the widespread acceptance of ideas like these within the universities, the media, the churches, not to mention the reflex habit of blaming the Jews themselves—as yesterday the Jews of Europe, today the Jews of Israel—for the depravity of their enemies.

And this was a habit, she had occasion to observe, infecting some of Israel's putative friends, too many of whom proved ready in moments of emergency to stand by in postures of niggling aloofness, or sentimental regret, or fastidious distaste, or pious exasperation, or anxious and irresolute despair. On these subjects, on the diseased nature of these attitudes, her own perfect lucidity sounded a rallying tocsin.

3

"The reward of being Jewish lies in defining oneself, not in being defined."

These words, at first rather strange (for who are the Jews if not history's most defined people, and what is Judaism but one of the world's most highly defined faiths?), sum up a credo. In writing them, Lucy Dawidowicz was polemicizing against the notion of Jewish existence as a matter only of fate, or of reaction. Such an idea, to which the sheer comprehensive antagonism documented in her own writings may inadvertently be thought to lend support, she wholly rejected; it offered, she wrote, "the torment [of being Jewish] without the gift, the infliction without the reward." If the reward, which in her own life she both seized and extended to others, lay in defining oneself, the gift lay "in possessing one's own heritage and in affirming one's existence on one's own ground." Rather than a mere existentialist assertion, her statement reflects a supported historical judgment, a considered attachment to the majesty and inner freedom of Jewish experience quite independent of the massiveness of the forces historically arrayed against it, and a principled position with regard to the Jewish future.

In her writings about the Nazi period this judgment informed her repeated insistence on the, despite everything, amazing phenomenon of Jewish resistance, the sometimes ordinary, sometimes heroic, sometimes petty, sometimes selfless refusal of individual Jews and of whole Jewish communities to bow to the edict that doomed them, their iron determination to make out of suffering an occasion (as she wrote about

xix

the Warsaw ghetto) of "solidarity and self-help, of succor and self-sacrifice." The principle of self-definition also shaped her approach to a radically different subject, that of American Jewry, a realm of historical experience which had been developing according to its own original lights and laws but which, precisely because of American society's bedrock condition of freedom, offered, she thought, still untold possibilities of Jewish cultural expression and creativity. ("At home in America," she observed in sentences that epitomized her steely but unapologetically championing view, "Jews are in every respect still in the process of learning to live in a pluralist society and to balance their Jewish identity with their Americanness. The drama of their three-centuries-old balancing act is a fascinating, even an inspiring, one.") And the same affirming idea similiarly animated all her efforts to preserve the gift and the reward of Jewishness for future generations.

As an American intellectual and as a Jew Lucy Dawidowicz made her own way, at her own pace; by temperament she was no joiner. Although in her last years she would come to be identified, and wholeheartedly to identify herself, as a neoconservative in politics (that is, vocally mindful of the blessings of liberty and American democracy), she arrived at this position only after an unrushable sifting of its implications. Nor, though she had written for *Commentary* magazine for decades, did she particularly think of herself, again until her last years and then again with perfect pride, as a comrade-in-arms of Norman Podhoretz and the "*Commentary* crowd." Which "crowd" she did belong to was a matter of her own idiosyncratic selectivity, though roughly speaking, in at least one relevant division within the Jewish community and among its spokesmen, her lot was with the "survivalists" and the "particularists" as against the "assimilationists" and the "universalists." More interestingly, though born into a secular family—she did not set foot in a synagogue before her early twenties—though steeped in secular Yiddish culture, and though married to a militantly secular Bundist, she became a practitioner of Judaism, keeping a kosher home, attending the synagogue, associating herself (in however critical or sometimes even captious a way) with the dictates, the rhythms, the impulses of Jewish religious life. Her love of Zion was, of course, complete.

As she grew older she grew more worried, and became more of a public activist, not a natural or comfortable role. At one point in the mid-1980s she made strenuous efforts over a period of many months to form a committee of Jewish intellectuals, academics, and other sympathetic public figures in order to oppose the anti-Israel (and anti-American) drift in American liberal opinion, including in liberal Jewish opinion; although in the end the organizational effort faltered, the issue continued to preoccupy her writing and her public speaking, and her conversation. As she could be a formidable field marshal and scold, many was the consequent public act performed by others that owed its inspiration or its execution to her mobilizing will.

More suited to her temperament was another initiative of those years, the Fund for the Translation of Jewish Literature. This project, whose first priority was the publication of some of the masterpieces of Yiddish letters, represented a return to the positive work of retrieval and transmission she had embarked upon decades earlier in *The Golden Tradition*. Into it she threw unremitting energy, single-handedly drafting the urgent statements ("What we do not retrieve and reclaim now may be permanently lost"), raising the money, forming the organization, inspiriting Ruth R. Wisse and others to oversee the actual commissioning, translating, and editing of the texts, negotiating with the publisher, and in general holding out a standard of discipline and excellence whose fruits can be assessed in the three beautiful volumes Schocken Books has already published in the Library of Yiddish Classics, and in those yet to come. Through these, at any rate, she meant at once to claim and to proffer the gift of the Jewish heritage, the reward of Jewish existence.

4

"I am probably the shortest person who has ever stood on this stage, and that includes any thirteen-year-old violin prodigy."

With this crack, delivered in the venerable concert hall of the 92nd

Street Y in New York, she opened her 1984 State of World Jewry Address, here published as "American Jews and Politics." Short she was, and trim only in calf and ankle, and, though touchy about many things, about these quick to laugh. Dogged, too, and blunt, and with her friends, as we may attest, sharp-tongued where for charity's sake she might have made do with euphemism or the even safer refuge of negligence or indifference. Until the very end Lucy had force and will power to burn, some of it vented on the exacting work of character analysis, that is, gossip and the improvement of our various deficiencies. For those she loved, advice was freely forthcoming whether solicited or not, and the rigor of her expectations fell upon us like a goad. She had a historian's memory for our failings, the record of our misdeeds, the unfulfilled charter of our promise; she had a writer's impulse to stipulate them. At the same time, no one whom she loved ever knew a more ardent or more loyal fan.

She liked to keep her personal accounts as square as her checkbook, which was very square indeed. She was full of judgment, and if her moral categorizings could sometimes seem a little loose—her highest compliment was *edel*, "refined," her favorite terms of dismissal a riff on "vulgar" that could take in "disgusting" and "repulsive" on their way downward—they compensated often enough in general accuracy for what in particular cases they may have lacked in nuance. It is possible that she was too preoccupied with the sadness of history, which amounted to the hard incontrovertible truths of conflict and oppression, and that she was herself too deeply scarred by historical knowledge, to be patient with some of the less exigent sorrows of everyday lives, the tears that are in things, the normal waywardnesses and delinquencies of normal hearts. She was capable, though, of hilarity, together with a certain innocent cynicism toward those too ostentatiously on the side of "life," especially if they also happened to sleep on pillows of money, health, security. She mistrusted the *sentiment* of nobility.

And she was a devotee of grace, an enthusiast of spectacle, a pursuer of transcendence: in her youth an acolyte of Keats, in her maturity she was mad for music, particularly grand opera, the grander the better, and with the pianist Menahem Pressler of her adored Beaux Arts Trio she formed a spiritually sustaining mutual admiration society. Her exuberance for the New York Mets, especially in the person of their sometime captain and first baseman, Keith Hernandez, was improbably romantic and infectious. Through these means and through others she made her necessary escapes from history, into realms untouchable by marauding time or by that passion for nullification against which she had commanded herself, with every ounce of mind and heart at her disposal, to stand.

Her husband, Szymon, a brand plucked from the fire of the Nazi war against the Jews, she fiercely loved and protected, and when he died of stomach cancer in 1979 she wrote in a private letter to friends about the vigil of his final months. She had kept a historian's record, day by day, a separate sheet for each day, meticulously searching for patterns, for coherence, for the meaning that would rescue from darkness: a record of his illness and its course, of his inexorable wasting, of the fight he waged to remain alert and articulate, of the medical treatment and its effects, of the purées she cooked and what he ate of them or failed to eat, of, finally, a frailty so complete that the doctors were unable even to find his "poor tiny veins." He died, as they both wished, at home; he was her responsibility.

Lucy mistrusted mere ideas, mere spirit; it was, she thought, rightly, the letter that giveth life. In her own life and in her writings she kept the letters, and gave *them* life, and therefore the everlasting spirit within them.

1
IN PURSUIT
OF MEMORY

WHAT IS THE USE OF JEWISH HISTORY?

Yitzhak Leibush Peretz, the great Yiddish writer, opens his essay "On History" with a dialogue in a Warsaw park. An acquaintance asks him why he looks downcast. Peretz replies: "Graetz has died." The man then inquires: "Oh, was he from hereabouts?" Peretz becomes indignant. He explains that Heinrich Graetz wrote the history of the Jews. "Oh, history," responds his friend, as if he had just swallowed a rotten egg. Just as Peretz is about to explode again, the man asks, quite innocently: "And what is the use of history?"

Graetz died in 1891, but the question put by Peretz's Jewish man-in-the-street still persists. Nowadays people ask: "What is the use of studying Jewish history?" Or: "What is the use of studying the Holocaust?" They mean by this question: What benefit can be derived from studying Jewish history and especially the Holocaust, a history of suffering and persecution? Jews are, after all, practical people, people who think of *tachlis*, of purpose and purposefulness. It is to be expected that people with a pragmatic outlook will belittle the value of history. Henry Ford, a man whose practicality changed the course of history, is remembered also as a philosopher of history. "History," he is reputed to have said, "is more or less bunk."

One conventional answer to the question concerning the use of history has been given from the days of Cicero through Voltaire down to Lewis Namier. History, we are told, is the *magistra vitae*, the teacher

3

of life. It instructs us about ourselves, our own people, and other peoples. The experience of the past will teach us how to confront the present and anticipate the future. This, then, is the practical benefit of history, aside from the sheer pleasure simply of reading history or the pursuit of knowledge for its own sake.

But what does the historian himself say about his own interest in history? The question here concerns not so much benefit as purpose and goal. The professional historian may reply that he has chosen his field because he likes it. He relishes the zest of chasing after documents and facts, the elation of discovery, the work of constructing or re-creating the past. The late Cecil Roth once explained that he became a historian "frankly for the pleasure of the thing." Still, no historian works only for the fun of it, no matter how much fun he gets out of it. Whether or not he acknowledges it, he has a larger purpose. The historian's pursuit of knowledge is also a pursuit of truth, and that truth is often put in the service of what the historian holds dear. Since time immemorial, history has been used to celebrate, legitimate, and validate. It has also been used, and especially in our own time, to denounce, impeach, and condemn.

Every people, every nation has used its history to justify itself in its own eyes and in the sight of the world. But surely no people has used its history for such a variety of national purposes as have the Jews. That may be simply because the Jews have the longest historical record of any people. They originated the idea of the God of history and they produced a written record of the past at least four centuries before Herodotus, who was called "the father of history" by those who were ignorant of, or indifferent to, the ancient lineage of Jewish civilization.

To appreciate the longevity of the Jewish historical record, one has but to recall that the Jews have their own written accounts of their origins deep down in the well of the past, to use Thomas Mann's lapidary phrase, whereas the French and Germans, much younger peoples, have to turn to Caesar and Tacitus for the history of their origins.

Memory is the very stuff that constitutes history. The earliest Jewish

4

records, the Five Books of Moses, resound with the word *z'chor*, with the concept of memory and remembrance. The Bible exhorts the Jews to "remember what Amalek did unto thee," to remember that destructive attack in the desert when they were famished and worn out from their flight out of Egypt. But the Bible also exhorts the Jews to "remember the days of old," to be mindful of God's Covenant with them and its great promise. Jewish history, from its very origins, has vibrated between these two poles—between the memory of the past and the hope for the future, between destruction and redemption. In our days, we observe, in close succession, Yom Hashoah, which commemorates the Holocaust, and Yom Haatzmaut, which celebrates Israel's independence.

Yet though the Jews have always been history-conscious, living with the dual perspective of catastrophe and deliverance in forward-moving time, they have, paradoxically, seldom been history-oriented. That is to say: in Jewish consciousness throughout the ages, the specific events of Jewish history have often been transformed into transcendent myths of history. We still relive those great myths. We reenact the redemption from Egypt, every year, at the *seder* during the festival of Passover. We sit in *sukkot* to comemorate the wandering in the desert, and we are taught that all of us were at Sinai when God gave the Torah. We fast and mourn on the Ninth of Av to mark the destruction of the Temple. And we rejoice during the festival of Hanukkah to celebrate the victory of the Maccabees and the rededication of the Temple.

The great historic myths that were fashioned out of historical reality and integrated into the living traditions of Judaism and of the Jewish people are the products of a process of selection whose criterion may have been the usefulness of their remembrance in serving a national Jewish purpose. For many centuries, those who determined how the history of the Jews' past was to be told had the power and the authority to do so—kings, prophets, priests, and, for well over fifteen hundred years thereafter, rabbis. It was they who molded Jewish historic consciousness out of the events of the past, appropriating history in the service of Jewish survival and of the survival of Judaism.

5

* * *

Jewish history begins with the mythic event of God's everlasting Covenant with Abraham and then proceeds on a theocentric course for many centuries. What happens in Jewish history is accounted for in terms of that Covenant. The triumphs and defeats of the Jewish people, their prosperity or their misery, are explained by the presence of the living God among them, Who guides their destiny. He rewards the Jews for their loyalty to the Covenant and for their adherence to His law. He punishes them for their disobedience and refractoriness. This history of the Jews, according to the traditional Jewish view, exists only within the framework of the Covenant and is not governed by the same laws of development that determine the history of other peoples.

This theocentric conception of history made the Jews continually conscious of their commitment and obligation to the Covenant. History was thus used as an adjunct to Judaism, as a means of reinforcing Judaism's authority. Josephus, in the introduction to *Jewish Antiquities*, sums up the function of Jewish history as told in Scripture:

> . . . the main lesson to be learned from this history by any who care to peruse it is that men who conform to the will of God, and do not venture to transgress laws that have been excellently laid down, prosper in all things beyond belief, and for their reward are offered by God felicity; whereas, in proportion as they depart from the strict observance of these laws, things otherwise practicable become impracticable, and whatever imaginary good thing they strive to do ends in irretrievable disasters.

Though Jewish history was believed to operate under the laws of God rather than of man and nature, the ancient Jewish historians nevertheless saw Jewish history as operating within the limits of historical time. In the period after the destruction of the First Temple, when the Jews were driven into Babylonian exile, the prophets who retold the history of the Jews offered their contemporaries solace with the promise of restoration, of a return to an earlier and happier status as their reward for steadfastness to the Covenant. There was, to be sure, a messianic element in the expectation of the Jews' return to Palestine, to resume political power under a king of the house of David, and to rebuild the Temple, but the messianic advent was foreseen within the bounds of history, when all peoples and nations would accept the teachings of the God of Israel.

The later course of Jewish history vindicated these prophetic expectations. Under Cyrus, the Jews did return to their land, and they did rebuild the Temple. This demonstrable fulfillment of prophecy in history would, in a later period, serve to support the tenability and credibility of still later messianic prophecies.

The conquest of Palestine by Alexander the Great and the succession of wars and political upheavals in the later period of the Second Temple gave rise to new sects among the Jews and an explosion of messianic beliefs. Rampant utopianism, apocalyptic visions, and eschatological fervency now infused Jewish political life as well as Jewish religious life. Division and dissension spread. The overheated religious atmosphere and the oppressive pagan occupations eventually set off the series of Jewish revolts and wars that culminated in the great war against the Romans and ultimately in the destruction of the Second Temple.

The Temple's destruction convulsed the course of Jewish history, and the tremors of that catastrophe agitated the subsequent centuries. Yet how extraordinary it is that except for Josephus, whom the Jews considered a traitor, no coherent Jewish account was ever produced to describe and explain the events leading up to and encompassing the destruction of the Second Temple. By contrast, to account for the fall of the First Temple over six hundred years earlier, the Bible gives us an abundance of historical interpretations.

To be sure, we have certain well-known fragments of explanation, which concur on one point: the catastrophe was to be blamed on the sins of the Jews. Both the Romans and their Jewish loyalists like Josephus believed that the destruction of the Second Temple was God's punishment for Jewish rebelliousness. Christians held that the Jews were punished because they denied Jesus as savior and messiah. Passages in the Talmud put the blame on Jewish sinfulness: *sin'at hinam*, "groundless hatred," was offered as the historical explanation for those terrible events. It is believed to refer, however enigmatically, to the profound divisions among the Jews at that time.

The rabbis turned their backs on history at that point, because no historical explanation would have served a useful national purpose. Consider the words of Simeon ben Gamaliel, who lived through the Hadrianic persecutions in the generation after the Temple's fall: "We too cherish the memory of our troubles, but what are we to do? For they are so numerous that if we came to write them down, we would not be able to do so." Then follows this dramatic and poignant sentence: "The dead flesh in a living person does not feel the scalpel." This stark image epitomizes the futility of historical explanation at a time of despair and trauma. The catastrophe had so burdened the Jews, by calling into question their fundamental beliefs about Divine Providence, that a historical explanation in realistic terms might have threatened their continued loyalty to Judaism.

Left without political and military resources, the Jews could not hope to regain their lost land and the remnants of their political power. How could they survive? Rabbi Yohanan ben Zakkai gave them the answer: Study Torah and observe the commandments. Each Jew through his own acts could thus bring about redemption and eventually change the course of history. The perfect observance of Judaism promised the abolishment of the Exile, the return of the Jews to their Holy Land, and the restoration of the Divine Presence in human history. Discouraged by their rabbinic leaders from seeking redress in the arena of politics and war, the Jews in effect withdrew from history and turned to metahistory.

Since the restoration of political power and the return of their sovereignty were beyond the political and military capacities of the Jews, the rabbis began to sketch out a concept of a personal messiah who, as an agent of God, would come to redeem His long-suffering people, defeat their enemies, and return them to Zion, where they would rebuild the Temple again. Thus, an era of earthly bliss, ennobled by religious and moral perfection, would be ushered in. This messianic belief became even more spiritualized as Jewish history seemed increasingly to move off the stage of the real world. The otherworldly elements of Judaism seemed to supplant the temporal ones and the universalist aspects transcended the Jewish national ones. As the messianic idea evolved, it no longer focused on a return to the reality of land and political power, but on the concept of a Messianic Age that would herald the End of Days, a time beyond history.

Of course, the Jews continued to exist in history, that is to say, they continued to live in this world. But they kept no record of this history. From the time Yohanan ben Zakkai reconvened the Sanhedrin in Yavneh after the destruction of the Second Temple until modern times, the talents of the Jews were applied not to history but to Torah, *halacha* (religious law), and esoteric mysticism, for such dedication was seen as the means of hastening the Messiah's coming. For nearly a thousand years the Jews ceased to write history.

Jewish history reemerged in the Middle Ages. The Jews were now more widely dispersed than they had been during the Second Temple period, more exposed than ever to a diversity of political and cultural circumstances and influences. Their geographic dispersion and the divergence of their experiences eventually divided them into two major communities—Sephardim and Ashkenazim. That diversity was reflected in the historical or pseudohistorical works, or rather fragments of works, that have survived from the ninth century onwards. From these we see that the uses of Jewish history were becoming more varied not only in terms of Jewish national purpose but also in matters of personal benefit.

These medieval documents were not history proper, but were composed in a variety of literary forms. There were genealogies and chronologies, hagiographies and martyrologies, fables, legends, anecdotes about the life and works of great rabbis. They included historical data, intermixed with fiction and liturgy, written in prose and sometimes in verse, in Hebrew and, increasingly, in Yiddish.

Some genealogies and chronologies were produced as polemics against the sect of Karaites, and were intended to validate the legitimacy of the Talmudic-rabbinic tradition which the Karaites denied.

9

History thereby became an instrument to enforce rabbinic authority but also, for the first time, took on an existence of its own, independent of Scripture, in a culture where study of the Torah had been the only sanctioned intellectual endeavor.

The Jewish medieval chronicles also told of recent events, of the persecutions which the Jews had endured during the Crusades. They offered accounts of pathos, depicting the powerless of the Jews, their sufferings, and their ultimate agonies. The chronicles described in horrible detail how in some cities the Christians slaughtered the Jews and also how, in other places, Jews took their own lives in dramatic acts of mass suicide, *al kiddush ha-Shem*, sanctifying God's name.

In these accounts, the traditional explanation for Jewish suffering— *mipnei hataeynu*, "because of our sins"—receded into the background, overshadowed by a newly formed collective consciousness of Jews as the unblemished sacrifices of a mass *akedah*, martyrs for their God and their faith. Stories of these martyrs were later incorporated into the liturgy, for such historical material reinforced the rabbis' teachings and served as *exempla*, models of piety for Jews to emulate.

This idealization of Jewish suffering and martyrdom particularly distinguishes *Sefer Yosifon*, a work destined to become the most widely read book of Jewish history for many centuries. Written in Hebrew by an unknown Italian Jew in the mid-tenth century, *Sefer Yosifon* was a popular reworking of Josephus's *The Jewish War*, with an admixture of Talmudic literature and contemporary oral traditions. In rendering the history of Jewish suffering, heroism, and catastrophe, *Sefer Yosifon* gave its readers a sense of the continuity of Jewish history and a feeling of contemporary relevance. Its narrative power made it a good read and a good cry, an indulgence not without its pleasures (as we all know from grand opera and soap opera alike). *Sefer Yosifon's* widespread popularity no doubt nourished that collective Jewish historical consciousness which the late Professor Salo W. Baron deplored and characterized with asperity as "the lachrymose conception of history."

That collective Jewish consciousness has been and remains—with justice, I think—one of the central myths of Jewish history, being an

10

essence distilled from real events and reinforced in nearly every Jewish generation until our own time by brute reality. The medieval emphasis on Jewish suffering and martyrdom was, in its way, a variation on the Biblical conception of Jewish history oscillating between the poles of destruction and redemption.

With the invention of printing, Jewish history continued on its course of diversification. The production of historical books was no longer in the exclusive purview of the rabbis. Laymen began to write history; the reading public grew larger. The sixteenth century witnessed the rise of an enormously popular printed Yiddish literature that combined history and legend—the *Melokhim-bukh*, the *Shmuel-bukh*, and soon thereafter, the *Maaseh-bukh* and then a Yiddish version of *Sefer Yosifon*. A mass audience of readers was being created, and the books they read, rich in history, diffused ever more widely a national sense of Jewish historical consciousness.

The great watershed was the sixteenth century, marking the end of Sephardi creativity and the rise of Ashkenazi hegemony. The expulsion from Spain, the persecutions and forcible conversions which brought to an end the era of Sephardi civilization, inaugurated a period of apocalyptic mysticism whose reverberations throughout the Jewish world were to be felt for more than a century to come. The rise of the Kabbalah and the publication of the Zohar alone are evidence of the dominant presence of mysticism as a force in Jewish life in the sixteenth century.

Yet, at the same time and occasionally even in the same place, influences of Renaissance humanism, rationalism, and secularism penetrated Jewish cultural and intellectual life. These conflicting claims of mysticism and reason were reflected in the historical works of that era.

The three works most widely known in the mid-sixteenth century were Solomon Ibn Verga's *Shevet Yehuda* (Staff of Judah), Samuel Usque's *Consolation for the Tribulations of Israel*, and Joseph Ha-Kohen's *Emek ha-Bakha* (Vale of Tears). All embodied the tradition of history as consolation, offering the promise of redemption. They also continued the medieval tradition of history as a series of *exempla*, by pre-

11

senting models of piety to help reinforce loyalty to Judaism. In some Italian communities, passages from *Emek ha-Bakha* used to be read, together with Lamentations, in the synagogues on the Ninth of Av.

But in the last quarter of that century, two heralds of what we would today call modern historiography made their appearance. One was a Sephardi historian, the other an Ashkenazi. Both crossed the threshold of modernity cautiously, even timidly. Azariah dei Rossi's work, *Meor Enayim* (Light to the Eyes), evinced the disparate influences of the Italian Renaissance and the Kabbalah. It was his innovation to combine wide-ranging erudition in Jewish and Christian sources with a critical evaluation of those sources. Nevertheless, he remained under the impact of the cataclysmic events of his lifetime. Even though he had the courage to question the historical accuracy of some rabbinic writings, he nevertheless believed that history had didactic value only for the Gentiles, not for the Jews. Jewish history, he held, was determined by divine law and was not subject to empirical causation.

The first Ashkenazi Jew to write history was David Gans, who lived most of his life in Prague. His major work *Tzemah David* (Offspring of David), published in 1592, was less erudite, less sophisticated, less rigorous in its use of sources than dei Rossi's. Yet his arguments on behalf of history have a modern ring. Reading history, Gans wrote, gives pleasure: "I hope to bring joy to householders who earn their bread in sorrow and by the sweat of their brow, so that after their toil and effort, they may rest from their labor by reading of matters old and new."

History teaches by experience, said Gans, and he thought it could help Jews in their everyday lives. By improving their knowledge of their own history and of world history, it would enable ordinary people to converse more easily with non-Jews whom they encountered. Perhaps he meant that familiarity with Jewish history would be useful to Jews in possible disputes with Christians. Thus, he offered the idea of history as national apologia, as a means of justifying Jews and Judaism, as a way of winning esteem from non-Jews and enhancing Jewish self-esteem.

But more interesting for our subject than dei Rossi's and Gans's ideas about the uses of history was the way the rabbis responded to them. In Venice, Padua, Rome, Ferrara, and several other Italian cities, the rabbis issued a ban on dei Rossi's book, on the ground that it presented "many new interpretations not thought of by our holy forefathers." An adult who wanted to read or study *Meor Enayim* had first to obtain written permission from his local rabbi. Joseph Caro, the Kabbalist and compiler of the *Shulhan Arukh*, was said to have ordered a ban on the book, but died before he signed it. Gans's *Tzemah David*, in contrast, enjoyed a favorable reception among the rabbis and a wide reading public among Ashkenazi Jewry. Gans had studied with Rabbi Moses Isserles in Prague, who had encouraged him to write history.

The difference between the Sephardim and Ashkenazim in their reception of these books reflected a difference in *halacha*, Jewish religious law. That difference was not a major issue, but it is nevertheless instructive. Caro's *Shulhan Arukh* had incorporated the principles and practices of Sephardi Jews. Isserles, meanwhile, who had been compiling a similar work, was eventually satisfied to publish only his glosses on Caro, which incorporated Ashkenazi practices.

Caro, drawing upon longstanding rabbinic traditions, forbade the reading of history, which he characterized as "tales of war"—a likely reference specifically to *Sefer Yosifon*—not only on the Sabbath but even on weekdays. Isserles, however, dissented modestly, and declared the prohibition valid only for works written in foreign languages, but not if they were written in the "holy tongue."

What can we conclude from these different rulings? Reeling under the impact of the catastrophic events of their time, the Sephardi rabbis in the sixteenth century responded to the expulsion from Spain in the same way the rabbis had reacted after the destruction of the Second Temple: they turned their backs on history, for it could serve no national use. Permeated by a belief that they had come to the end of the Jewish history in this world, steeped in apocalyptic mysticism, the Sephardi rabbis looked to the coming of the Messiah and the End of Days.

The Ashkenazim, in contrast, then faced the world with optimism and confidence. That era was called the Golden Age of Ashkenazi Jewry and would last until 1648, when Chmielnicki's Cossack uprising triggered a terrible massacre of Jews. But until then, through the sixteenth century and into the seventeenth, material well-being went hand in hand with extensive Talmudic learning in Eastern Europe. *Yeshivot* flourished and, astonishingly, also a compatible rationalist humanism that derived from the Italian Renaissance.

Perhaps, too, the manifest devotion of the Ashkenazi community to Judaism and to traditional learning gave the rabbis the confidence to permit and even encourage secular study. Certainly, Rabbi Moses Isserles, who was known for his interest in cultivating science and scholarship, played a key role in the cultural openness of the Ashkenazi Jews.

But just a century later, after the Third Catastrophe—*der driter khurbn*—as the Yiddish chronicles called the Chmielnicki massacres, history was no longer a significant factor in Jewish intellectual life. Only metahistory remained, for the terrible events of 1648–49 justified the medieval conception of the Jews as blameless martyrs sanctifying God's name.

In the eighteenth century Jewish history became the province and the ideological instrument, not of Jewish scholars, but of Christians—a subject which is itself of considerable historical curiosity. In any case, however, it was not before the beginning of the nineteenth century that Jews resumed writing their own history. That was when modern historical scholarship—history as we know it today—burst upon Europe's cultural scene. Jewish historians soon mastered the methods of the then-new history and became part of the new wave of critical historical studies.

Modern historiography was a product of Europe's social and political transformations following the Enlightenment and the French Revolution. The nation-state and nationalism were in the ascendancy. Henceforth, history would no longer serve as an auxiliary of the universal church, nor would Christianity any longer be the central subject

14

of universal history. The political state had replaced religion as the prime historical mover.

For Jews, these consequences were radical and transforming. In Western and Central Europe, eighteenth-century rationalism and Enlightenment had already begun to erode the commitment to Judaism and Jewish law. Then, the nation-state and nationalism began to erode the Jews' commitment to the Jewish people.

Western Jews who grew up in this new world, who attended universities or whose economic successes had catapulted them out of traditional Jewish society, no longer looked to Judaism as the center of their personal or communal existence. The pursuit of emancipation, of civic and social equality, became their religion and driving motive. For some, however, the study of Judaism itself, or, as it was called then, *Wissenschaft des Judentums*, became a means through which they hoped to attain emancipation.

The first programmatic statement to that effect appeared in 1822, under the auspices of the Verein für Cultur und Wissenschaft der Juden, the first incarnation of several generations of organizations devoted to Jewish scholarship. In this pioneering document, the author argued that the scientific study of Judaism "must decide on the merits or demerits of the Jews, their fitness or unfitness to be given the same status and respect as other citizens."

This meant that critical scholarly study of Judaism's history would be used to demonstrate to the guardians of the German state and its culture that the claims of the Jews for citizenship and equal political rights were justified by the high level of past Jewish achievements. Thus, the founders of *Wissenschaft des Judentums* invented a new national purpose for Jewish history: to improve the political position of the Jews, to hasten their emancipation.

Those apologetics differed from David Gans's idea that Jewish history could help Jewish self-esteem. Gans wanted to enhance the status of Jews *and* Judaism, while *Wissenschaft des Judentums* hoped, as it turned out, to enhance the status of Jews, at the price of their Judaism.

For the young men who formed that first society, *Wissenschaft des Judentums* was intended also for internal Jewish education, for a process

15

Leopold Zunz characterized as "inner emancipation." The inner world of the Jews, according to the members of the Verein, had to be brought into harmony with the scientific spirit of the times. These young men, alienated from Judaism and the Jewish community, undertook to use Jewish history to hasten Jewish assimilation. Thus, for the first time in Jewish historiography, Jewish history was enlisted in an enterprise which, while serving the political and social interests of the Western Jews at that time, no longer looked to a Jewish future.

In that milieu in Germany, Judaism appeared to be a sinking ship. In 1822, Isaac Marcus Jost, who was to write the first modern history of the Jews, expressed bleak pessimism about Judaism's viability. "I am not a friend of desertion," he wrote to a friend, "but the history of our times makes it universal and justifies it." He himself had come to believe that Prussia and other German states were right to deny political equality so long as the Jews failed to assimilate and intermarry. In his letter, Jost argued that young Jews were right to forsake Judaism, for only then they could "attain freedom, a sense of national belonging, patriotism, and service to the state, the highest qualities of mortal men."

But what kind of Jewish history could a man write who believed that Judaism had come to the end of the line, and who vindicated its apostates? Jost's history, a pioneering work in methodology and critical treatment of sources, had been written to prove that the Jews were "peaceful citizens and faithful subjects," even though he himself believed that their faith was backward, superstitious, and arrogant. Graetz later said of Jost: "He tore to shreds the heroic drama of thousands of years."

What Jost's history lacked was *ahavat yisrael*, that distinctive Jewish concept of love of one's people, which entails not only a sense of identity with the Jewish past and an involvement in its present, but also a commitment to a Jewish future. None of the great themes of Jewish metahistory—God's Covenant with the Jews, the cycle of destruction and deliverance, the martyrdom of the Jewish people for God's name, the promise of redemption—found a place in Jost's work.

These themes only barely surfaced in the more distinguished scholarship of Jost's friend, Leopold Zunz. Like Jost, Zunz had turned to Jewish scholarship as a weapon in the struggle for political emancipation and to justify the revisions in Jewish practice undertaken by Reform Judaism. But after a while, even Reform Judaism ceased to interest him. One understands the force of the philosopher Hermann Cohen's view of Zunz: "He could have been a great historian, and was nothing but an antiquarian." For if interest in the Jewish past is not sustained by concern for the future, then Jewish history loses its animating power, its very life.

In the early 1850s, a mutual friend introduced Zunz to Heinrich Graetz, saying that Graetz was planning to publish a history of the Jews. "Another history of the Jews!" Zunz exclaimed with acerbity. "Another history," Graetz retorted, "but this time a *Jewish* history!"

Graetz's history restored a Jewish perspective to Jewish history. He rescued the Jewish past from the hands of Christian theologians and historians and also from assimilationist Jewish reformers. "The Christian conception of history," Graetz wrote, "fully denies to Judaism any history." The Christian tendency to issue "a death certificate" to Jewish history was merely self-serving. Graetz believed that Jewish historians urgently needed "to vindicate the right of Jewish history" and "to present its tenacious and indestructible character." He took that obligation upon himself.

Graetz was convinced of the "enduring faculty of the Jewish race, which defied so many persecutions." In response to Christians of his time who argued, as Arnold Toynbee would a century later, that Judaism was merely an archaic or fossilized remnant of an irrelevant past, Graetz held that the Jewish people was an extraordinary phenomenon, which, though it dated from "hoary antiquity," still possessed "youthful vigor." Himself a believing Jew, he asserted that he heeded "the voice of God which speaks in Jewish history, in Jewish law, and in the Jewish people."

Graetz used Jewish history in a new way: to give his Jewish readers renewed pride in being part of the Jewish people and in its past. He strove to communicate a sense of the dignity and creativity of the

17

Jews as a people and to demonstrate through his history that Judaism and its culture were still viable. As for his Christian readers, Graetz hoped they would find in his work a depiction of the Jewish past as it had existed in its historic reality. He wanted Christians to see Judaism, not as a vestige of the denial of Christ, but as the animating and continuously creative force in the life and culture of the Jewish people.

Graetz was our first modern historian. In the nineteenth century, with the spread of universal education, history became the discipline through which love of one's country and people was taught. Graetz was of this school of national history. The Jewish version of patriotism is *ahavat yisrael.*

Graetz's name became a byword among the rising generation of Jewish writers, intellectuals, and scholars throughout Europe—even if Peretz's acquaintance in Warsaw had not heard of him. Graetz's most distinguished recruit to Jewish history was Simon Dubnow.

While preparing an obituary study of Graetz's life and work, Dubnow made the most momentous decision of his life. "My aim in life," he wrote in his diary, "has become clarified: to spread historical knowledge about Jewry and particularly to work on the history of the Russian Jews. I have become a missionary of history."

Unlike Graetz, Dubnow was a secularist, but somehow he saw in Jewish history a mystic force that had ensured, and would continue to ensure, Jewish survival. In a justly celebrated essay, Dubnow intimated that Jewish history—the history itself, not just the written account—might help usher in a better world, for the understanding that it would bring could lead to the elimination of intolerance and prejudice. "The future task of Jewish history will prove as sublime as was the mission of the Jewish people in the past," he wrote.

Dubnow had been opposed to the idea of Zionism and had argued instead for a national ideology which he called Diaspora nationalism. His most forceful professional antagonist was Yitzhak Fritz Baer, whose brilliant essay *Galut* is in part a polemic against Dubnow's ideas. Baer, a passionate Zionist, looked to Jewish history to uphold and validate Jewish claims before mankind, that is, to justify the Jews' political

18

claim to Palestine. His Zionism assumed the dimensions of religious messianism. "There is a power," Baer wrote, "that lifts the Jewish people out of the realm of all causal history," for "our place in the world is not to be measured by the measure of his world. Our history follows its own laws. . . ." Thus spoke Baer, upholding a view of Jewish history that had its origins in the Bible and had all but died out in modern times.

Baer wrote those words just before the darkness of the Holocaust enveloped the European Jews. Since then, the course of Jewish history has continued its ancient pattern, oscillating between the poles of destruction and deliverance: the Holocaust and the rise of Israel; the liquidation of the Jewish communities in Arab lands and the miracle of the Six-Day War; the destruction of Jewish life in the Soviet Union and the deliverance of those Jews from Communist bondage.

Whether we are believers or skeptics about providential destiny, we must admit that Baer was right: Jewish history follows its own laws. And also Dubnow was right: Jewish history, however dark and catastrophic, has in it the potential for Jewish survival. This sense of Jewish history and destiny is what every Jew who cares about the survival of his people feels in his bones, even if he does not know the dates and events, even if he has never heard of Graetz.

The same is true also for the Jewish historian. Some people think that the professional historian's personal commitments—to his people, his country, his religion, his language—undermine his professional objectivity. Not so. Not so, as long as historians respect the integrity of their sources and adhere strictly to the principles of sound scholarship. Personal commitments do not distort, but instead they enrich, historical writing.

Except for the few practitioners of *Wissenschaft des Judentums* whose work was warped by their estrangement from Jews and Judaism, Jewish historians from ancient times until today have produced their work not just for the sake of intellectual satisfaction or professional accomplishment, but rather out of the desire to use Jewish history as an instrument for Jewish survival. Historians too are captivated not just by the great events of Jewish history, but by its great myths as well.

19

— 2 —

HISTORY AS AUTOBIOGRAPHY: TELLING A LIFE

I n mid-August 1938, I embarked on a year-long journey to Poland that my family and friends thought was reckless, even quixotic. At twenty-three, a native New Yorker, with a B.A. from Hunter College and a year of graduate study in English literature at Columbia, I set out for Vilna. I had received a fellowship for a year's study in Jewish history and the Yiddish language at the Yiddish Scientific Institute—*der yidisher visnshaftlekher institut*—YIVO, headquartered in Vilna, where it had been founded. Vilna, even as late as 1938, still laid claim to being the cultural capital of Jewish Eastern Europe, still prided itself on being the Jerusalem of Lithuania, the name which, so it was said, Napoleon gave it in the summer of 1812.

The year 1938 was not auspicious for travel to Eastern Europe for business or pleasure. The guns of war were muzzled, but the threat of war poisoned the air as if the suffocating aroma of sulphur had already been unloosed. In March Adolf Hitler had invaded Austria and annexed it. Then he turned on Czechoslovakia under the pretext of protecting the "rights" of the German-speaking population who had lived for centuries in a part of Bohemia called Sudetenland. In August, when I sailed for Poland, the Czech crisis, which had flared and then died down, was starting to heat up again. No, the summer of 1938 was definitely not an auspicious time to go to Poland.

20

Indeed, the Jewish traffic had long been moving in the opposite direction. Central and Eastern Europe had become a vast prison house from which Jews wished to escape. Those lucky enough to get visas headed for Europe's exits. At just that time I was starting out on my reverse, perverse journey. Years later, the novelist Isaac Bashevis Singer tried to fathom my state of mind. He himself had fled Poland in 1935 and come to the United States. Puzzling over my recklessness or imprudence, as he saw it, he at last found an explanation that satisfied him. "I," he said, "was a Polish Jew and I thought anything could happen. You were an American Jew and you thought nothing could happen."

To be sure, American confidence and American breeziness contributed to my decision to go to Poland. Those bad old days were, in at least one respect, like our times. People everywhere in the world craved American citizenship, and, even if they could not get a visa, they still blessed America for its generosity to the world. In those days, a native American with an American passport in his pocket felt rich and secure abroad, no matter what his condition at home. Every American abroad felt rich, for even in the days of the Depression, the United States was still a land of plenitude, at least compared to Europe. In those days, Jewish families in America, however pinched and needy, were still sending money and goods to their less fortunate relatives in the old country.

In those days, when the lawlessness of the Nazi, fascist, and semi-fascist states eroded what little security their citizens had ever enjoyed, when the tyranny of the Communist dictatorship terrorized the peoples of the Soviet Union, to be carrying an American passport was like wearing a suit of armor. Jews especially, and the immigrant generation from Eastern Europe particularly, appreciated America's protectiveness, for they knew that in their lifetime no country had ever been better to its Jewish citizens than the United States. Being an American was itself enough to give anyone a bushelful of courage.

Yet my going to Poland was not mere youthful American bravado. It was more akin to a convention of another sort—the traditional passage from youth to adulthood, the quest to seek one's purpose in

21

life. It was quite simply my coming of age, even if, at twenty-three, somewhat late.

That journey of mine forms the starting point of my *From That Place and Time*. It is a memoir and not an autobiography, a distinction that is not as distinct as it might be. The word "memoir," the dictionary tells us, was first used in 1659, to define a "record of events, a history treating of matters from the personal knowledge of the writer or with reference to particular sources of information." But within fourteen years, the word "memoir" took on the meaning of "an autobiographical record," though—I note this as a curiosity—the actual word "auto-biography" did not come into the language until early in the nine-teenth century. After a while, the memoir took on the plural form and the distinction between memoir/memoirs and autobiography be-came further blurred.

In his book *Design and Truth in Autobiography*, Roy Pascal offers a serviceable distinction between these two related genres of literary composition. "In the autobiography proper," he writes, "attention is focused on the self, in the memoir or reminiscence on others." Georg Misch, in his now classic work, *History of Autobiography in Antiquity*, distinguishes autobiography from memoir in terms of man's relation to the world. Autobiography, he says, represents the active relation-ship, the writing of people who have shaped events. The memoir represents the passive relationship, the writing of those who were observers of the events they recount. Yet any memoir or autobiog-raphy, whether its mode is active or passive, if it is more than merely a vehicle of gossip, offers at the least glimpses of the society in which the writer lived and accounts of the events which he witnessed.

Memoirist and autobiographer both depend on memory, and mem-ory is the foundation of public history. The memoirist and the au-tobiographer resemble the historian in that they undertake to recall and to reconstruct the past. Leon Edel, whose biography of Henry James is one of the great works of literature, has testified that "the writing of lives is a department of history and is closely related to the discoveries of history." It is the substance of history which gives both the memoir and the autobiography dignity and weight. The great autobiographies and memoirs of literature have been written by people who were the makers of history and shakers of the world. But even those who were mere spectators of history can use the memoir to record the historic events they have witnessed.

I called my book a memoir and not an autobiography because I would not dare claim to have had a role, however minor, in the making of history. I have no such pretension. It is in fact just the reverse: the world's public events served as a calendar for the private events of my own life. Even my earliest memory is a date in history. It is of a street celebration on New York's Lower East Side after the United States entered the First World War. An effigy of the kaiser was strung high above the street, suspended between the tenement buildings on either side. I remember music and dancing. It is a fitting memory for war, filled with ambiguity, frightening yet exhilarating, the child's terror at the effigy eased somehow by the pleasure of the music and the dancing. Many years later, the Depression and the Moscow Trials became events and milestones in my personal life. The Depression determined how my family lived for many years. The Moscow Trials ruptured many of my friendships, but led me to new ones. I would not have become the person I am without the intervention of the great events of history in my personal affairs. That is what I have implied in the title of this essay, "History as Autobiography."

Mallarmé once wrote that "the world exists to be put in a book." It was my wish to put in a book the world in which I lived for a year just before it was destroyed in the fire and ashes of the Holocaust. For I was one of the last people who saw Vilna when it was still the Jerusalem of Lithuania.

Vilna no longer exists. On its site stands a place identified on the maps as Vilnius, a Lithuanian city. The Vilnius that one reads about in today's papers bears little resemblance to the Vilna I knew. Most Jews there now are not natives of Vilna, but people who came from other places in Lithuania and from the Soviet Union. Few of them are literate in Jewish matters, though many are impelled by a poignant desire to recover a Jewish past they never knew. Reportedly, many of those still there wish desperately to leave for Israel. The Vilna that I knew, the Jerusalem of Lithuania described in Jewish annals, now lies buried, like Troy and Carthage, beneath the debris of history, interred beneath layers of death and destruction which the Russians, the Lithuanians, and the Germans in succession piled upon it.

Vilna exists now only in history, only in memory. One of the last people to have seen Vilna, I have been haunted by the compelling Jewish obligation to remember. I wished, to use Jules Michelet's poignant words, "to make the silences of history speak," to bestow on Vilna and its Jews a posthumous life. I felt it was my duty to resurrect it, if I could, by recreating the life in that world capital of the realm of Yiddish, as I had known it in the last year of its authentic life.

To be sure, I saw it with American eyes, but these were not just curious eyes looking for exotica in an alien world. At twenty-three I already belonged to two worlds, having been educated in two cultures. Still half in love with Keats and English poetry, I was being drawn inexorably, during those terrible years of the 1930s, into the turbulent vortex of Jewish life. I was moved by Jewish sorrows, gripped by the drama of Jewish experience. I went to Vilna not as a tourist but as a Jew, to search out the continuities of Jewish history, the connections between my world and that which my parents had left behind.

Still, being American gave me a different perspective, a distance that encouraged objectivity. Always I was sensitive to the differences that emerged between me and the rest of Vilna's Jews. After all, my American passport was not the only thing that set me apart from them. My American heritage and my life experiences contrived effectively to differentiate me from them, for their lot had been the First World War and German occupation, famine, poverty, homelessness.

My being American gave me singular access to Jewish Vilna. Everyone I met was determined to initiate me into the mysteries of Vilna, to instruct me in Vilna's history and customs, to guide me to places of interest and to present me to people of accomplishment. I met many of Vilna's Jewish luminaries, its leading citizens and political figures, its scholars, intellectuals, and writers. I had unusual oppor-

tunities to explore Jewish Vilna's lower depths, encountering desti-
tution and poverty beyond the imagination even of one who had grown
up in the America of the Great Depression.

Being in Vilna I now experienced on my own skin what it was like
to be a Jew in Poland, learning at first hand what before I had known
only from books and newspapers. I saw for myself the violence of anti-
Semitism on the street and in the university and felt the cruelty of
anti-Semitism in the economy as it deprived Jews of the means of
their livelihood. Everywhere the commanding presence of the Catholic Church was visible, not just as a religious force but as a political
one, the core of Polish nationalism and even, alas, the moral authority
for anti-Semitism. The Polish government and Polish political life
were dominated by the Right, which ranged from near-fascist to outright fascist, which was almost universally anti-Semitic, and given to
violence.

Vilna's crooked streets, with their worn cobblestones and their
picturesque arches, were the ubiquitous landmarks of the city's distant
past. But just as enduring as any architectural relic was the abiding
presence in Vilna of Jewish history, a history of faith and learning
and matters of the spirit. Vilna was the city of that powerful eighteenth-century Talmudic mind, Vilna Gaon; it was the stronghold of
rabbinic Judaism, the fortress that withstood the assault of Hasidism.
Modern Hebrew literature had originated in Vilna and Yiddish literature thrived there. In Vilna the Zionist movement experienced its
first stirrings and there too the Jewish labor movement and the Jewish
Socialist Bund had their origins. In Vilna, even as late as 1938, one
could still witness the powerful and passionate conflict between tradition and modernity in the Jewish community. In Vilna I lived at
the heart of Jewish history.

History written from the inside, from the perspective of the participant
or the participant-observer, conveys an immediacy that cannot always
be captured when history is written from documents alone. That kind
of immediacy I tried to introduce in my first book—*The Golden Tradition: Jewish Life and Thought in Eastern Europe*. It consists of auto-

25

biographies, memoirs, and letters of some sixty persons, as well as reminiscences about them. In my introduction, I quote a philosopher of history who characterizes the memory of the individual as "the germinal cell of history."

When I began writing my memoir, I was astonished to find how much the memoirist's methods resemble those of the historian. Both must start with reliable sources and documentation. The raw data then have to be authenticated and corroborated. Thereafter, historian and memoirist alike must select, extracting from the welter of gathered materials those that are essential to describe and explain the past as it really happened. The process of selection is inextricably associated with the search for coherence and meaning, whether it be in an account of a distant time or in an account of one's own life.

At first blush, it would seem that the memoirist needs no documentary sources or corroborative evidence, for he is, after all, relying on the authority of his memory. Yet memory alone may not prove sufficiently comprehensive or dependably precise. For, as each one of us can testify, though we remember, we also misremember and, even worse, we forget.

Even when memory operates in good order, we have all experienced those moments when, as the saying goes, it deceives us. Our ability to remember and our capacity to forget are still not well understood. Freud hypothesizes that forgetting is purposeful, motivated by the wish to repress the memories of unpleasant episodes in one's life.

Still, as we all know from experience, forgotten and repressed material can be retrieved and memory can be prompted. Victor Hugo noted that "nothing awakens reminiscence like an odor." Proust depicted the hypnotic power of sensory recall at the moment he sipped the tea in which he had soaked a crumb of his *petite madeleine.* Any taste, smell, sound, touch, and sight may become a magical cue to awaken a past one had thought beyond recall.

In summoning up the past, we often must contend with gaps in our memories. We tend to fill in those gaps with a connective tissue of imagined facts. We imagine that we remember and we remember our imaginings as if they were real events of the past. Who can tell where authentic memory ends and where imaginative reconstruction begins? André Maurois once said that "memory is a great artist." A contemporary psychologist puts it this way: "We fill up the lowlands of our memories from the highlands of our imaginations."

Consequently, since memory needs prompting and since the process of remembering may involve a process of refabrication, the memoirist needs documents to serve as the signposts on the route to historical accuracy and to discipline his flights of fancy. For however authoritative the voice of memory, a recounting of the past which relies only on unchecked and uncorroborated memory will be imperfect, incomplete, not quite the true record of the historical past. Without exception, the autobiographies and memoirs that have enriched our historical literature have made use of supporting documents—daily logs, appointment books, diaries, letters, photographs, public and private papers.

Since I knew that I could not rely just on my memory, that without documentary support I could never write a memoir about my year in Vilna sufficiently rich in detail to interest an American reader, I despaired of ever doing so. For all I had at my disposal were memories and a bare handful of souvenirs. I had kept no diary of how I spent my days. To be sure, I knew that I could prompt my memory by turning to books and newspapers of that time and place. Still, that kind of memoir, based mainly on memory and re-creative imagination, could become a hybrid, part fiction, part memory, not quite history, not quite the way it really was.

But, as Jews like to say, God will provide. Around 1985, my oldest friend unearthed a cache of letters which I had written to her during that year in Vilna. Soon after, my sister turned up a similar bundle of letters, richly detailed and charged with the wonder of my experiences. The idea of writing the memoir now became more practicable. For these letters, so providentially rescued from dust, together with a handful of autographed books and photographs, were the only keepsakes, as it were, of my year in Vilna. Back in 1939, I had not planned it that way.

The reason I had none of the tourist's usual mementos lay in the circumstances of my departure from Vilna. Late in August 1939, I had gone with friends on a short vacation. We were staying at a riverside village six kilometers from Vilna. On Wednesday, August 23, 1939, we set off early to spend the day at the beach. Toward evening, when we returned to our lodgings, we were greeted by a great hubbub and I found urgent telephone messages to call Vilna. Only then did we learn that on that very day the Germans and the Russians announced they had signed a nonaggression pact. When I telephoned Vilna, I was told that a special-delivery letter had arrived from the American consul, advising that if I intended to return home, I had better do so soon, for it might prove impossible later.

The next morning we set out for Vilna and found that the Polish government had already requisitioned all transport—taxis, the few private cars, trucks, horses, and wagons. We had to walk the six kilometers back to the city. There, panic reigned. The Polish army had begun to call up the reserves. Husbands and wives, parents and sons were everywhere engaged in tearful farewells. People were buying up food. At home, Zelig Kalmanovich, one of YIVO's directors, and his wife, Rivele, dearer to me than my own parents had ever been, pleaded with me to leave. They felt that war would come any day. They had few illusions, having lived their lives on familiar terms with war, revolution, and hardship. When I said I wanted to stay and share their fate, they spoke harshly to me. I would be a burden, another mouth to feed, another body to care for.

We reached a compromise. I would go to Warsaw, but just to see the consul, just to get some reliable information. I left some of my things behind and took a night train, arriving in Warsaw the morning of August 25. The American consul and my friends in Warsaw urged me to leave. There was no longer any doubt that Hitler would invade. And so, heartsick and stricken with guilt, I decided that I would have to go.

But where to? My return ticket on a Polish transatlantic liner that was to have sailed from Gdynia, Poland's port, was probably worthless. Gdynia was already closed to commercial traffic. The ships, it was rumored, had been requisitioned. Still, I reasoned, if a ship were to leave, it would stop en route westward at Copenhagen. So Copenhagen became my destination, a port city from which I might get passage home.

On Saturday evening, August 26, I left by train for Berlin, where I was to change for Denmark. The train was filled with Poles, all deep in despair. At Poznan, on the Polish-German border, the Poles got off; Germans boarded the train, all in a mood of high martial spirits. An official of the German consulate at Poznan, who had been recalled home, took a seat in my compartment. We talked through the night. War would come, he assured me. He was just as certain that Germany would win the war. I did not tell him I was Jewish. I flaunted my Americanness.

Sunday morning, the train pulled into the Schlesischer Bahnhof in Berlin. As we entered the city, all we could see was a sea of soldiers, waves of Nazi flags, and the equipage of war. Cannons were mounted on the tracks at the station's entrance. The city was gripped by war frenzy. The cheers, the shouts, the rousing songs left no doubt of the German will to conquer.

My traveling companion, the German consular official, responding to my feminine helplessness, managed to snare a taxi for me. The driver had to inch the car through the masses of soldiers and hysterical crowds to reach the Stattner station on the other side of Berlin, where I just barely made the train to Copenhagen.

Five days later, on September 1, 1939, the armed forces of National Socialist Germany invaded Poland. Two days later, England and France declared war on Germany. On September 16, I sailed for home. On September 17, the Russians invaded Poland from the east.

The story of my flight from Vilna is a tale of drama. In trying to reconstruct those desperate days at the end of August 1939, with their intimations of war and destruction, I came to realize that the memoirist inhabits a region that belongs nearly as much to the art of fiction as to the craft of history. He is obligated to be faithful to the past not only by making it authentic but also by rendering it lifelike. I wanted

29

to re-create Jewish Vilna as it really was in the last year of its existence, and to do so without sentimentality, remaining faithful to the reality and to my own feelings.

Was it possible? How can one separate the present remembering self from the past remembered self? Any memoir or autobiography is likely to show signs of double exposure, for the past, even when it is accurately reconstructed and corroborated by documents, is nevertheless filtered through the memoirist's present consciousness. While I was writing, I was often reminded of a painting by Chagall, called *Dream Village*, which he did in Paris in 1929 and which I had seen in a lovely museum in San Antonio.

In the center foreground a vase filled with an enormous bunch of roses stands on a small table before an open window. Beyond the window lies, not the reality of a Paris street, but Chagall's dream village, the crooked little houses of Vitebsk, the sun and the moon, and the figures of a young man and a girl, dreamy, wispy, yet still touching ground, not yet afloat, not yet unloosed from reality. *Dream Village* is a powerful evocation, yet it verges perilously close to sentimentality, an artist's threnody for a past irretrievably gone. Already a successful artist in Paris in 1929, Chagall was painting his memories of Vitebsk as it had been before the First World War, filtered through his present consciousness of how the Bolshevik Revolution had destroyed Vitebsk as he knew it.

How much greater is the distance which the Holocaust created between the past and present, and how much more difficult it is to traverse that terrain. The terrible finality of the murder of the European Jews and their disappearance from history darken our memories and cloud our visions of the past. In trying to bridge that abyss between past and present, the memoirist is obliged to arm himself against sentimentality, to guard against nostalgia. I was constantly aware of the desire to idealize that destroyed world. I tried to discipline myself to portray Vilna as it was, without retouching, without removing the warts and blotches of historical reality.

Yet at the same time, I felt that I needed to hone the skills of a storyteller if I wanted to bring to life the people I was describing.

30

History, it used to be said, is not only a science but also an art. One of the great masters of narrative style, Thomas Babington Macaulay, claims that history is sometimes fiction, sometimes theory, and that a good historian "must possess an imagination sufficiently powerful to make his narrative affecting and picturesque." The great German historian Theodor Mommsen describes imagination as the mother of history as well as of poetry. And according to R. G. Collingwood, the English philosopher of history, without imagination "the historian would have no narrative to adorn."

The idea of my memoir began with the wish to bring Vilna back to life. But as I pursued the idea, I realized that the story I wanted to tell did not end with my flight from Vilna. The threads of my life thereafter continued to be woven into a web of experience whose pattern, which I did not recognize then but discerned only later, formed a design of thematic unity and continuity. It was as if I was living in a story whose coherence I could not perceive or appreciate until the distance of time intervened. I might say, to use terms which describe the structure of fiction, that the crisis of my story was created by the imminence of war and my flight from Vilna, while my story's denouement or resolution came in the postwar years. Between the crisis and the denouement, the terrible passage of the war intervened.

Those years, from 1940 to 1946, form the second part of my memoir. They were years rich in catastrophic history. We who lived in the safety of the United States, sheltered from the disasters that had overtaken the European Jews, were nevertheless beset by the turbulence of world events. Obsessively we followed the course of the war across the ocean. Our very existence hung on its outcome and on it depended the fate of the European Jews. Consciousness of the war always intruded into our everyday existence, always persisted, even in moments of intense private joy.

In the early years, the course of the war, in Europe especially, but also in the Pacific, presaged disaster. In 1941, the Soviet Union, Hitler's ally for two years, overnight became Hitler's victim. National Socialist Germany controlled nearly all of Europe. Even the Allied landings on North Africa in November 1942 brought little elation,

31

for no sooner had the troops landed than they were locked in bitterly fought battles. Only when the Russians at last drove the Germans from Stalingrad in February 1943 did the tide begin to turn. But even as the military news improved, the news about the European Jews gave us little to hope for. That news filtered in bit by bit, despite the barriers of German censorship and the breakdown of communication with those under German occupation.

With each passing year that the Allied armed forces failed to breach Hitler's Fortress Europe and failed to get a foothold on the terrain of Europe, our despair intensified. In the spring of 1943 we learned of the uprising in the Warsaw ghetto. By the time the Allied forces landed in Normandy, more than a year had passed since the Warsaw ghetto smoldered into ruins. We knew that the Allied troops had arrived too late to rescue the European Jews. Most of the three million Polish Jews had already been murdered in Treblinka, Majdanek, Sobibór, Bełżec, and Auschwitz.

In those years I worked at YIVO in New York. This is how it came about. Back in 1925, shortly after the YIVO had been established in Vilna, an American branch was organized in New York, mainly as a fund-raising arm for Vilna. But soon the American branch attracted a group of distinguished Jewish scholars—all originally from Eastern Europe—who participated in the YIVO's scholarly activities. It was the American branch which had made possible my year in Vilna.

Early in 1940 Max Weinreich, one of YIVO's founders in Vilna and the only one of its three directors who survived, a polymath of international renown, especially noted as a linguist, arrived in New York. He persuaded the American branch to operate as the YIVO's headquarters for the duration of the war, with himself as research director. In his plans, he stipulated that he wanted me to work for him. My year in Vilna had qualified me. In Max Weinreich's eyes, I represented the connection between the European past and the American present, the possibility of YIVO's continuity in America.

In those years, YIVO became a center for refugee scholars, writers, and communal leaders from Eastern Europe. With many of them I made new and enduring friendships. At that time too, while working at YIVO, I returned to Columbia, with Max Weinreich's encouragement, to complete my unfinished master's degree. Back in 1937 English literature had been my chosen field. Now I enrolled in Jewish history, studying with the master of Jewish erudition, Professor Salo W. Baron.

In those years, Max Weinreich, who had once studied in Germany and earned his doctorate at the University of Marburg, became preoccupied with the role of German professors who had lent their scholarly authority to legitimate the Nazi regime and its anti-Semitic policies. His remarkable book, *Hitler's Professors*, was published in April 1946, the first work ever to document the complicity of the learned professions in the destruction of the European Jews.

Meanwhile, early in 1945, shortly after American forces entered Frankfurt, we learned that part of the Vilna YIVO library and archives had been found in that city. The story of how some of the holdings of the YIVO library and of other great European Jewish libraries reached Frankfurt is another chapter in the unedifying record of German scholars in Hitler's Germany.

It was in Frankfurt that Alfred Rosenberg, Hitler's chief ideologue, had established the Institut zur Erforschung der Judenfrage, a pseudo-scholarly institution dedicated to anti-Jewish studies. Rosenberg intended to enlist German scholars to apply the honored methods of German scholarship to prove that the Jews were indeed as corrupting and evil as the Nazis claimed. Frankfurt became the site of Rosenberg's institute because, a few years earlier, its mayor had confiscated the magnificent Judaica collection of the municipal library.

The Frankfurt collection became the cornerstone of Rosenberg's anti-Jewish research organization and spurred him to even greater efforts of bibliokleptomania. He confiscated the libraries of the Berlin Jewish community, the Breslau Rabbinical Seminary, the Vienna Jewish community, and the Vienna Rabbinical Seminary. In 1941, after the Germans invaded the Soviet Union, Rosenberg set up a special-duty task force, Einsatzstab Reichsleiter Rosenberg für die besetzten Gebiete—Reich Leader Rosenberg's Special Task Force for the Occupied Areas—to scour the European continent for more Jewish libraries. They seized the libraries of the Alliance Israélite Universelle and the École Rabbinique in Paris and the Rosenthaliana collection in Amsterdam. Later they came to Vilna. They took as their booty portions of several important libraries in the city, including the Strashun Library and, of course, YIVO's library and archives.

In 1945, in the rubble of Frankfurt, American forces found the remains of the Institut zur Erforschung der Judenfrage with its library, among them also portions of YIVO's Vilna library and archives. When we learned of this extraordinary find, we submitted to the State Department and to the Office of Military Government, United States (OMGUS) in Germany our documented claims that the New York YIVO was the rightful heir of the property of the YIVO in Vilna. It was then already clear that YIVO would never return to Vilna.

Early in 1946, the late Koppel Pinson, a professor of German history and a close associate of YIVO during the war years, then education director for the Joint Distribution Committee (JDC) in occupied Germany, believing that my knowledge of Yiddish and of East European Jewry would be useful, urged me to join him with the JDC in Munich. Even more persuasive was the prompting from within me, summoning me not to Vilna, for I knew it no longer existed, but to the survivors, to be with those whom I felt I had abandoned in 1939. And so once again in my life, I embarked on a chimerical journey.

The American Joint Distribution Committee signed me on as an education officer. The third and last part of my memoir describes my work in Germany from mid-1946 until the end of 1947, first in Munich, then in Offenbach—both places in the American zone of occupied Germany. I wore an American army officer's uniform, with AJDC insignia. Much of that time I spent with Jews who had survived Hitler, who had survived the German gas chambers and the SS mass-shooting squads, who had lain concealed in bunkers or who had fought with the partisans in the forests. Some among them had survived the Soviet slave-labor camps and then, after the war, had fled from Poland's ungovernable anti-Semitism. The Jewish survivors rejected the name

34

"displaced persons," with which the American occupiers designated those who did not wish to return to their homelands. The Jewish survivors referred to themselves instead as the *she'erit ha-pleta*, the saving remnant.

As far as I know, only one book has been written about them— Leo W. Schwarz's *The Redeemers*, long out of print. Perhaps historians have not been attracted to studying the survivors because their story is like a "time-out" in history, hardly more than a passageway between past and future, from the ashes and rubble of a thousand years of Jewish life in Europe toward new worlds and new lives. Yet the *she'erit ha-pleta*, so it seems to me, from their liberation in 1945 until 1953, when the last "displaced persons" camps were finally closed down, stood at the very center of Jewish history, even—it might be said— in the eye of world history.

In Germany, in the daily rounds of their lives, their memories haunted their days and disturbed their sleep. They lived at swords' point with the Ukrainians and the Balts, who had been Nazi collaborators. From time to time, I would hear of, and once I actually saw, their violent eruptions of revenge in the camps or on the streets of German cities. Nevertheless, the will to live prevailed among the *she'erit ha-pleta* and soon they began to lead normal lives, though camp existence could hardly have been described as normal. They got married, had children, created new families. They themselves established their own camp institutions—schools and newspapers, theaters and political parties.

For the time they lived in Germany, they were the wards of the American army and of the JDC. They had to be housed, fed, clothed, cared for medically. While others saw to their basic wants, it was our task in JDC's education and cultural departments to provide texts, pencils, and composition books for the children in the camp schools, newsprint for the camp newspapers, books for camp libraries, art supplies, musical instruments, sheet music, records, and resources for cultural activities.

Soon after liberation, a group of Jewish survivors had set up a series of local historical commissions in the expectation that they could supply evidence to upcoming trials of German war criminals. These commissions undertook to gather testimonies of the terrible experiences which the Jews had endured under the Germans. They hoped thereby to create and preserve the historical record of how the Germans had murdered the European Jews. In Munich, a handful of survivors from Poland and Lithuania established the Central Historical Commission to advise and encourage the amateur historical societies in collecting and recording testimonies and to coordinate their work. The commission even published a journal, *Fun letstn khurbn,* "Out of Our Most Recent Catastrophe."

The men who organized the Central Historical Commission became my friends. I was able to help them, using the resources of the JDC and even of the United States Army, from whom we obtained the use of a Linotype machine on which to set their journal. It turned out to be in the very plant that had published the official Nazi paper, the *Völkischer Beobachter.*

The Central Historical Commission and its affiliates gathered thousands of eyewitness testimonies. After the commission's staff emigrated, their archive of testimonies was desposited with Yad Vashem in Jerusalem.

Working in occupied Germany among the survivors was an emotional experience, but for me the most intense personal drama involved the remnants of the YIVO library which had been found in Frankfurt. My work for the JDC had brought me into contact with the Offenbach Archival Depot, which operated under the Restitution Branch of OMGUS's Economics Division. There, at Offenbach, just across the river from Frankfurt, in an enormous warehouse that had belonged to the I. G. Farben chemical-industrial enterprises, were now located the Jewish books, archives, and ceremonial objects which the Germans had seized from Jews all over Europe. Now the American military authorities were trying to return these treasures to their rightful owners as rapidly as they could.

Many months before I had come, Professor Pinson had borrowed from the Offenbach depot a few thousand nonvaluable books—Yiddish fiction and other popular works—for use in the camp libraries. As JDC education officer, it became my task to follow up on that arrangement. But soon I became involved in the restitution of the YIVO library.

When I first arrived in February 1947 at the Offenbach Archival Depot, a considerable portion of YIVO property had already been identified. But in the course of my work for JDC, we found a great deal more among the 300,000 or so still-unidentified books and archival materials. As a consequence of that discovery, I asked for, and eventually received, permission from the JDC to work at Offenbach to complete the identification of YIVO property. I stayed there until June, when my work was successfully completed and I witnessed the removal from the depot of some 420 cases of books and archives to the YIVO Institute in New York.

That experience was for me like a dream come true. All through the war years I had been obsessed by recurring fantasies that I might find, even rescue, some of my lost Vilna friends. Finally, I had, in a very tangible way, rescued a part of Vilna, even if it consisted just of inanimate objects—books, mere pieces of paper, the tatters and shards of a civilization.

But in the course of my melancholy work, I also learned that one could not restore the murdered past to life. One could never put Vilna together again. I came to realize that all we can ever do is to remember and, each according to his ability, to create out of our memories lasting monuments of remembrance—poems and stories, memoirs and history. It is the only way through which the past, irrevocably destroyed, can survive.

— 3 —

IN BERLIN
AGAIN

I n October 1985 I went to Berlin for the third time in my life.
My first visit, on Sunday, August 27, 1939, had lasted barely
two hours. I had arrived by train from Warsaw and was en route
to Copenhagen. The date was not notable or memorable, except that
it happened to be just four days after Vyacheslav Molotov and Joachim
von Ribbentrop, to the shock of the whole world, had signed a nonaggression pact between the Soviet Union and National Socialist
Germany. No one knew it then, but only four days later the Germans
would invade Poland.

My train pulled into the Schlesischer Bahnhof. Cannons were
mounted at the entrance to the station, trained on the tracks. Everywhere within sight was an endless sea of soldiers and Nazi flags, with
the equipage of war—cavalry, tanks, cannons—rising like heavy
swells above the human tide. My taxi had to inch its way to reach
the Stattner station on the other side of Berlin.

Notwithstanding the protection of my American passport and the
bravado of youth, I was frightened by the massive German military
presence. The atmosphere was thick with swagger, bluster, and bul-
lying. Despair tempered my rage against the Germans. One did not
need to be a political expert to know that war was inevitable, or a
military expert to know that Poland was no match for Germany.

Those two hours in Berlin were my only firsthand encounter with National Socialist Germany.

The second time I came to Berlin was in February 1947. Now I wore an American army uniform whose blue-and-white chevrons with the letters AJDC identified me as an officer with the American Joint Distribution Committee, the leading Jewish relief organization. The JDC then operated in the American and British zones of occupied Germany under the aegis of the United Nations Relief and Rehabilitation Agency (UNRRA). Its task was to care for the Jewish displaced persons, the survivors of Hitler's war against the Jews.

Berlin was not my regular station, but JDC business took me there. As everywhere in Germany, I photographed with grim satisfaction the ruins and wreckage that survived as monuments to Hitler's Thousand-Year Reich. It was especially gladdening to me to photograph Berlin, for the devastation there had been even more massive than in Frankfurt or Munich. The rage against the Germans which agitated every fiber in my body was released at the felicific vistas of burned-out hulks of buildings, tottering skeletons of houses, the shards and rubble to which the Third Reich had been reduced.

My work for JDC often brought me into contact with Germans, from whom I needed to get services and materials so that we could provide the necessary educational and cultural supplies to the Jewish survivors. As if on cue, every German I encountered, without exception, in an unvarying and predictable routine, volunteered that he knew nothing about the murder of the Jews. All swore innocence; none had ever been a National Socialist. They were as craven in defeat as they had been insolent in victory. I liked to watch them scrounge and scramble for cast-off American cigarette butts.

At the end of 1947, when I had completed my service with the JDC, I returned home to New York. I never again visited Germany until October 1985. For forty years I had never bought German products. Some people I knew still believed in the existence of that "other" Germany, the Germany of Goethe, Schiller, Kant, and Bach. But for me there was only one—the Germany of Hitler, Himmler, and Heydrich, the Germany that had conceived, planned, organized, and carried out the systematic murder of six million European Jews, the Germany that had turned Europe into a vast Jewish necropolis.

Why, then, did I return to Berlin almost forty years later?

The occasion was a scholarly conference about the life of the Jews in National Socialist Germany in the years between 1933 and 1939. It was organized by the Leo Baeck Institute (LBI), which in the thirty years of its existence has dedicated itself to preserving, through research and publication, the historical past of German-speaking Jewry. By traveling to Berlin for its first public and collective appearance in Germany, the LBI hoped to tell the Germans how the Jewish community had responded to the persecution which the German dictatorship had unloosed against it. This return of the Jewish exiles, refugees, and survivors of National Socialist Germany to confront the Germans with that terrible past seemed to me a momentous occasion, a minidrama of Jewish history. And so I was disposed to have a part in it, at least as a witness.

Yet the very thought of returning to Germany unnerved me. I feared that spoken German would grate on my ears with the resonance of Nazi-*Deutsch*. I feared I would encounter Germans old enough to have been Nazi party members, to have relished the anti-Semitic propaganda in the *Völkischer Beobachter* and *Der Stürmer*, to have set a torch to a Jewish synagogue in 1938, to have volunteered for action in an *Einsatzgruppe* to murder Jews in Eastern Europe, to have joined an SS Death's-Head unit administering Zyklon B in a death camp.

A young friend, no doubt disapproving of my indecisiveness, suggested that I was mired in the past, unresponsive to contemporary realities. "Why not take a look at Berlin today?" he asked. "It stands at the center of Europe, at a crossroads of East and West." And so I decided to go, to try to see the place not only through the lens of the past but for what it is today.

Long before I set foot in Berlin I was preoccupied by the problem of reconciling past and present. How could I be an objective observer in the land of the murderers of the Jews? Could I ever forget that wherever I walked, I trod on ashes?

Unexpectedly, West Berlin's cityscape came to my aid. Right after I checked into my hotel I went to have a look at downtown Berlin. I walked to the Kurfürstendamm, that broad boulevard with its department stores, boutiques, movie houses, pubs, cafés displaying an abundance of pastries. It was a gloomy overcast Sunday afternoon, with a chill in the air, yet the street was alive with people, noisy with traffic and human voices, bright with lights and the glare of neon advertisements atop the buildings. Nearly everything looked contemporary, built of steel and glass, shiny and glittery.

Unlike other European cities, West Berlin offers few relics of its historical past for the sightseer to explore. The extensive Allied bombings, beginning in 1940 in retaliation for the London blitz and accelerating thereafter into the major strikes in February 1945, destroyed much of the center. Then came the intensive Soviet artillery barrages, followed by street-by-street fighting, which reduced much of what is now West Berlin to a vast stretch of rubble. Even the trees are postwar plantings, for the Battle of Berlin left the earth parched and scorched. As West Berlin was being rebuilt, many rickety structures of earlier times were bulldozed out of existence.

The division of the city between East and West further contributed to the erasing of the architectural past. In August 1961, in response to the massive flight of Germans from the East, the Communists erected the infamous twenty-nine-mile-long wall along the boundary lines, with its few heavily guarded crossing points. The construction of the wall soon brought changes also in the landscape on the western side. Many old buildings near the wall were torn down and on their site several spectacular buildings have been erected that form an emerging cultural center.

Back on the Kurfürstendamm, the flow of vehicular traffic was ceaseless. The sidewalks were crowded with promenaders, window-shoppers, girl-watchers, mostly young people strolling in couples or in small groups. They were, from their appearance, a varied lot—sporting fur coats or leather jackets, punk hair styles or cropped cuts,

41

boots or high heels, jeans or heavy winter skirts. Following them, eavesdropping, I felt like a voyeur.

What I expected to see or hear I can't now imagine. But it was the youthfulness of the crowds that disconcerted and even disoriented me. These were not the Germans I had expected to confront. All of them were obviously born after 1945 and most were probably born after the Berlin Wall was erected. They were ordinary young people, too young to be charged with the burden of Germany's terrible history. They were not the ghosts of the Nazi past.

Perhaps it is only in Berlin that one gets this sense of discontinuity. There, indeed, it is nothing new. As far back as 1821 Heine wrote that it was very difficult to see ghosts in Berlin: "The town contains so little of old days, and it is so new. . . ." So little has remained of many old neighborhoods that one hears the same anecdotes repeated time and again about exiles and refugees who have returned to Berlin to look for their childhood homes and cannot find them. Sometimes even the streets have changed beyond recognition or even disappeared.

Still, there are buildings that have remained intact, that go back even before World War I. They are massive, solidly constructed, with exterior architectural ornaments of the kind that builders can no longer afford. The windows are high and wide, bespeaking spacious high-ceilinged apartments. Walking on such a street, I heard a piano being played. Suddenly I felt the presence of ghosts. I imagined that once upon a time, a prosperous Jewish family lived there. I could see the heavy Biedermeier furniture, the large dining-room table, the china closet with its fine pieces, the dark velvet drapes and portières. In the parlor, at the piano, the teenage daughter of the household, a Shulamith with dark braids and a white pinafore, was practicing her scales.

Who lives in that house now and whose golden-haired daughter Margarete practices her scales there now? Who appropriated the furniture, the piano, and the household effects after the Jewish owners were deported? Antique dealers in Berlin, so I was told, are now buying up the backlog of stolen Jewish property that had been stashed away for decades, and are said to be getting good prices for old prints, fine art, silver, china, and porcelain figurines.

Among West Berlin's surviving remnants, mute testimony to worse times gone by, surely the most dramatic is what is left of the old Kaiser-Wilhelm-Gedächtniskirche (Kaiser Wilhelm's Memorial Church) just off the Kurfürstendamm on Breitscheidplatz. A neo-Romanesque church built in 1895 to memorialize Wilhelm I, it is now a hollow shell, its once proud tower a broken stump. The Berliners decided to preserve this ruin as a memorial to the havoc and horror of war. What Germans think, as they strain to penetrate the darkness of the gutted church, I don't know. Perhaps they reflect bitterly on the Allied bombing—or perhaps, remembering the past or what they learned of the past, they ponder the destruction which National Socialist Germany unloosed on all Europe.

But when one enters the *new* Kaiser-Wilhelm-Gedächtniskirche, an austerely modern octagonal structure erected alongside the old one, there is no doubting what one remembers and on what one meditates. On the back wall, to the left of the entrance, is a thirteenth-century Spanish sculpture of the Crucifixion, spare and sorrowful. It is dedicated "To the Evangelical Martyrs: In the Years 1933–1945."

The next day I went sightseeing. My guide was a *Gymnasium* teacher of history and literature, a young German from the Rhineland, obsessed with the history of his people, with the Nazi past. He takes his students to visit the synagogue on Pestalozzistrasse, which was destroyed in November 1938 but has since been restored. He shows them the sights he showed me.

Our first stop was in suburban Berlin, long a fashionable lakeside resort with lovely beaches and promenades. It is still an elegant neighborhood. We stopped on a quiet street, Am Grossen Wannsee, where the privacy of the houses and their fine grounds is secured by stone walls and iron gates. The day was gray and drizzly; the street was strewn with fallen yellow leaves. No one was about. At number 56–58 we read the memorial plaque embedded in the exterior wall:

In diesem Haus fand im Januar 1942 die berücktigte Wannsee-Konferenz statt.

*Dem Gedenken der durch Nationalsozialistische Gewaltherrschaft um-
gekommenen Jüdische Mitmenschen.*

[In this building in January 1942 the infamous Wannsee Conference took place.

In memory of Jewish fellow men murdered by National Socialist
despotism.]

Here, in this secluded villa, once known as the Polizei-Palais, Reinhard Heydrich, second to Heinrich Himmler in the SS, convened the
Wannsee Conference. They were altogether fifteen at this meeting,
counting Heydrich and his assistant Adolf Eichmann, and they represented the second-command level of the state ministries and of the
Nazi party's ideological and killing apparatus. The main item on the
agenda was how to coordinate the efforts of the various agencies
involved in carrying out the murder of the Jews. They did not call it
murder; they used the code name, "The Final Solution of the Jewish
Question." The meeting lasted less than two hours, after which drinks
and lunch were served.

The minutes of that meeting, which Eichmann prepared, were
found among the mountains of documents retrieved by the Allies from
the rubble of the Third Reich. Those minutes were used by the prosecution in the trial of the major German war criminals in Nuremberg
and later at Eichmann's trial in Jerusalem. They were vital evidence
in the effort to document how Hitler's Germany had planned, organized, and carried out the murder of the Jews.

Nowadays the building at Am Grossen Wannsee 56–58 is used for
more beneficent purposes, but the gate was locked and no one answered the bell. All we could do was look through the iron grates.
The house was set back about a hundred feet from the gate, but its
porticoed entrance was clearly visible at the end of an arbored drive-
way. It was elegant and serene, enshrouded in silence. I visualized the
sleek black limousines driving in, the chauffeurs opening the car doors
for their prestigious passengers, saluting. I pictured the conferees

44

emerging from the cars, stiff and erect in their black uniforms and polished boots, walking toward the portico. There, I suppose, Eichmann stood, waiting to greet his guests.

It was an eerie exercise in imagination, for this quiet house betrayed no sign of the evil function it once served. It was merely a building whose appearance was incongruous with its history. It was no memorial site for the six million murdered Jews, nor was it haunted by their ghosts. Like the tormented dead of ancient legends, the six million never rest in any one place, but are present everywhere the record of history is preserved.

Later we went to Levetzowstrasse, at the corner of Jagowstrasse, in Moabit, a middle-class residential neighborhood that reminded me of streets in Queens in New York City. Jews had lived in this section of Berlin and at this corner the Levetzowstrasse synagogue once stood. It had been burned during the *Kristallnacht* pogrom in November 1938, but in 1941 it served as a *Sammellager*, an assembly camp, from which the Jews of Berlin were deported. In October 1941, when they began to be rounded up, they were brought here, to Levetzowstrasse. From this assembly camp they were taken to the Moabit railroad station just nearby. The trains then brought them to the ghettos of Lodz, Riga, and Minsk. In 1942, when the gassing facilities at Auschwitz had been put into operation, the train transports went directly to the camp. In time, additional assembly points were set up in other places in Berlin. Altogether, sixty-three death transports left from Berlin with over 35,000 Jews.

A playground now occupies the site of the Levetzowstrasse synagogue, but a plaque has been erected which memorializes the synagogue's destruction and the deportation of the Jews. At the Grünewald railroad station, another place from which Berlin Jews were deported, there is also a memorial tablet.

Afterward we went to Gedenkstätte Plötzensee, a prison and place of execution in northwest Berlin, now a somewhat macabre museum and also a memorial. "To the Victims of the Hitler Dictatorship in the Years 1933–1945." Here about 2,500 Berliners were hanged, some because a neighbor informed police that they had listened to forbidden

Allied broadcasts, others because they had belonged to underground resistance groups, still others because they had participated in the failed assassination attempt against Hitler on July 20, 1944. Busloads of schoolchildren are regularly brought here to study the documents on exhibit—the charges and verdicts of the Volksgericht (People's Court)—and to gape at the execution chamber. Plötzensee is also on the itinerary of Berlin tour buses.

To tell Plötzensee's ugly history, the Berlin Information Center has produced a thirty-two-page illustrated brochure in German, French, English, Spanish, and Turkish (for the substantial Turkish segment of Germany's foreign workers). Answering its own question—"Do we really want to know this today?"—the brochure refers to the horrible deeds committed by the SS. To illustrate, it cites the following passage from Himmler's speech to his top SS officers on October 4, 1943, surely one of the most grisly texts in the annals of National Socialist Germany:

I also want to make reference before you here, in complete frankness, to a really grave matter. Among ourselves, this once, it shall be uttered quite frankly; but in public we will never speak of it. . . . I am referring to the evacuation of the Jews, the annihilation of the Jewish people. This is one of those things that are easily said. "The Jewish people is going to be annihilated," says every party member. "Sure, it's in our program, elimination of the Jews, annihilation—we'll take care of it." And then they all come trudging, eighty million worthy Germans, and each one has his one decent Jew. Sure, the others are swine, but this one is an A-1 Jew. Of all those who talk this way, not one has seen it happen, not one has been through it. Most of you must know what it means to see a hundred corpses lie side by side, or five hundred, or a thousand. To have stuck this out and—excepting cases of human weakness—to have kept our integrity, that is what has made us hard. In our history, this is an unwritten and never-to-be-written page of glory. . . .

46

That evening the LBI opened its conference at the Otto-Braun-Saal of the Staatsbibliothek, an attractive auditorium in Berlin's architecturally stunning public research library. Many of the nearly five hundred seats were occupied by West Berlin's political dignitaries and notable intellectuals. The press and the TV cameras swarmed over the hall, especially to cover Helmut Kohl, chancellor of the Federal Republic, who was to address the conference. After the blunders of Bitburg in May 1985, his speech was awaited with curiosity, apprehension, and even hostility.

This time, the chancellor committed no blunders. Speaking in a low-keyed colorless drone that is, so I was told, his habitual form of address, he delivered a talk that was right and fitting. It may be said that he wanted to exploit this opportunity to speak to a Jewish audience, but with barely 5,000 Jews in West Berlin and fewer than 30,000 in all of West Germany, Kohl has no Jewish constituency to appeal to. He was in fact addressing not only the Jews in the hall but, through the television cameras and the press, his countrymen.

He began by welcoming the LBI's decision to meet in Berlin, and then he said:

Never can we undo the injustice and evil of the past. But we can, we must, and we want to ponder it—what happened, how it came to happen, and how we must try to master it. And from this we must draw a lesson for the future.

He then unfolded a minihistory of National Socialist Germany's assault against the Jews, starting with the boycott of Jewish businesses on April 1, 1933, and continuing date by date, episode by episode, to the terrible end. It was an elementary lesson in history, unimaginative, unreflective, impersonal. When he completed his mournful chronicle, he said: "We are ashamed as Germans, because the National Socialist crimes were committed in the German name. We are

47

ashamed as human beings. . . ." Kohl's talk was carried by all German television stations and reported in the press all over Germany. *

To be sure, the passages I have quoted have the ring of ceremonial public rhetoric, of a kind to which no weight is given, especially not in a nation founded by Otto von Bismarck, who once declared that "the great questions of the time are not decided by speeches and majority decisions . . . but by iron and blood." Nevertheless, public rhetoric reflects political reality and civic values. Even in Weimar, no political leader would have ventured publicly to come to the defense of the Jews.

Later in the week, after the conference had ended, I continued my tour of Berlin. I began with an exhibition at the Staatsbibliothek, cosponsored with the LBI, "In the Catacombs: Jewish Publishers in Germany, 1933–1938." Mounted by the Deutsche Literaturarchiv of Marburg, largely from its own holdings, the exhibit depicted how Jewish publishers coped with the restrictions and limitations which the Nazis imposed on them. The glass cases displaying the Jewish books, journals, and papers issued in those terrible times, with photographs of the publishers, their authors, and accompanying documents, formed a wide circle around the large room. On the walls themselves were hung reproductions of the contemporary German press, with its virulent and still-intimidating anti-Semitic headlines, some of them in heavy red ink, and poster-sized enlargements of official National Socialist laws and regulations against the Jewish community, and especially against Jewish publishers and writers. The very arrangement—the wall displays surrounding, encircling the glass cases—conveyed the sense of siege under which Jewish publishers and writers lived and worked in National Socialist Germany so long as they were permitted to live.

Afterward I explored the spacious Staatsbibliothek. I looked up my name in the catalogue and found several of my books, including the

---

* As far as I know, except for a brief piece I wrote for the *Wall Street Journal,* no American newspapers carried an account of these proceedings, nor did any Jewish press service here, in England, or in Israel.

original English and the German translation of *The War Against the Jews 1933–1945.* I looked up other Jewish historians. Their works were all in the library. Then I came upon the exhibition room of the Mendelssohn Archive, which, I learned, is a collection on which the Staatsbibliothek's music department especially prides itself. The archive includes not only the compositions and papers of Felix Mendelssohn Bartholdy, but also documents, art work, and artifacts of the whole Mendelssohn family, going back to Felix's grandfather, Moses Mendelssohn. In 1979, on the occasion of the 250th anniversary of his birth, the Staatsbibliothek had mounted an impressive exhibit, "Moses Mendelssohn: His Life and Work," whose catalogue is still in print.

From the Staatsbibliothek I walked to the Reichstag. The route goes along the Berlin Wall,* from Potsdamer Platz past the Brandenburg Gate, on Ebertstrasse, named for the first president of the German republic. Since the Communists first erected the Wall in 1961, they have massively reinforced it. The Wall's function is not to keep Westerners out of East Berlin but to lock the Easterners in. In this respect it is now virtually unassailable, standing thirteen feet high, topped by oversize concrete tubing whose diameter is much too wide for any handhold. Behind the wall lies a 160-foot no-man's-land of concrete and grassy plots. It is not entirely a wasteland, for it is enlivened, so to speak, by watchtowers, tank traps, patrol dogs, searchlights, and a sixteen-foot-deep ditch. To ensure that the Wall is escape-proof, the eastern side of the no-man's-land is further secured by an electrified fence.

In contrast to the watchtowers and armed guards on the eastern side, the West Berlin authorities have provided on their side observation platforms for tourists who want to look over the Wall into East Berlin. Kiosks at Postdamer Platz sell postcards and souvenirs of the Wall. Wherever it is accessible, the west side of the Wall is scribbled with graffiti, some of them like the graffiti in the New York subways,

---

*The present essay was published in 1986, three years before the destruction of the Berlin Wall and the events leading to the unification of Germany.—ED.

but some political—*Weg mit dem roten Nazi-Regime* (Away with the red Nazi regime); *Wer Mauer, hat's not* (Who builds a wall, must need one). In my walk I passed an enormous graffito in red paint, each letter about three feet high, immortalizing John F. Kennedy's declamation *"Ich bin ein Berliner."* At several places simple memorials— wooden crosses, plaques, floral wreaths—marked the sites where people trying to flee from the East had been shot down. Since the Wall was first erected, seventy-two persons have been killed by the Communists for attempting to escape the prison that is East Germany.

The Reichstag stands literally with its back to the Wall, between Scheidemannstrasse, named for the first chancellor of the Weimar Republic, and the Spree, whose western bank demarcates the East-West border. One of Berlin's most imposing buildings, the Reichstag was first damaged in the fire of February 27, 1933, when its large assembly hall was gutted and its glass dome shattered. That fire, whose origins are still disputed by historians, gave Hitler's cabinet the excuse to impose emergency decrees suspending all the basic liberties which the Weimar constitution had guaranteed. When the Reichstag finally convened on March 23, 1933, it was in the Kroll Opera House, and there the Enabling Act was passed that gave Hitler the power to issue emergency legislation without recourse to the legislature. Hitler thereafter had little use for the Reichstag building.

During the Battle of Berlin in 1945, the Reichstag, at the very center of the shelling and fighting, was devastated. Its restoration began in 1957 and was completed in 1971. Except for the glass dome, which was not replaced, the exterior now looks as it did in 1894. Inside, however, except for assembly halls and conference rooms used occasionally by some ministries and legislative groups, the Reichstag has been converted into an enormous permanent exhibit entitled "Fragen an die deutsche Geschichte" (Questions Put to German History), which first opened in 1974. Since then, about 640,000 persons have visited the exhibit every year.

The exhibit combines the latest in audiovisual technology, stylish graphics, photography, and old-fashioned historical materials—dates, names, facts, statistics—to offer a survey course in German history from 1800 until the present. I chose to look at only two of the seven chronological sections—"The Weimar Republic: 1919–1933" and "The Third Reich: 1933–1945."

No museum show has ever gripped me so. Walking from one display to the next, I felt entrapped in a history which I was compelled to reexperience. Drawn into the maelstrom of that history, I moved from one display to the next as the past unfolded before my eyes with relentless inevitability. At times I was possessed by a surreal desire to stop the course of events, to turn it back, or freeze it where it was. But I continued on, a sleepwalker in the toils of a nightmare. I witnessed the unraveling of the Weimar Republic, the rise of the National Socialist party, the collapse of democracy, the mounting violence, the terror, the inexorable anti-Semitism.

The fate of the Jews ran as a thread through the exhibit—photographs, placards, charts. Then I came to a display with an enormous six-pointed yellow star superimposed on a map of Europe. It gave the statistics of the annihilation of the European Jews, country by country, totaling five to six million. The catalogue for the exhibit, 456 pages of texts, photographs, documents, diagrams, and maps, contained comparable material. One passage explained that the murder of the Jews, "like the attainment of *Lebensraum* for the 'German master race,' was an ultimate professed war aim."

Then I approached what seemed to be a cave, barely illuminated by the images on a small television screen. People leaned against the walls or sat on the floor in front of the screen. An unseen voice provided the running historical commentary for newsfilm clips of the Hitler era. As I entered, the speaker was describing the anti-Jewish program of the Hitler regime—the exclusion of the Jews from the civil service, the Nuremberg laws, *Kristallnacht*. The screen showed the synagogues of Germany going up in flames. The voice intoned these words: *"Und dann kommt der Krieg. Es war auch ein Krieg gegen die Juden"* ("And then came the war. It was also a war against the Jews").

The images continued to flicker on the screen, but I could no longer see them. My eyes were blurred by tears. I went out to find a corner where I might try to control myself but a wave of hysteria swept over me. The old rage returned. The six million Jewish dead could not be restored to life. No atonement was commensurate with the crime.

Back in the hotel, after my emotion had abated, I tried to sort out my feelings. The exhibit had released the tension building within me ever since I had arrived in Berlin. Though I knew and had long known that the National Socialist regime expired in the rubble which I so happily photographed in Berlin nearly forty years earlier, contemporary Germany nevertheless had no real presence for me, for my consciousness of Germany as National Socialist Germany totally preempted any other idea. What knowledge of postwar Germany I had accumulated over the years remained stored in a remote corner of my brain, unassimilated, undigested. No wonder I was discomposed by the acknowledgments of shame and guilt which I had encountered in public places and on public occasions.

I felt like a morbid Rip Van Winkle, awakened to a reality I had slept through all these years. Could I have really supposed that the Berlin of 1985 was a continuation of the Berlin of 1935? Could I have thought that the Germans on the street were the same Germans who had jeered at Jews on the streets of Berlin in 1938? Of course I did not believe that Germans were a killer species among the nations of the world, like the killer whale among mammals, a race whose murderous instincts were inbred and immutable, who killed and would always kill. (This is in fact what many Frenchmen used to think, as John Colville notes in his recently published wartime diaries, *The Fringes of Power*.) Yet though I did not believe in inborn German murderousness, I knew that German anti-Semitism had been an integral part of German society and its culture for centuries. I was skeptical that in my lifetime it could be eradicated.

There was another reason why I resisted the reality of contemporary Germany. Would not an acknowledgment that Nazi Germany is now a closed chapter in history mean, or be taken to mean, that the murder of the six million European Jews is similarly a closed chapter, to be stored away in the historical file cabinet? Does not such an admission sanction the lapse of memory into forgetfulness? But the parallel, I soon realized, was misleading, for the place of Nazi Germany in history is not the same as the place of the murder of the European Jews. One belongs to a transient past, the other to an enduring past.

Hitler's Germany lasted twelve years. It came into existence on January 30, 1933, supplanting the Weimar Republic, which then was relegated to the annals of the past. It, in turn, was supplanted by the two postwar Germanies. The entire edifice of National Socialist Germany, with all its political, social, and cultural institutions, disintegrated into the dust of the past. Except for the murder of the European Jews, Nazi Germany left no lasting heritage.

The perpetration of the murder of the six million European Jews occupied an even shorter stretch of time than the twelve years of Hitler's Germany, yet, as an event in history, it has no *terminus ad quem*. It did not cease to exist as a historical and moral reality, even when the killing ceased, nor was it supplanted by anything else. Its historicity belongs to the timeless present, like any fundamental scientific truth. One might say that the murder of the European Jews is forever lodged in history's throat. The murder of the European Jews may be compared to the destruction by the ancient Romans of the Temple in Jerusalem—both are historical events that have not receded into the past but continue to remain alive in human, and especially Jewish, consciousness—while the Hitler regime may be likened to the reign of Titus, a historical event that belongs only to the domain of the past.

Yet even conceding the pastness of Nazi Germany, how are we to resolve our nagging doubts about the survival, in other forms, of Nazism in Germany today? What of the former citizens of Hitler's Reich who are still what they once were—nationalists, militarists, racists, anti-Semites, who have not renounced their old ideas, prejudices, and habits? What influence have they had on their children and grandchildren? What potential do they provide for the reemergence of a murderous Germany?

For an answer we must turn once more to history, to chart the course of events in Germany over the last forty years. By looking backward from today to April 1945, when National Socialist Germany collapsed, we may hope to discern whether and to what degree Germany has changed from what it was.

Back in the 1950s, even into the 1960s, no one could yet tell whether Germany's collapse in 1945 had brought an end as well to those characteristics of German society that had shaped its politics and governments for over a century. Like many people I knew, I had little confidence that the short term would bring a lasting change. I used closely to scrutinize every anti-Semitic incident reported from Germany, to examine every utterance as if under a magnifying glass, in search of signs of that deadly disease which had caused the murder of six million Jews. But the longer perspective of forty years has made it easier to see that the great disjuncture in modern German history came not in 1933 with Hitler's advent as führer but in 1945, with the end of his dictatorship.

It was then, in 1945, that the course of German history changed. Three things happened to produce that change. First of all, defeat brought the Germans face to face at last with the unspeakable crimes their country had perpetrated. That confrontation was made possible when the Allied armies first came upon the camps with the dead piled high and the living nearly dead. Then the International Military Tribunal at Nuremberg, established by the victorious Allies, began its hearings in November 1945 with the trial of twenty-two major war criminals. Twelve subsequent trials were held before Nuremberg tribunals for a wide variety of war crimes—medical crimes, the murders committed by the *Einsatzgruppen*, the complicity of the state ministries and the armed services in war crimes, and the participation of industrialists in the exploitation of slave labor.

Public revelation of the immensity and monstrosity of Germany's crimes forced most Germans, whether they had once been enthusiastic Nazis, merely obedient citizens, or inner émigrés, to retreat into shame, guilt, and revulsion. Thomas Mann summed up that response in *Doctor Faustus*, through the words of his most sympathetic character:

Germany had become a thick-walled underground torture chamber, converted into one by a profligate dictatorship vowed to nihilism from its beginnings on. Now the torture chamber had been broken open, open lies our shame before the eyes of the world. Foreign commissions inspect those incredible photographs everywhere displayed, and tell their countrymen that what they have seen surpassed in horribleness anything the human imagination can conceive.

In those days there was much talk of Germany's "unmastered past"— as if such a past could then have been mastered.

Secondly, whether they tried to confront the past or to evade it, most Germans realized that their country had become the pariah of the nations, that everywhere in the world other peoples looked upon them as a nation of murderers, beyond the civilized pale. Even if they were not motivated by moral revulsion against the Nazi past, they knew that they had to make postwar Germany a different kind of country from prewar Germany.

Thirdly, the victorious Allies, especially the Americans, undertook to "reeducate" the Germans, to teach them the fundamentals of political democracy and the essentials of civil liberty. Already in 1945, the Allied occupiers, hoping to prepare for an independent and, in time, democratic postwar Germany, established "denazification courts" to try and to punish former Nazis. Those found guilty of substantial participation in Nazi institutions were sentenced to prison terms; less important Nazis were fined. Most were barred from political activity and excluded from employment in the public sector.

To be sure, denazification proceedings were not popular with Germans who wanted to gloss over the past. When, in 1946, the Americans turned over responsibility for these proceedings to the Germans themselves, the German public seemed more hostile to the denazifiers than to the former Nazis. Indeed, in the first decade after the war, the denazification courts amnestied many Nazis or quashed their cases. These unreconstructed Nazis tried to return to political life, to restore *their* good old days. Some began forming neo-Nazi parties. In 1949, in the first Bundestag elections in the newly constituted Federal Republic of Germany, several such parties managed to win a total of 9 percent of the vote, 37 seats out of 402. In those days, we were certain that renazification was a greater likelihood in Germany than denazification.

Potentially, the most dangerous of those neo-Nazi parties was the Socialist Reich party (SRP) in Lower Saxony, whose leaders were former Nazis, some of whom had been interned during the Allied occupation. One had openly defied the ban on his participating in any political activity. In 1951 the SRP received 11 percent of the vote in Lower Saxony, electing sixteen delegates to the state's legislature. Within the year, however, West Germany's government moved to have the party declared unconstitutional, on the ground that it was a successor organization to the Nazi party. Its followers then rallied to another neo-Nazi party, but three years later, in state elections in Lower Saxony, that party received less than 4 percent of the vote and soon after petered out.

Ten years later a new neo-Nazi party emerged, the National Democratic party of Germany (NPD), winning nearly 10 percent of votes in state elections in 1966. Yet this threat too fizzled out in 1969, when the party received less than 5 percent of the vote in the federal election, failing to win a single seat in the Bundestag. Since then, the neo-Nazis have barely mustered 1 percent of the vote in West Germany's communal, municipal, state, and Bundestag elections.

With the virtual disappearance of neo-Nazi parties, the era of anti-Semitism in German political history has come to an end. For the first time in over a century, German political parties no longer appeal for votes with anti-Semitic planks and programs.

Forty years is, in the long run, merely the twinkling of an eye. Nevertheless, it is a time span of generations. In those forty years, the Federal Republic of Germany has become a successful model of a democratic country. It has evolved a stable two-party system which has, in turn, produced stable governments. The government formed under Konrad Adenauer in 1949 stayed in power for seventeen years—

three years longer than the entire lifetime of Weimar. The government formed under Willy Brandt in 1969 stayed in power for thirteen years— one year longer than the entire lifetime of Hitler's Reich.

Unlike Weimar, the West German government has the support of the German people. Voter turnout has increased over the decades. In 1950, only 53 percent of respondents in a public-opinion poll thought it was better for a country to have several political parties than one, and as many as 24 percent actually favored a one-party system. In 1979, the responses to the same questions were, respectively, 90 percent and 4 percent. In 1955, only 30 percent of respondents expressed support for Germany's constitution; in 1978, 70 percent did so. Respect for civil liberties has increased too, though not to the same degree. *

Once the Federal Republic came into being in 1949, anti-Semitism lost its political legitimacy. Just then, however, a rash of anti-Semitic incidents erupted all over the country. But in a response unprecedented in German history, government officials, political-party leaders, church dignitaries, and intellectuals spoke out unequivocally. Chancellor Adenauer declared that "as Germans and Christians we have a duty to repair the wrongs committed against the Jews and strongly to oppose the anti-Semitic outbreaks."

Two years later, on September 27, 1951, Adenauer announced in the Bundestag his government's readiness to enter into negotiations with Israel and with representatives of Jews in the Diaspora regarding material reparations. "Unspeakable crimes," he said, "were perpetrated in the name of the German people which impose on us the obligation to make moral and material amends." In a year's time, agreements were concluded which provided for the payment of nearly $1 billion in reparations to Israel and to the Conference on Jewish Material Claims Against Germany, an organization representing Jewish communal organizations outside Israel.

---

*The best survey of German public opinion on these questions is Frederick Weil, "The Imperfectly Mastered Past: Anti-Semitism in West Germany Since the Holocaust," *New German Critique* 20 (Spring–Summer, 1980), pp. 135–153. It has been republished as a pamphlet by the Anti-Defamation League.

The sense of shame for the crimes of National Socialist Germany, the feeling of obligation to make amends for the past, and the political imperative to combat anti-Semitism in the present have been evident in the words and deeds of most of West Germany's political leaders over the last four decades.

It is true that exceptions upset the general practice. Some elected officials and party functionaries do occasionally speak in accents appropriate to National Socialist Germany. But their anti-Semitic remarks invariably elicit outraged counterstatements and eventually have to be retracted. Recently a spokesman for the Christian Social Union, the Bavarian wing of the Christian Democratic party, said that Jews show up "whenever money tinkles in German cash registers." Quickly the Christian Social Union dissociated itself from the words of its spokesman and he himself later had to apologize. Shortly thereafter the Christian Democratic mayor of a small town in North Rhine–Westphalia said that "a few rich Jews"should be slaughtered in order to balance the town's budget. He was pressured by the CDU to resign.

Both incidents, widely reported and nationally discussed, prompted a debate in the Bundestag on the danger of recurrent anti-Semitism. A few days later, at a ceremony marking Brotherhood Week, organized by the Association for Christian-Jewish Cooperation in Bonn, Richard von Weizsäcker, West Germany's president, in an appeal to world Jewish public opinion, apologized for the anti-Semitic remarks.

Some eighty-nine extremist right-wing organizations still operate in West Germany. Altogether they have about 22,100 members, of whom 6,100 belong to the NPD, still the largest neo-Nazi group. But anti-Semitism no longer shapes public policy or government action. Indeed, in order to constrain neo-Nazi propaganda which denies that National Socialist Germany ever murdered six million European Jews (popularly known as the "Auschwitz lies"), the Bundestag last year enacted legislation making that denial punishable by law.

No one can deny that anti-Semitism remains a disturbing presence in Germany, the more disturbing precisely because it is Germany. But it expresses itself primarily, as elsewhere in the West, in personal attitudes, opinions, and feelings. Countless polls and surveys seek to elicit the German public's attitudes toward Jews, their feelings about Hitler and National Socialism, and the level of their commitment to democratic institutions. Here are some of their findings. In 1954, a survey showed that 15 percent of Germans "would vote for a man like Hitler"; in 1961, only 5 percent said they would. In 1962, a public-opinion poll conducted among Germans aged sixteen to eighteen asked whether some Jews had only themselves to blame for what happened to them during the Hitler era. Sixteen percent replied in the affirmative. More than twenty years later, only 5 percent said yes to the same question. Most Germans, when asked about their sympathies in Middle Eastern matters, if they have an opinion at all, are favorably inclined toward Israel. Only a small percentage has pro-Arab sympathies.

From the welter of polls and statistics one concludes, first, that a substantial segment of Germans—anywhere from 15 to 30 percent of the population—still harbors anti-Semitic attitudes, some overt, some latent, and, second, that with each passing decade the proportion of anti-Semitic responses declines. Predictably, anti-Jewish prejudice remains stronger among older and less educated Germans, among those who are the survivors of National Socialism, and among those who were not raised and educated in the changed political milieu of the Federal Republic.

While younger Germans are less susceptible to the traditional anti-Semitic sterotypes, pockets of them have succumbed to other variants. "Skinheads," lower-class unemployed young people, given to violence and driven by resentment, direct their rage against the Jews who—so they think—have everything they do not. In Germany this variant is also known as *"Fussball"* anti-Semitism because it has erupted at soccer games; when fortified by beer, skinheads scream vicious anti-Semitic slogans at the opposing team.

More visible than skinhead anti-Semitism among younger Germans is the anti-Semitism of the Left, which turns up in the media and the arts. It is also politically more mischievous, concentrating as it does on hatred of Israel and Zionism in the familiar strains of the propaganda one associates with the UN, the Third World, and the Soviet Union.

During a recent debate in the Frankfurt City Council, an SPD faction leader denounced Menachem Begin as "a murderer, fascist, and terrorist." Like the anti-Semites of the Right, he later apologized.

Borrowing from Soviet anti-Semitism, the German Left likes to compare Israel with National Socialist Germany, while assigning to the Palestinian Arabs the role of the Jewish victims. In East Berlin, that is everyday propaganda. (There, even the murder of the European Jews is a nonsubject.) One might have thought that in West Germany, intellectuals would know enough history to see the Nazi-Israel comparison as a species of gallows humor. Alas, they do not. Wolfgang Bergmann's film *Schatten der Zukunft* (Shadow of the Future), which has been shown on prime-time German television, is dead serious in presenting this "version" of the Israel-Arab conflict.

Like their counterparts elsewhere, German left-wing anti-Semites often claim that they are "only" anti-Zionist, "only" criticizing Israel. Their real complaint, however, is that "normal" anti-Semitism is taboo in Germany, and that they cannot make anti-Semitic remarks without being accused of wanting to put Jews in gas chambers. Their anti-Semitism, in other words, takes the form of an openly expressed resentment at the fact that they are not permitted to be anti-Semitic.

The most notorious example of Left anti-Semitism in Germany has been the late Rainer Werner Fassbinder's play *Garbage, City, and Death*, whose aborted production in Frankfurt on October 31, 1985, set off a loud controversy. Fassbinder had dramatized a novel by Gerhard Zwerenz, a best-selling left-wing writer, which had itself provoked charges of anti-Semitism when it appeared in 1973 on account of its ugly pornographic portrayal of a greedy and unscrupulous Jew. In Fassbinder's version, the anti-Semitism is even more blatant. The Jewish real-estate speculator has no name or personal identity; he is called, Brechtian-style, "The Rich Jew." His parents were murdered in the gas chambers, and the characters in the play think it a shame that he was not murdered as well. One of them puts it this way:

He sucks us dry, the Jew does. He drinks our blood and puts us in the wrong because he's a Jew and we are guilty. . . . But the

Jew is guilty, for he makes us guilty, just because he's here. If he'd stayed where he came from or if they had gassed him, I could sleep better today. They forgot to gas him. That's no joke. That's how I think inside me.

Like Fassbinder's characters, the Germans who cannot come to terms with National Socialist crimes want desperately to forget them. Consequently, the evocation of the Nazi past has unloosed among them an anti-Semitic temper that cuts across generational lines and political differences. Germans who cannot stand to remember the past, who resent having to feel guilty about it, blame the Jews for keeping it alive. Such feelings, which have now become overt, surfaced most visibly during the Bitburg episode.

But blaming the Jews for keeping alive the memory of National Socialist crimes is, like other anti-Semitic charges, a canard. In Germany that memory is preserved by other Germans, those for whom remembrance of the past is a form of expiation for the crimes committed by their country, by their fathers and grandfathers. It is *their* way of coming to terms with themselves. Germans, not Jews, marked the fortieth anniversary of *Kristallnacht* in the Federal Republic by commemorative gatherings, silent marches, radio and TV programs, and religious services. An estimated twenty million West Germans and Berliners saw the American TV film *Holocaust* on German regional television in 1979. (Polls taken at the time reported that 68 percent of the viewers responded favorably.) Just lately, hundreds of West Berliners crowded into a theater for the premiere of Claude Lanzmann's nine-and-a-half hour documentary, *Shoah*.

The interest in things Jewish expresses itself in many ways among Germans who wish to master their past. Thousands, for instance, belong to local societies for Christian-Jewish Cooperation, an organization which conducts educational activities among young Germans. Hundreds of thousands have visited Israel. After the United States and Israel, Germany is one of the largest publishers of serious books on Jewish subjects—even books about the murder of the European

Jews. Lectures and courses about Jewish history and culture sponsored by Jewish institutions attract nearly as many Germans as Jews. The Jüdische Gemeinde in Berlin, for instance, offers an extensive adult-education program, which, several board members told me, Germans attend in large numbers.

In 1963, the city of Cologne mounted a major exhibit, "Monumenta Judaica," depicting two thousand years of Jewish history on the Rhine. It was opened by then–Bundestag President Eugen Gerstenmaier and it attracted tens of thousands of visitors from all over Germany. Last November the Berlinische Galerie presented an exhibit of German-Jewish art which had been collected by the Leo Baeck Institute in New York. The reviewer for *Der Tagesspiegel*, Berlin's most respected newspaper, wrote of this exhibit:

If someone should ask what we [Germans] lack today—intellectually, culturally, in terms of human decency and cultural history—I would point to the row of paintings here. . . . This is doubtless the most important cultural-historical exhibit that Berlin has confronted since the war. It displays a major portion of that intellectual substance that was cold-bloodedly murdered, while the city silently tolerated it. . . . One leaves the exhibit with a mixture of shame, shamefacedness, rage, and historical admiration.

The desire on the part of Germans to learn more about Jews and Jewish civilization is, it seems to me, a form of moral education. It is as if, by acquiring rational knowledge and a firmer grasp on the historical reality of Jews and Judaism, they might thereby hope to exorcise the demonic image of the Jew which Nazi propaganda implanted in the German consciousness.

This, finally, is what I came to see in my third visit to Berlin.

2

IN PURSUIT

OF TRUTH

4

HOW THEY TEACH
THE HOLOCAUST

A scandal erupted in 1988 when the United States Department of Education rejected an application for a $70,000 grant to disseminate *Facing History and Ourselves*, a privately produced curriculum to teach junior-high-school students about the Holocaust. It seems that an outside reviewer for the department had criticized the curriculum for failing to present the viewpoints of the Nazis and the Ku Klux Klan. Though the department denied that its decision had been determined by the outside reviewer—or, as the curriculum's supporters charged, by the negative opinion of the conservative activist Phyllis Schlafly—Congressman Ted Weiss (New York) invoked his status as the son of Jewish refugees from Nazism to air the matter before his congressional subcommittee. After hearing testimony from the author of *Facing History*, who was also the executive director of the foundation distributing it, the subcommittee concluded that "the peer-review process had been subverted by opponents of Holocaust education."

During the ensuing controversy, in which charges of right-wing conspiracy and anti-Semitic intent were hurled at the Department of Education, the editor of an educational newsletter invited me to write a piece defending *Facing History*. I never did so, for my own reading of the curriculum persuaded me that the Department of Education had ample reason to turn down the grant application. Putatively a curriculum to teach the Holocaust, *Facing History* was also a vehicle for instructing thirteen-year-olds in civil disobedience and indoctrinating them with propaganda for nuclear disarmament.

My unexpected finding shocked me and aroused my curiosity. How, in fact, *was* the history of the murder of the European Jews being handled in secondary schools in the United States? The decentralized nature of the American educational system makes it very difficult to find out in exactly how many districts the subject is taught, what precisely is taught, for how long a period, or with what effect. What we do know is that, for an event of such historical magnitude and moral import, the Holocaust as a subject has yet to earn a full place in secondary-school education.

Of course, history itself is under general beleaguerment in the secondary schools. A 1988 survey by the Bradley Commission found that at least half the students in elementary and secondary schools do not study any world history or Western civilization at all. Today, fewer than twenty states require more than the usual one year of American history for graduation. Instead of history, most schools now offer a subject called "global studies" or "world civilizations," an omnium-gatherum of pop anthropology, sociology, geography, history, and art appreciation, characterized by one historian as a "globe-trotting survey of dozens of societies on every continent."

History is also being squeezed out to make room for subject matter demanded by special-interest groups. Blacks have called for teaching about the role of blacks in American history and culture, and Hispanics, Native Americans, and women have followed suit, giving rise to what has irreverently been labeled "oppression studies." The original psychological rationale for these studies—that they would foster pupils' self-esteem—has now been superseded by an ideological rationale which preaches the equality of all cultures and attacks the "hegemony" of Western civilization and its "Eurocentric" character. In either case, the time and space that could be devoted to studying the murder of the European Jews shrink even more. And lobbying efforts by Holocaust survivors, which intentionally or not often reinforce the impression that the Holocaust is nothing more than the

Jewish branch of oppression studies, cannot always compete with other more fashionable or better organized "causes."

There has also been outright opposition to teaching about the murder of the European Jews. Back in 1977, when the New York City Board of Education introduced its own curriculum for a mandatory unit called *The Holocaust: A Study of Genocide*, M. T. Mehdi, head of the American Arab Relations Committee, decried it as "an attempt by the Zionists to use the city educational system for their evil propaganda purposes." The president of the German-American Committee for Greater New York said, "It creates a bad atmosphere toward German-Americans in this country" and added that "there is no real proof that the Holocaust actually did happen." The New York Association of Black Educators objected on the grounds that the topic was irrelevant to black students. In Philadelphia, where preparations were under way to introduce a similar course, a Lutheran minister worried that the schools were not teaching other instances of genocide; besides, the Holocaust curriculum made it appear "that genocide was a Teutonic phenomenon." Early this year, parents of a student in a suburban Chicago junior high school protested against such instruction on the ground that the Holocaust was a "myth."

Still, despite indifference and opposition, the history of the murder of the European Jews *is* gradually being given some place in the secondary-school curriculum. As far as I have been able to ascertain, it is now incorporated in the "Global Studies" or "World Cultures" courses of at least seven state education departments (California, Connecticut, Illinois, New Jersey, New York, Ohio, Pennsylvania), and in the curricula of many large-city boards of education (Atlanta, Baltimore, Des Moines, Los Angeles, Milwaukee, Minneapolis, New York City, Philadelphia, Pittsburgh) and of many dozens, perhaps even hundreds, of local boards, mostly in suburban communities of large cities. Studied in the context of totalitarianism in Europe (Nazism, fascism, and communism) and of World War II, and sometimes also as part of the American history curriculum for the period, the subject is commonly offered in grade 10 (age fifteen), occasionally in grade

11. Some schools teach the subject as early as middle-school grades 8 and 9 (ages thirteen and fourteen).

The teaching unit ranges from two to ten periods, or longer if student interest warrants. In New York State, where instruction is mandatory, the Regents high-school examinations in Global Studies (formerly Social Studies) and in American History, which students are required to pass for graduation, regularly include one question on the subject.

Most school boards or departments of education produce their own curricula, which develop material briefly sketched in world-history textbooks. (These days the textbooks adopted by major school systems usually contain a couple of pages about the Holocaust, though the information may not always be coherent or even correct.) Course outlines are organized into teaching units, supplemented with teaching aids, and fleshed out with reading materials consisting largely of bowdlerized borrowings from books, magazines, and newspapers. Curricula produced for use in individual schools are usually little more than a batch of mimeographed pages stapled together, while big-city or statewide curricula are more elaborate products of committees, consultants, review boards, graphic designers, and printing presses.*

School districts sometimes provide training programs to familiarize their teachers with the new course material. Schools and teachers can also avail themselves of outside resources. Social Studies School Service, a commercial company, distributes a "World History" catalogue with five pages of listings of books and videocassettes on Hitler, Nazism, the Holocaust, and genocide—twice as many as those on the French Revolution. The company also issues a thirty-two-page catalogue, *Teaching the Holocaust: Resources and Materials*, a macabre cornucopia of books at all grade levels, curricula, teaching guides, atlases, charts, videocassettes, sound filmstrips, photo aids, posters, simulation games, crossword puzzles, cartoon assignments, and quizzes.

Teachers can also make use of Jewish institutional resources. Ac-

---

*As a basis for this essay I collected twenty-five curricula, itemized in the Appendix at the end of the chapter.

cording to the U.S. Holocaust Memorial Council in Washington, there are no fewer than nineteen Holocaust museums in the United States, forty-eight resource centers, thirty-four archival facilities, twelve memorials, and twenty-six research institutes.

The twenty-five curricula I have examined undertake to do two things: first, to give pupils basic information and, second, to provide appropriate moral education. They are better at the first task than at the second, and better at describing what happened than explaining why it happened.

Most curricula plunge right into the story of Hitler's Germany; a few provide some background on the Weimar Republic, presumably to explain Hitler's rise to power. Though all curricula discuss Nazi anti-Semitism, preferring generic terms like "racism" and "prejudice" instead of the specific "anti-Semitism," fifteen of the twenty-five never even suggest that anti-Semitism had a history *before* Hitler. Of those that do, barely a handful present coherent historical accounts, however brief.

A small number of curricula include lessons which survey the pre-Nazi history of Jews in Europe, presumably to humanize the image of the Jews depicted in Nazi propaganda. In schools with a considerable Jewish population, these lessons may function also as homage to a destroyed community and culture.

Some readings, like those in the New York State curriculum, are informative and stimulating. Others, like the New Jersey *Student Anthology*, are overloaded with junk items from popular culture. With few exceptions, the English language is mutilated in most curricula and errors turn up everywhere—errors grammatical as well as typographical, misspellings of names, wrong titles, sloppy mistakes—which reflect prevailing educational standards.

Nor are errors of basic fact and interpretation all that uncommon. Thus, the California *History–Social Science Framework* seeks "to engage students in thinking about why one of the world's most civilized nations participated in the systematic murder of millions of innocent people, mainly because of their religious identity." One would have thought that by now educators would know the Nazis determined who was a Jew not by religion but by the spurious criterion of "race." A more egregious distortion of fact appears in the New York City Board of Education curriculum, *The Holocaust*, of 1988 (not the same as the more substantial curriculum which the board issued in 1979). Two short excerpts from Hitler's *Mein Kampf* are presented "to show that racist hatred extends to all groups that are 'others.' " The first sets forth Hitler's ideas on the mental inferiority of blacks, but omits from the quoted passage a key sentence in which Hitler asserts that only Jews regard blacks as equals of whites. The second excerpt is one of Hitler's more benign statements about the Jews—that they lack their own culture. The curriculum thereby makes a travesty of Hitler's views, creating the impression that blacks and not Jews were his primary targets.

A grave error of omission occurs in those curricula which include a lesson on "World Responses" or "Resistance, Rescue, and Intervention," where the United States is routinely charged with indifference to the fate of the Jews during the war or accused of "doing nothing" to help them. These curricula never mention that the United States committed enormous resources of men and material to fight the Germans, and that only the American military presence made possible the defeat and collapse of the Nazi dictatorship. No curriculum cites the belief of U.S. government and military officials that the only way to stop the murder of the Jews was to defeat Hitler on the battlefield. Nor does any curriculum connect the inability of the Allies to accomplish that task sooner with the rapid disarmament of the 1920s and 1930s. By such omissions, these curricula fail properly to place the events of the Holocaust in the context of World War II.

As for the teaching of moral lessons, all the curricula come to pretty much the same general conclusion, with the variations among them apparent only in their rhetoric. Santayana's words, that "[t]hose who cannot remember the past are condemned to repeat it," are widely quoted, or misquoted. A cruder version of the same idea turns up as: "So that it will never happen again." Most curricula also aim (in the words of one) "to teach students the inevitable consequences of hatred, prejudice, bigotry, and scapegoating." They try to instill respect for racial, religious, and cultural differences, and to foster a commitment to democratic values. A bare handful discuss the sanctity of human life (the Michigan/Bolkosky curriculum is a heartening example). Most focus on "individual responsibility" as against "obedience to authority" as keys to moral behavior.

Besides lectures, readings, films, and discussions, most of the curricula use simulation games or role-playing to teach their moral lessons. Students play Gestapo, concentration camp, and Nuremberg Trial. They act out the roles of murderers, victims, judges. These exercises have been known to produce unprecedented emotional tensions in the classroom, among some students arousing fear, panic, and overidentification with Jewish victims and, among others, releasing sadomasochistic urges, violent responses, and overidentification with the murderers.

The testimony of classroom experience is too fragmentary and subjective to allow judgments about how any particular curriculum translates into effective classroom teaching. But the texts themselves reveal their shortcomings. Though most recite the facts, they do not stress the centrality of premeditated mass murder as an instrument of policy. But the more serious failure, to which I have already alluded, is the omission of the history of anti-Semitism—and especially its roots in Christian doctrine—as necessary background to the murder of the European Jews. To be sure, Christianity cannot be held responsible for Hitler, but the Nazis would not have succeeded in disseminating their brand of racist anti-Semitism had they not been confident of the pervasiveness, firmness, and durability of Christian hatred of Jews. Anti-Semitism, in the words of the late Ben Halpern, is "the name of a cumulative *tradition* of hostility."

Trying to teach adolescents about the roots of anti-Semitism in Christianity, however, even in the secular schools of a secular state, is like leading a tourist party across crocodile territory. How do teachers who may themselves be believing Christians explain this history to children from observant Christian homes? How will parents react when

their children tell them what they have learned about Christian persecution of the Jews? Clearly a desire not to offend is the reason most
curricula detour around the subject. The Pennsylvania/Grobman curriculum, which does include an excellent lesson on the history of
Christian anti-Semitism, cautions that "some students (and some
teachers as well) may have difficulty accepting the injustices which
have occurred during the centuries in the name of religion, particularly
if that religion is their own." The New Jersey curriculum takes the
problem directly into the classroom for discussion: "Many people feel
that a crucial part of growth is our response to uncomfortable new
knowledge about things we cherish. How do you respond to the charge
that organized Christianity might have played a major role in the
historic mistreatment of Jews?"

Is it at all possible to improve instruction on this painful subject?
In the first two decades after the war, Catholics and Protestants alike,
horror-struck and guilt-ridden by the terrible evidence of the murder
of the six million, acknowledged that their church teachings had
provided the bedrock of anti-Semitism. Some institutions took steps
to excise what Jews called the "doctrine of contempt" in church
teachings. Liberal Protestant groups renounced proselytism and accepted Judaism as an equal sister religion. But the most dramatic and
radical breakthrough came when the Catholic Church, after a long
and bitter debate during the Second Vatican Council in the years
1962–65, removed the charge of "deicide" from ancient and modern
Jews. In those days there was also much discussion about revising the
textbooks used in Catholic parochial and Protestant denominational
schools.

Now, more than a generation later, it appears that those post–
World War II teachings have not filtered down with equal effectiveness
to local churches and parishes. The fundamental question still remains
of whether it is at all possible to eradicate anti-Semitism from Christian
teaching without, as the radical theologian Rosemary Ruether has
written, "destroying the whole structure." In any case, Christian re-
morse over the murder of European Jews has long since dissipated.
Not only is the old hatred of the Jews still to be found in fundamental

Christian texts, but new layers of anti-Semitism have accreted, as hatred of Jews now disguises itself in anti-Zionist rhetoric and anti-Israel propaganda. These days liberal Christians rarely respond to expressions of anti-Semitism, no matter how irrational or ugly.

One wonders whether any Christian educators, scholars, and theologians would be willing to try to solve this problem. It would be a daunting task to create a teaching guide for a short series of lessons about the history of Christian anti-Semitism for use in a Holocaust curriculum and to do so without suppressing the facts, without hypocrisy, and yet preserving the integrity of Christian faith and its doctrines.

Omitting all references to Christian anti-Semitism is one way some curricula avoid the sensitivities of the subject. The more acceptable and common pedagogic strategy is to generalize the highly particular nature and history of anti-Semitism by subsuming (and camouflaging) it under general rubrics like scapegoating, prejudice, and bigotry. (As Sir Francis Bacon noted nearly four hundred years ago, "the spacious liberty of generalities" has always been more appealing than "the inclosures of particularity.")

The concept of scapegoating is easy to transmit. Every child is familiar with the experience, whether as victim or as victimizer, and knows how easy it is to heap blame on an innocent and helpless creature for whatever has gone wrong. A variation on the scapegoat theory appears in *Facing History*, which explains that "hatred of Jews invariably reflects larger crises in society which directly affect the lives of all," and that "the resurgence of anti-Semitism points to a resurgence of other forms of intolerance and hatred." These abstract words suggest that hatred of the Jews is not a thing in itself, but a symptom of "larger" troubles, though no explanation is given as to why the Jews, rather than dervishes, for instance, are consistently chosen as the scapegoat.

The curricula similarly resort to the concept of prejudice, a generic term for hostile prejudgments of people and groups. Some curricula, determined to teach the irrationality of prejudice, even invent the notion of arbitrary prejudice, directed, for example, against left-handed or red-haired people. A common classroom activity involves singling out children with specific characteristics like blue eyes or long hair and then having the whole class act out nasty forms of prejudiced behavior against them. The trouble with this kind of universalization is that it once again ignores the particular religious and historical roots that nurture specific prejudices. It certainly does not explain the distinctive character and history of anti-Semitism.

In studying prejudice or any other generic substitute for anti-Semitism, most curricula focus on individual attitudes, beliefs, and opinions rather than their embodiment in public policy and law. This approach conceives of prejudice as a psychological or mental-health problem, a disease that can be cured: if only every bigot could be put on the analyst's couch, prejudice would be eliminated from society. The failure to distinguish between individual behavior and state policies may be attributable to the relatively benign American experience of anti-Semitism, which, with few exceptions, has been a history of individual prejudices expressed through words and acts in the private sector of society. Yet anti-Semitism as public policy is an essential aspect of what the Holocaust was about, and it too has a history. Whenever anti-Semitism has become the instrument of authority, and been incorporated in the very structure of government, Jews have been deprived of their rights, their property, and ultimately their lives. It happened when the medieval Church agitated the faithful against Jews during the Crusades; it happened when modern European nation-states denied Jews their equal rights and citizenship; it manifested itself in the anti-Semitic goals and platforms of political parties in nineteenth- and twentieth-century European countries and in the enactment of anti-Jewish legislation.

Curricula commonly ask their students whether "it" could happen here and even give their own answer: Yes, it could happen here. But these curricula do not instruct their students in the fundamental differences between, on the one side, our pluralist democracy and constitutional government, ruled by law, and, on the other side, the authoritarian or totalitarian governments of Europe that legitimated

74

discrimination against and persecution of Jews. One wonders whether students learn about those fundamental differences *anywhere* in their high-school education.

There is still another way of deemphasizing the role of anti-Semitism in the murder of the Jews—by categorizing this particular crime as an act of genocide, a crime which can be committed against any people, nation, or race. Both the concept and the word (combining the Greek *genos*, meaning "race" or "descent," and a Latin suffix, meaning "kill" or "slay") were invented by Raphael Lemkin, a Polish Jew, most of whose family was murdered in Warsaw by the Germans during the war. Lemkin wanted the word to become a generic term that would define a crime in international law, and indeed as such it was encoded in the Genocide Convention which the United Nations adopted in 1949.

The concept of genocide—an act "committed with intent to destroy . . . a national, ethnical, racial or religious group"—has since become widely debased, and today groups of all sorts clamor for recognition as victims of genocide. Browsing among the curricula, I found few setting any qualifications for eligibility. Thus, the Cleveland Heights, Ohio, World History curriculum enumerates as victims "of 20th-century genocide . . . the Ibos, the Armenians, and the Indonesian Chinese." The New Jersey curriculum encourages students "to probe the concept of genocide," and cites as one historical example "the plight of the contemporary 'boat people.' " The authors of the Connecticut curriculum, altogether altering the original meaning, define genocide as "all official actions *to harm*, in whole or in part, various types of human groups" (emphasis added). According to the Connecticut curriculum, victims of genocide include North American Indians, South and Central American Indians, and the aboriginal peoples in Australia. This curriculum, which bears the imprimatur of the state's commissioner of education, also accuses "Americans" of having committed genocide, asserting that the American "army sometimes deliberately spread smallpox" among the Indians.

These farfetched instances surely reflect in some cases the attitudes of the "hate-America" crowd, but they are used also as a pedagogical device. By enumerating supposedly analogous cases, the curricula can make the issue "relevant" by deflecting attention from the Jews as the sole or most prominent victims of genocide. The New York City curriculum of 1979, for instance, copes with the problem by having it both ways. In an early chapter it lists, in addition to the murder of the Jews, four other examples of imputed genocide: (1) the treatment of American Indians; (2) the treatment of blacks during the slave era in the United States; (3) the slaughter and deportations of the Armenian people by the Turks; and (4) the reported murders of tens of thousands of Ugandans who opposed Idi Amin's dictatorship during the 1970s. Then in a later chapter the authors reverse themselves and at last make a crucial distinction: "While there have been many instances of genocide . . . , the total annihilation of a people was not an officially sanctioned purpose of a national government as it was in Nazi Germany." By this standard, only the slaughter of the Armenians possibly qualifies as an example of genocide comparable to the Holocaust.

Besides accumulating such imprecise and often tendentious analogies, some curricula enlarge the list of victims of Nazi genocide to include those whom the Nazis never intended to wipe out. The Pennsylvania/Grobman curriculum is one of several which instance homosexuals and members of the Jehovah's Witnesses, though there is no historical evidence that the Nazis ever planned to exterminate these as groups. To be sure, the Nazis put homosexuals in concentration camps and identified them with pink traingles, proposing to "reeducate" them to function in "normal" society. And Jehovah's Witnesses (*Bibelforscher* in Germany), who refused to recognize the authority of the Nazi state, were likewise sent to concentration camps (and identified by purple triangles) for a term limited to two months. Both groups were incarcerated together with other categories of prisoners whom the Germans did not intend to murder: criminals (green triangle); antisocials—beggars, vagrants, prostitutes, and the like (black triangle); and political prisoners (red triangle). Many of these inmates, including the Jehovah's Witnesses and homosexuals, unable to withstand the hardships of forced labor, became ill and died for lack of medical care. Moreover, as the war progressed, the camp regimen became ever more brutal, and non-Jewish inmates too weak or ill to work were routinely sent to their deaths. But none of this was part of a Nazi program to eliminate the group in question.

The lack of precision in the curricula may reflect the imprecision in the text of the Genocide Convention itself. Though it was designed to prevent and punish the crime of murder of a whole people, such as was committed against the Jews, the Convention does not once use the word "murder." "Killing" is the operative word. Nor is the word "murder" used with much frequency in the curricula. The more commonly invoked words tend to be abstractions—destruction, annihilation, extermination, and, of course, genocide. Though many curricula include a lesson on the Nuremberg trials in which they discuss crimes against humanity, they hardly ever discuss the crime of murder. Why?

Since the beginning of time, murder with malice aforethought has been outlawed and punished by every people and state, damned by every religion, forever unredeemed and unredeemable. Yet despite the clear understandings handed down from ancient cultures and incorporated in modern law, many people today embrace a relativistic attitude toward murder. Some denounce capital punishment for the crime of murder as if the penalty itself were murder. Others insist that instead of rushing to condemn we should seek out the "root causes" in our social system that lead murderers to commit their crimes. It seems to follow, then, that we should convict "society" instead. This moral climate may account for a serious lapse in most Holocaust curricula—the failure to impart any moral lesson about the specific crime of murder, in this case mass murder.

As for the moral lessons in which the Holocaust curricula *do* abound, these are often inappropriate to the subject.

A few curricula offer exercises in outright political indoctrination in currently fashionable causes. Thus, the New Jersey *Student Anthology* ingeniously applies the history of the Holocaust to "the American

77

civil-rights movement and other social-action groups" and, going even further afield, to "the experiences of Maryknolls in El Salvador," all of which "raise old questions about how we should respond to new oppression." Needless to say, the curriculum does not spell out just how the history of the Holocaust applies to these movements.

In the Pennsylvania/Grobman curriculum, a lesson entitled "Nazi Fascism and the Modern Totalitarian State" assigns the students to "research the value of war toys sold annually in the United States" and to "discuss if this says anything about our culture." Another activity in the same lesson asks students to find out if there are local facilities "which provide land for 'war games.' " These classroom activities reflect the influence of the "peace-education" movement which successfully penetrated the school curriculum in the 1980s.

The most blatant example of that influence appears in *Facing History*'s last chapter, "Facing Today and the Future." Claiming that "continued adult denial of the information regarding potential nuclear annihilation is harmful to our students," *Facing History* finds a parallel between the Holocaust and a "potential nuclear holocaust" in that "the explanations educators give for perpetuating the silence about nuclear issues are the same as those given for avoiding a confrontation with the Holocaust." At chapter's end, the authors disclose their activist agenda by offering to make available to teachers and students a list of groups dealing with "issues of the nuclear world of today."

But the lesson most frequently taught by these curricula is political in a more indirect way. It centers on the theme of moral choice, the obligation of each person to be responsible for his own actions. Usually the curricula pose the problem in either/or terms: conforming (which is immoral) or resisting (moral), obeying authority (bad) or following the dictates of one's conscience (good). The standard examples are two famous court cases in which the defendant invoked "superior orders": Adolf Eichmann at his trial in Jerusalem in 1961 and Lieutenant William L. Calley at his court-martial for having shot to death unarmed Vietnamese civilians at My Lai in 1968.

In citing the "superior-orders" defense, however, the curricula erect a man of straw. This defense was specifically repudiated in Article 8 of the Charter of the International Military Tribunal of August 8, 1945, which the Allied governments created to try the major Nazi war criminals. Rejected in international law, it was denied at both Eichmann's and Calley's trials. The curricula which refer to those cases have confused the discredited legal argument of obedience to superior orders with the concept of obedience as a trait of character. Eichmann claimed he was merely an obedient officer performing his duty and the authors of *Facing History* take him at his word, believing, along with Hannah Arendt, that he was a faceless example of the "banality of evil." But Eichmann was in fact a fanatically committed Nazi, zealous in pursuit of Nazi goals, and enterprising in facilitating the murder of the Jews.

The longest chapter in *Facing History*, "Preparing for Obedience," which undertakes to teach its students that obedience and conformity are not morally admirable qualities, opens with the ominous statement that "obedience is one of the critical ingredients of a totalitarian society." But as anyone knows who has studied totalitarian societies, the critical ingredient of these societies is not obedience, but terror. It is terror that elicits obedience under duress, even to unjust laws.

According to a study guide for a film which *Facing History* and many other curricula include in their course, "[o]bedience to the law is not necessarily the determinant of a moral person." That message of moral relativism has reached the students using the curriculum; in the diary in which they are required to enter their reactions one of them wrote, "From the course I've learned that there is not just one right and one wrong answer." This is a message that might have been useful to students in prewar Germany, the most flagrantly authoritarian society in all the West. But do American children, who have been raised in unprecedented freedom and permissiveness, need to be instructed in the virtues of disobedience?

Some curricula teach that following one's "conscience" is morally superior to obeying one's parent or the just laws of society. None recommends that students read Plato's *Crito*, where they might come upon Socrates' refusal to accept his friends' plan to organize his escape from prison: "Do you imagine that a city can continue to exist and

79

not be turned upside down, if the legal judgments which are pronounced in it have no force, but are nullified and destroyed by private persons?" Nor does any curriculum question the reliability of conscience as a guide to distinguishing between good and bad, right and wrong. The voice of conscience may sometimes sound loud and clear, but not necessarily at all times and under all circumstances. Furthermore, the consciences of different people within the same society or in different societies vary widely.

Conscience can be especially unreliable when it comes to moral questions which we have never before faced or imagined and for which we lack the wisdom to choose an honorable course of action. The Jews who lived under Hitler's rule were confronted with cruel dilemmas, forced to make difficult, even impossible, choices about matters of life and death for which conscience could offer no direction and the past could give no guidance. Yet many high-school curricula frivolously suggest role-playing exercises in which students imagine how they would behave if confronted with such dilemmas. What kind of answers can come from American children who think of the Gestapo as the name of a game?

If conscience is not a satisfactory guide to moral behavior in times of duress, and if one is compelled to live in a society with unjust laws, by what standard then should people be guided? My own answer is simple: We turn to a more authoritative law, to the fundamental moral code of our civilization and of the three great religions whose basic text is the Jewish Bible. We turn to the Sixth Commandment, which prescribes: "Thou shalt not murder." This, in my view, is *the* primary lesson of the Holocaust.

In the public schools, teaching moral standards as they are incorporated in the Ten Commandments (or even in just one commandment) would, so I am told, constitute a violation of the doctrine of the separation of church and state. If that is so, something is clearly wrong with both our system of education and our standards of morality.

The failure of American schools to teach effectively has become a national scandal. Surveys and studies continue to report that large numbers of pupils cannot read well enough to comprehend a simple text, that they cannot write a straight sentence, perform everyday arithmetical tasks, locate a foreign country on a map. Yet the unending flow of criticism does not mean that we should abandon the entire educational enterprise. Similarly, this disheartening survey of secondary-school Holocaust curricula is not intended to undermine the legitimacy of teaching about the murder of the European Jews. Of the curricula currently in use, two, each quite different in its treatment— Michigan/Bolkosky's A Holocaust Curriculum: Life Unworthy of Life and New York State's Teaching About the Holocaust and Genocide— are excellent. They, at least, can serve as the basis for reconsidering how this thorny subject can be taught with integrity and without political exploitation.

APPENDIX

The following list of curricula is arranged by states, but includes a separate listing for New York City. Staff members of the Anti-Defamation League helped me obtain some; others, collected by the Jewish Education Service of North America, are available at the Library of Hebrew Union College-Jewish Institute of Religion in New York City.

California: (1) California State Board of Education, Model Curriculum for Human Rights and Genocide (1988, 66 pp., printed). Sections of this curriculum have been excerpted from the Connecticut State Department of Education curriculum, Human Rights: The Struggle for Freedom, Dignity, and Equality. (2) California State Board of Education, History-Social Science Framework for California Public Schools Kindergarten Through Grade Twelve (1988, 122 pp., printed) places the teaching of the Holocaust within grade 10. (3) Los Angeles Unified School District, Instructional Planning Division, The Holocaust: An Instructional Guide (1979, 67 pp.).

Connecticut: State of Connecticut, Department of Education, Human Rights: The Struggle for Freedom, Dignity, and Equality (1987, 90 pp.).

Georgia: Fulton County (Atlanta): (1) Riverwood High School, Holocaust and Human Rights (1989, 55 pp., processed). (2) Northside High School, Study Unit on the Holocaust (n.d., 16 pp., processed), for grade 7.

Illinois (1) Champaign Community Unit School District #4, Middle School Holocaust Curriculum (January 1990, 28 pp., processed), for grade 8. (2) Board

81

of Education of the City of Chicago, *The Holocaust: A Teacher Resource Unit: Grade 8* (1990, 68 pp., processed). (3) Evanston, *Teachers' Guide to the Holocaust* (1977, 38 pp., processed).

Iowa: Des Moines Independent Community School District and the Community Relations Commission of the Jewish Federation of Greater Des Moines, *A Study of the Holocaust* (2nd ed., 1984, processed); 2 vols.: *Teacher Guide* (19 pp.), *Student Handbook* (58 + 41 pp.).

Maryland: Baltimore, Baltimore City Public Schools, Office of Social Studies, *The Holocaust* (1979, 116 pp., processed).

Massachusetts: Margot Stern Strom and William S. Parsons, *Facing History and Ourselves: Holocaust and Human Behavior* (Watertown, Mass.: Intentional Educations, 1982, 400 pp., printed, ill.). An eight-to-ten-week unit, for grade 8 or 9. Privately produced for sale, nationally distributed.

Michigan: Sidney M. Bolkosky, Betty Rotberg Ellisa, David Harris, *A Holocaust Curriculum: Life Unworthy of Life: An 18-Lesson Instructional Unit* (Farmington Hills, Mich., The Center for the Study of the Child, 1987). Consists of: *Instructor's Manual* (216 pp., printed, ill.), *Student Textbook* (318 pp., printed, ill., in looseleaf binder), and a 60-minute videotape of interviews with Holocaust survivors, boxed. Privately produced for sale, nationally distributed.

New Jersey: Richard F. Flaim and Edwin W. Reynolds, Jr., eds., *The Holocaust and Genocide: A Search for Conscience: A Curriculum Guide* (Vineland, N.J., Board of Education and the Anti-Defamation League of B'nai B'rith, 1983, 183 pp., processed). A six-unit curriculum. A companion volume, Harry Furman, ed., subtitled *A Student Anthology* (217 pp.), was "developed under the auspices of the State of New Jersey Department of Education." Both volumes bear the imprimatur of New Jersey's then governor, Thomas H. Kean. Teaneck High School uses these materials in grade 9 "World History" and "World Cultures Program."

New York State: The University of the State of New York, the State Education Department Bureau of Curriculum Development, *Teaching About the Holocaust and Genocide: The Human Rights Series* (1985–86, 3 vols., 66 pp., 323 pp., 166 pp., printed). A two-week course of study.

New York City: (1) Board of Education of the City of New York, Division of Curriculum and Instruction, *The Holocaust: A Study of Genocide* (1979, reprinted 1985, 587 pp., printed). May be used as a unit of two to five weeks and also for longer units and elective courses. (2) New York City Board of Education, Division of Curriculum and Instruction, Social Studies Unit, *The Holocaust* (1988, 66 pp., processed). A two-week unit. (3) Ira Zornberg, *Classroom Strategies for Teaching About the Holocaust: 10 Lessons for Classroom Use* (1983, Anti-Defamation League of B'nai B'rith, 91 pp., processed). Nationally distributed. (4) Karen Shawn, *The End of Innocence: Anne Frank and the Holocaust* (1989, Anti-Defamation League of B'nai B'rith, 102 pp., ill., printed). Nationally distributed. A five-lesson unit.

Ohio: (1) Leatrice B. Rabinsky and Carol Danks, eds., *The Holocaust: Prejudice Unleashed* (1989, State of Ohio, Materials and Curriculum Committee of the Ohio Council on Holocaust Education, printed, ill., nine individually paged and bound booklets assembled in a looseleaf binder and boxed). A ten-lesson unit. (2) Board of Education, Cleveland Heights-University Heights City School District, *Modern World History* (1979, 39 pp., processed). Includes an optional unit on the Holocaust.

Pennsylvania: (1) Gary Grobman, *The Holocaust: A Guide for Pennsylvania Teachers* (Harrisburg, Pa.: The Pennsylvania Jewish Coalition, 1990, 166 pp., printed). The Pennsylvania Department of Education has approved this curriculum for distribution free of charge to each school district in the state. (2) Philadelphia, Instructional Series of the School District of Philadelphia, *The Holocaust: A Teacher Resource* (1977, 129 pp., printed). (3) Mt. Lebanon (Pittsburgh) School District, nine untitled pages on teaching the Holocaust in required social-studies courses, grades 7, 10, and 11 (1988, processed). (4) Upper St. Clair (Pittsburgh) Public Schools, a two-to-three-week unit in a social-studies course, "World War II and Holocaust" (n.d., processed).

LIES ABOUT
THE HOLOCAUST

Historians are always engaged in reinterpreting the past. They do so sometimes on the basis of newly found documentary sources, sometimes by reconsidering the known data from a different political position, or by taking into account a different time span, or by employing a new methodology. Every historical subject has undergone revision as each new generation rewrites the history of the past in the light of its own perspectives and values. But the *term* "revisionism" has applied specifically to dissident positions which are at variance with mainstream history on several subjects from the Civil War on. Three of these subjects have been politicized beyond the limits of historical truth—World War I, World War II, and the cold war (and there is a new subject, the war in Vietnam, now in the making).

In these three instances, revisionists, more ideological than academic in their approach, have tried to refute the prevailing views as to who was to blame for the outbreak of war. Using—and sometimes abusing—historical data, World War I revisionists have tried to prove that Germany was not to blame, or was less to blame than England. World War II revisionists have traveled the same route, picturing Fanklin D. Roosevelt as the arch-villain. Cold-war revisionists have blamed the United States and absolved the Soviet Union for having initiated the cold war.

World War I revisionism was launched late in the 1920s with Sidney

B. Fay's *The Origins of the World War*, which gave some historical dignity to what was more often a political and ideological issue. On the Right, conservatives and isolationists blamed England for the war and whitewashed Germany. On the Left, the Communists and their splinter groups attributed the origins of the war to the conspiratorial manipulations of the munitions-makers and the financiers. In Germany itself, the historical debate continued from the end of World War I until long past the end of World War II, but by now it would seem to have been put to rest by Fritz Fischer's definitive work, *Germany's War Aims in the First World War* (1961, English edition 1967).

As for World War II, the universal revulsion against the Third Reich and the open record of its belligerency did not create a hospitable climate for revisionism. Even in postwar Germany, where diehard Nazis continued to believe in the cause, they nevertheless did not dare to defend the Third Reich openly. The first—and still the only—revisionist work on World War II by a reputable historian was A. J. P. Taylor's mischievous book, *The Origins of the Second World War* (1961). There Taylor argued that Hitler had not planned a general war, and that the conflict, far from being premeditated, was "a mistake, the result on both sides of diplomatic blunders." Still, though Hitler was like other statesmen of his time in the conduct of his diplomatic affairs, Taylor explicitly declared that he outdid them all "in wicked deeds."

Historians everywhere roundly attacked Taylor for the book's conceptual perversity and its methodological flaws, but his book soon became the banner under which a swarm of Nazi apologists, cranks, and anti-Semites rallied. In twenty years' time, indeed, the allegations advanced by Taylor would come to appear mild and innocuous, for by 1980 one would find it being argued by so-called revisionists not only that Hitler's Germany was not to blame for World War II, but that the murder of six million European Jews by the Nazis had never taken place, that the Holocaust was a hoax invented by the Jews. Most shocking of all, these gross and malicious falsifications, far from being attacked and repudiated, have gained a respectful hearing in academic historical institutions in the United States.

85

*   *   *

In the same year that Taylor's book was published, 1961, a revisionist work appeared in Germany, written by an American, David L. Hoggan. The book had originated as a Harvard doctoral dissertation done in 1948, but it was revised, expanded, and Nazified in the ensuing years. Unable to find an American or a bona fide German publisher, Hoggan gave his manuscript to a known Nazi publisher. *

Hoggan's dissertation, according to one of his Harvard advisers, had been "no more than a solid, conscientious piece of work, critical of Polish and British policies in 1939, but not beyond what the evidence would tolerate." Thirteen years later, as published, it had turned into an apologia for Nazi Germany in which the English were portrayed as warmongers, the Poles as the real provokers of the war, and Hitler as the angel of peace. (The book also contained a short section on the Jews, arguing that from 1933 to 1938 the Third Reich treated its Jews more generously than Poland had.)

To support his outrageous claims, Hoggan tampered with sources, distorting and misreading those that did not fit his theories and prejudices, glossing over those that conflicted with them, and altogether ignoring those that actually confuted them. Nor, according to the president of the Association of German Historians, did he shrink from forgery. † One noted German historian summed up Hoggan's work as follows: "Rarely have so many inane and unwarranted theses, allegations, and 'conclusions' . . . been crammed into a volume written under the guise of history."

---

*Der erzwungene Krieg: Die Ursachen und Urheber des 2. Weltkriegs (The Imposed War: The Origins and Originators of World War II), translated from the English by M.E. Narjes and H. Grabert (Verlag der Deutschen Hochschullehrer-Zeitung, 1961); reviewed by Gerhard L. Weinberg in the American Historical Review, 68, 1 (October 1962), pp. 104–105. Weinberg's sharply critical review, noting the publisher's Nazi connections, provoked angry letters from Hoggan and his supporters. Their false assertions eventually elicited letters from several eminent American historians who wished to dissociate themselves from Hoggan's work.

†Helmut Krausnick, director of the Institute for Contemporary History in Munich, raised the charge of forgery in a foreword to Hermann Graml's lengthy critique of Hoggan, published in Geschichte in Wissenschaft und Unterricht, August 1963.

86

How had a once "solid, conscientious piece of work" metamorphosed into this rubbish of Nazi apologetics? The credit for the reverse alchemy belongs to the late Harry Elmer Barnes, presumptive doyen of American isolationist historians, guru to fledgling libertarians, and patron saint of neo-Nazi cranks and crackpots in search of academic legitimacy.

Harry Elmer Barnes (1889–1968) was an American historian and sociologist of wide-ranging interests and knowledge, whose career as a professor and then as a journalist was aborted by his contentiousness and his cavalier disregard not only for accuracy but also for truth. He produced no original scholarly work, but synthesized information from his vast reading in a series of prolix and repetitive works on the history of Western civilization. By his own account, however, the "subject of war responsibility" occupied more of his time than any other theme.

In the 1920s Barnes became a World War I revisionist and was soon possessed by the idea that "vested political and historical interests" were behind the "official" accounts of Germany's responsibility for the outbreak of the war. The rabid energy which this notion provoked in him sustained Barnes as a revisionist into the period of World War II. As early as 1937, already a fanatical Roosevelt-hater, he described himself as a "noninterventionist." His rage against Roosevelt became still more intensified after Pearl Harbor—for which Barnes held Roosevelt responsible—and America's entry into the war.

Barnes's obsessions with warmongering conspiracies in government and in the historical profession held him in thrall until the end of his life. His writing grew ever more shrill, irresponsible, and irrational. (Finding few outlets to publish his polemical pieces, he felt compelled to have them privately printed.) People who had once held him in regard ceased to pay heed as he grew progressively paranoid, seeing sinister plots and powerful enemies everywhere. He began to write about the "historical blackout," that is, about a conspiracy to prevent him from publicizing his isolationist views. Here is a sample from one of the earlier articles:

It is no exaggeration to say that the American Smearbund, operating through newspaper editors and columnists, "hatchet-men" book reviewers, radio commentators, pressure-group intrigue and espionage, and academic pressures and fears, has accomplished about as much in the way of intimidating honest intellectuals in this country as Hitler, Goebbels, Himmler, the Gestapo, and concentration camps were able to do in Nazi Germany. *

By now a calcified isolationist, Barnes opposed America's involvement in Korea and soon found himself in the company not only of right-wing isolationists, ex-America Firsters, and Nazi apologists, but also of radical libertarians devoted to laissez-faire in the economy, noninterference by the state in domestic affairs, and isolationism (non-intervention) in foreign affairs. In this period Barnes became acquainted with one James J. Martin and wrote an introduction to Martin's oddball history of "individualist anarchism," published by the Libertarian Book Club in New York. It was at this time that Barnes became interested in Hoggan's dissertation and over the years guided him straight into Nazi apologetics.

As the years progressed, Barnes's hold on political reality continued to slip. He had begun his isolationist-revisionist career by whitewashing Kaiser Wilhelm's Germany and ended up by whitewashing Hitler's. In 1962 Barnes already doubted that the Third Reich had committed any atrocities or murder. In a privately printed pamphlet, *Blasting the Historical Blackout*, which praised A. J. P. Taylor's book, if with some reservations (he thought Hoggan's was better), Barnes alluded to what he called the "alleged wartime crimes of Germany": "Even assuming that all the charges ever made against the Nazis by anybody of reasonable sanity and responsibility are true, the Allies do not come off

---

* "Revisionism and the Historical Blackout," which appeared originally as the lead article in *Perpetual War for Perpetual Peace* (1953), a massive compendium which Barnes edited and privately financed. The book was filled with isolationist and anti-Roosevelt material.

much, if any, better." Then, with the shamelessness of a habitual liar, he charged that the sufferings of the Germans who had been expelled from Czech and Polish border areas after World War II and returned to Germany were "obviously far more hideous and prolonged than those of the Jews said to have been exterminated in great numbers by the Nazis."

Four years later, in 1966, in another rambling and paranoid piece, "Revisionism: A Key to Peace," published in a short-lived libertarian journal, Barnes for all practical purposes denied that Hitler's Germany had committed mass murder. The following sentence is an elaboration of the one I quoted earlier:

> Even if one were to accept the most extreme and exaggerated indictment of Hitler and the National Socialists for their activities after 1939 made by anybody fit to remain outside a mental hospital, it is almost alarmingly easy to demonstrate that the atrocities of the Allies in the same period were more numerous as to victims and were carried out for the most part by methods more brutal and painful than alleged extermination in gas ovens.

In those days, even the neo-Nazis in Germany were circumspect in their journal, *Nation Europa* (which also published Barnes's articles), not daring to deny the facts of mass murder altogether but simply minimizing them. Only a certain Paul Rassinier in France was sufficiently divorced from reality to deny that the Third Reich had murdered the Jews.

Rassinier, once a Communist, then a socialist, had been interned in Buchenwald during the war, and afterward flipflopped into a rabid anti-Semite. In 1949 he published a book claiming the atrocities committed in the Nazi camps had been grossly exaggerated by the survivors. If any Jews had been murdered, Rassinier said, it was the Jewish *kapos* in the camps who had killed them. The book was widely denounced in France. Later Rassinier sued a newspaper editor for having called him a fascist; he was, he insisted, an anarchist. But the

89

Paris court ruled against Rassinier on the ground that his book expressed ideas "identical with those proclaimed by the neo-Nazis."

In 1964 Rassinier wrote another book, *Le Drame des Juifs Européens*, an incoherent assemblage of arguments rehashed from the storehouse of anti-Semitic writings. Rassinier had one new wrinkle: arithmomania. He came up with the weird calculation that precisely 4,416,108 of the six million Jews said to have been murdered were actually alive and that the rest had probably not been killed by the Germans anyway. Around this time Barnes and Rassinier met, the rendezvous having been arranged by Mabel Narjes of Hamburg, cotranslator of Hoggan's *Der erzwungene Krieg*.

Rassinier and Barnes obviously had much in common; Barnes undertook to translate Rassinier's book into English, * and also reviewed Rassinier for the American public, or at least for those most likely to be interested—the readers of the *American Mercury*. (Founded as an iconoclastic journal in 1924 by H. L. Mencken, the *American Mercury* deteriorated after Mencken's resignation in 1933 and eventually became just an anti-Semitic rag.) Here is Barnes at his unpitiable worst:

> . . . the courageous author [Rassinier] lays the chief blame for misrepresentation on those whom we must call the swindlers of the crematoria, the Israeli politicians who derive billions of marks from nonexistent, mythical, and imaginary cadavers, whose numbers have been reckoned in an unusually distorted and dishonest manner.[†]

Rassinier died in 1967 and Barnes a year later, but their fanaticism continued to inspire others in their quest for legitimacy. In 1969, a 119-page book, *The Myth of the Six Million*, by "Anonymous," ap-

---

The Drama of the European Jews, 1975. It was dedicated to "James J. Martin & the late Harry Elmer Barnes: Pioneers in Revisionist History." The publisher was an anti-Semitic outfit in Silver Spring, Maryland; it was distributed also by Liberty Bell Publications, run by a former Nazi working out of Reedy, West Virginia.

[†]"Zionist Fraud," reprinted in an appendix to *The Myth of the Six Million*, about which more below.

peared, with an introduction paying tribute to Barnes as "one of America's greatest historians." The introduction was written pseudonymously by Willis A. Carto, head of Liberty Lobby, the best-financed anti-Semitic organization in the United States, which operates out of Washington, D.C. *The Myth of the Six Million* was published by a Liberty Lobby subsidiary, Noontide Press. (*American Mercury* is also part of the interlocking network funded by Liberty Lobby.)

In his introduction, Carto explained that "Anonymous" was a college professor who wished to protect his standing in the academic community by hiding his identity. It appears likely that the author was none other than David L. Hoggan, for in 1969 he sued Noontide Press for damages, claiming authorship of *The Myth of the Six Million*. The litigation dragged on until 1973, when the plaintiff withdrew his complaint. (Perhaps Carto settled out of court.) In 1974 a new edition of *The Myth of the Six Million* appeared, still authored by "Anonymous."

The Myth of the Six Million undertook to disprove all the evidence of the murder of the European Jews and to discredit all eyewitness testimony, including that of Rudolf Hoess, SS commandant at Auschwitz, and Kurt Gerstein, the SS officer who delivered the poison gas to Bełzec and Treblinka. The author of *The Myth of the Six Million* did much the same thing that the author of *Der erzwungene Krieg* had done: distorting and faking some sources, suppressing others, and inventing still others. One example will suffice, as it is an item that turns up repeatedly in anti-Semitic tracts.

Benedikt Kautsky, an Austrian socialist, had been interned in Buchenwald and was later a slave laborer in Auschwitz. In his memoirs, *Teufel und Verdammte*, Kautsky wrote:

> I should now like briefly to refer to the gas chambers. Though I did not see them myself, they have been described to me by so many trustworthy people that I have no hesitation in reproducing their testimony.

The neo-Nazis cite Kautsky, with the appropriate bibliographical references including the correct page number, but falsify the passage so that he appears to corroborate their claim that there were no gas chambers.

We may not think much of Hoggan's anonymous scribbling, but the booklet was well received in his circles. In England a pamphlet, *Did the Six Million Really Die?*, which drew heavily upon *The Myth of the Six Million*, was put forward as a historical work, published by a so-called Historical Review Press in Surrey; the author was advertised as one Richard E. Harwood, "a specialist in political and diplomatic aspects of the Second World War" who was "with the University of London." Actually he was Richard Verrall, editor of *Spearhead* magazine, unofficial organ of the National Front, an English racist group.

By now the neo-Nazis had regularly begun to exploit terms like "historical review" and "revisionism" in an effort to get attention in respectable circles. In New York a splinter group of the pro-Nazi German-American National Congress hit on the idea of a Revisionist Press to publish pseudoscholarly materials. They concealed their identity behind a post-office box number first in Brooklyn, then in Rochelle Park, New Jersey. In 1973 this Revisionist Press reprinted as a small book Barnes's paranoid essay, "Revisionism: A Key to Peace," from which I quoted earlier.

The neo-Nazi bid for academic reputability took a great leap forward when word got around that a professor at Northwestern University named Arthur R. Butz had published a book called *The Hoax of the Twentieth Century*, the hoax being the "Holocaust legend." Butz's book, published in 1976 by the Historical Review Press in Surrey—Harwood/Verrall's publisher—confidently argued that the Jews of Europe had not been "exterminated and that there was no German attempt to exterminate them." Butz—an associate professor of electrical engineering and computer sciences—was convinced that all the Jews said to have been murdered were still alive and he undertook to prove it, his expertise in computers no doubt standing him in good stead.

In his review of the assorted neo-Nazi writings on this subject, Butz gave good grades only to Rassinier, though he did not find him entirely accurate or reliable. Butz dismissed *The Myth of the Six Million* as "terrible," but considered Harwood's *Did the Six Million Really Die?* "quite good" (perhaps because the two authors shared the same publisher). As examples of "leading extermination mythologists," Butz lumped together Gerald Reitlinger (*The Final Solution*), Raul Hilberg (*The Destruction of the European Jews*), and me (*The War Against the Jews*).

The news of Butz's extracurricular career as an anti-Semitic scholar percolated from England back to Northwestern, and finally an account in the *New York Times* in late January 1977 raised Butz to national notoriety. His presence at Northwestern embarrassed the university, especially as its Jewish contributors threatened to withhold their financial support. The faculty, for its part, held firmly to the principle of academic freedom and the right of tenure. (Nowadays teaching at a university appears to be widely considered a fundamental civil right, like free speech or the right to bear arms.)

To demonstrate that Northwestern did not approve of Butz's views, the university administration prompted its history department to organize a series of lectures which would confirm that six million European Jews had indeed been murdered. These lectures, delivered by three Jews and a philo-Semite, were published in a booklet, *The Dimensions of the Holocaust* (1977), and distributed to show that the university stood foursquare on the side of honor and decency. As one of the four lecturers at Northwestern, I argued in private with some members of the faculty and the administration that the university's response was inadequate, for it seemed to me that they regarded the affair merely as an unfortunate incident affecting Jewish sensibilities. In fact, in their public statements the university's president and provost had treated the Butz scandal as a Jewish family sorrow, "a contemptible insult to the dead and the bereaved." No one at this great center of learning seemed to regard Butz's absurdities as an offense against historical truth, a matter supposedly of concern to an intellectual and academic community.

That same year, 1977, *Hitler's War* by David Irving came out. Irving, an English journalist with strong German sympathies and a record of disregard for verity or verification, argued in this book that the murder of the European Jews—whose historicity he did not deny— was Himmler's doing, and that Hitler was in fact innocent of those terrible deeds. Because Irving did not dispute the historical reality that the Jews were murdered, his work found no acceptance in the anti-Semitic canon.

Butz was the one who became a celebrity, even lecturing before an audience brought together by remnant supporters of the late Grand Mufti of Jerusalem (a Nazi collaborator). His book has been distributed in the United States by Carto's Noontide Press and by practically every other enterprising anti-Semitic group. One of Butz's "academic" sponsors has been Dr. Austin J. App, who used to teach English at LaSalle College in Philadelphia and claims to have been associated with Barnes. App's Nazi sympathies and anti-Semitic activities date back to the early 1940s; a prolific pamphleteer, he himself is the author of a thirty-nine-page effusion, *The Six Million Swindle*, which he has peddled along with the collected works of Butz, Harwood, and Hoggan.

In Germany, Udo Walendy, a Nazi in good standing from the old days, translated Butz (*Der Jahrhundert Betrug*) and published his version through a "revisionist" press which he operates. Walendy has his own wrinkle: he claims that the photographs of barely living camp inmates or of dead and rotted cadavers are "fake atrocity photographs."

France has had its equivalent of Butz in the person of Robert Faurisson, who until last year was an associate professor of French literature at the University of Lyon-2. In 1978 Faurisson began to write articles asserting that the "alleged gas chambers and the alleged genocide are one and the same lie . . . which is largely of Zionist origin." Furthermore, said Faurisson, "the participants in this lie . . . distort the purpose and nature of revisionist research." Faurisson's articles created such a furor that the university suspended him, a development which prompted all sorts of "civil libertarians" to come to his defense. Among them was Jean-Gabriel Cohn-Bendit, brother of Danny the Red of the 1968 Paris student riots. Cohn-Bendit, according to Faurisson, wrote to express his support: "Let's fight to destroy those gas chambers which are shown to tourists in the camps where one knows now there hadn't been any at all." * From this country, Noam Chomsky outdid even himself to sign an appeal in defense of Faurisson's civil rights.†

In Australia Butz's book had a profound and unhinging effect on John Bennett, a Melbourne lawyer, for many years secretary of the regional Council for Civil Liberties. Converted by Butz, Bennett distributed about two hundred copies of the book and thousands of copies of Faurisson's articles to persons in Australian public life. Early in 1979, Bennett began to speak of the murder of the European Jews as "a gigantic lie" created by "Zionist Holocaust propaganda" to make people support Israel. Several of his sensational letters-to-the-editor were published in leading Australian papers. The subsequent uproar soon brought about his dismissal from the Council for Civil Liberties. In the wake of this unfortunate episode, the Embassy of the Federal Republic of Germany, working together with Melbourne's Jewish community, mounted an exhibit on the Holocaust intended to remind those who had forgotten, or to inform those who never knew, that the Third Reich had undertaken to destroy the European Jews and by 1945 had indeed succeeded.

Meanwhile, back in the United States, the Revisionist Press in Brooklyn had published a small book called *The Revisionist Historians and German War Guilt*. Its author was Warren B. Morris, Jr. holder of a doctorate from Oklahoma State University for an undistinguished dissertation on a minor nineteenth-century German diplomat.

The idea for *The Revisionist Historians and German War Guilt*, Morris acknowledged in his preface, came from the Revisionist Press itself and Morris expressed his appreciation also to Austin J. App, author of *The Six Million Swindle*. Morris set himself the task of determining

---

*Faurisson, in his "Right of Reply," *Le Monde*, March 29, 1979.
†In a letter to me, September 18, 1980, Chomsky expressed complete agnosticism on the subject of whether or not Faurisson's views were "horrendous," saying that he was not sufficiently involved in the issue to pursue or evaluate it.

who was right—the "revisionists" or the "traditionalists"—on such matters as the destruction of the European Jews, aspects of Hitler's foreign policy, and the legitimacy of the Nuremberg trials. On the Jews his "revisionists" were Butz, Rassinier, App, and Harwood. (Hoggan was his "revisionist" on Hitler's foreign policy.) The "traditionalists" included Reitlinger, Hilberg, and me. Morris noticed that we were all Jewish, but thought it "only natural" for Jews "to have been in the forefront of Holocaust studies" because "they or their relatives suffered under Nazi persecution of the Jews."

After weighing the findings of Butz and company and comparing them with those of the "traditionalists," Morris reluctantly concluded that "Rassinier, Butz, App, Harwood, and other revisionists have failed to discredit the traditional accounts of the Nazi efforts to exterminate the Jews." *Ipse dixit.* Yet Morris still rendered their due to the Revisionist Press and his friend Dr. App. Even if the "revisionists" had failed "to prove their most important arguments," he wrote, "by forcing historians to reconsider their evaluation of Nazi policy toward the Jews," they have "indeed done a very valuable service to scholarship."

In one of the more astonishing episodes of the story being unfolded here, the June 1980 issue of the *American Historical Review*, the journal of the American Historical Association, the preeminent professional organization of America historians, published a respectful review of Morris's book. * How this sly attempt to give academic legitimacy to the outpourings of a variety of neo-Nazis and anti-Semites came to be offered for review in the first place, and how it came to be assigned for review two years after its publication, is a bit of a mystery. One might have thought that a knowledgeable book-review editor would promptly have seen its worthlessness and that a competent historian would have disdained to review it. (The book is a 141-page reproduction of a sloppy typescript, priced at $44.95.) As to the review itself, it was "agnostic" and impartial to the point of vacancy.

---

*The review was written by Birdsall Scrymser Viault, of Winthrop College.

As the ranks of the pseudoscholars swelled, Willis Carto hit on the idea of creating an Institute of Historical Review, using the resources of Liberty Lobby and its network. In 1979 this institute convoked a "Revisionist Convention" on the Northrup College campus in Los Angeles. Papers were read by Butz, Faurisson, App, and Walendy, arguing that there had been no Holocaust and no gas chambers; that all the camp photographs had been faked; that the Jews (alas) were still alive. The assemblage also heard speeches by Carto, John Bennett (who came all the way from Melbourne), and Devin Garrity, president of the right-wing publishing house Devin-Adair.

The convention was dedicated to the memory of Harry Elmer Barnes; its opening speaker was none other than James J. Martin, Barnes's protégé from the 1950s. In 1964 Martin had produced a two-volume, 1,337-page compendium, published by Devin-Adair, which charged that between 1931 and 1941 American liberals had undergone a conspiratorial changeover from peace advocacy to war advocacy. (A reviewer summed up this "goulash of quotation, summary, and editorial comment" as "a scholarly disaster.") Now Martin has inherited Barnes's laurels and has been installed in the neo-Nazi pantheon as the "dean of historical revisionist scholars." He is the director of Ralph Myles Publishers, a firm which publishes revisionist books, some more fascist than academic. He also operates in the more rarefied atmosphere of the libertarians, where Right and Left sometimes bed together even if they don't always see eye to eye. Cato Institute, a libertarian outfit based in San Francisco, subsidized by the Koch Foundation (which supports the Libertarian party), recently published a collection of Barnes's more paranoid essays with a foreword by Martin. *

At the 1979 revisionist convention, Carto announced that in 1980 the Institute of Historical Review would launch a quarterly, *Journal of Historical Review*. It was delivered as promised, with a lead article by Butz and other pieces by Faurisson, App, Walendy, and their ilk. A second issue followed, with similar contents, and a second con-

---

* *Revisionism: A Key to Peace and Other Essays*, Cato Paper No. 12, 1980.

vention was held in August at Pomona College, Claremont, California, this one dedicated to Rassinier's memory. Mabel Narjes, Hoggan's translator, who had brought Barnes and Rassinier together many years before, was flown over from Hamburg to speak about that historic encounter. Martin read a paper summarizing his forthcoming book on genocide, the publication of which one can await only with anxiety.

Does any of this matter? Would any sensible and decent person be taken in by the absurd and malicious lie that Hitler's Germany never murdered six million Jews? Who would believe the monstrous falsehood that there were no gas chambers at Auschwitz? As it turns out, these are not just rhetorical questions.

While I was writing this article, a man associated with the Larry King radio show, a national network talk program, called to ask if I would debate with Faurisson. When I replied indignantly that Faurisson should not be provided with a platform for his monomania, the man mildly inquired why I was against discussing "controversial" matters on the radio. I in turn asked *him* if he thought the murder of the European Jews was a "controversial" matter. Had it not been established to his satisfaction as a historical fact? "I don't know," he answered. "I wasn't around at the time. I'm only thirty years old."

Perhaps it is not so hard after all to befuddle the ignorant, especially on Jewish matters, to which they are, at best, indifferent. Yet would Americans give a respectful hearing to someone who insisted that slavery had never existed in the United States, that blacks invented the story in order to get preferential treatment and federal aid, or that blacks had actually owned all the plantations? Somehow one doubts it.

Nor is it only the ignorant and the ill-informed who are involved here. The established academic and historical institutions of the United States, who should be the first to safeguard the truth of the past as it happened, have instead given respectful consideration to the most blatant falsifications of the recent past. The mindless review of Morris's tract in the *American Historical Review* is just one egregious example. Another is the response of the Organization of American

Historians (OAH) to the *Journal of Historical Review*, the new quarterly of the "revisionists."

In the spring of 1980, each of the twelve thousand members of the OAH received a complimentary copy of the inaugural issue of the *Journal*. A half-minute perusal should have sufficed to show that it was nothing more than a potpourri of anti-Semitic propaganda camouflaged to look like a learned journal. Some OAH members, in fact, protested the sale of the OAH membership list to neo-Nazis; others felt that, in the interests of intellectual freedom, the mailing list should be available to all. The OAH executive secretary responded to this division of opinion with irreproachable objectivity; he proposed to provide his executive board with "an analysis of the *JHR* as a historical publication," which analysis to "be developed by well-qualified historians," who would "focus on the credentials of the contributors and the use of evidence." Then, well-armed with a well-grounded analysis of this rubbish by well-qualified historians, the OAH's executive board would duly report to its members. *

Report what, is not quite clear. Perhaps that the neo-Nazis did not have proper academic credentials, or that they failed to use primary sources? Again one wonders: would the OAH have reacted the same way to a pseudoscholarly journal pushing KKK propaganda?

One turns with relief to the French historians. At the time of the Faurisson affair, thirty-four of France's leading historians issued a declaration attesting to the historical truth of the Holocaust and protesting the Nazi attempt to erase the past. † The concluding paragraph of the declaration could well serve as a guide to American historians:

Everyone is free to interpret a phenomenon like the Hitlerite genocide according to his own philosophy. Everyone is free to compare it with other enterprises of murder committed earlier,

---

* "Journal of Historical Review," *OAH Newsletter*, 8, 1 (July 1980), pp. 14–15.
† The full text of the declaration, with a list of all its signatories, appeared in *Le Monde*, February 21, 1979.

at the same time, later. Everyone is free to offer such or such kind of explanation; everyone is free, to the limit, to imagine or to dream that these monstrous deeds did not take place. Unfortunately they did take place and no one can deny their existence without committing an outrage on the truth. It is not necessary to ask how *technically* such mass murder was possible. It was technically possible, seeing that it took place. That is the required point of departure of every historical inquiry on this subject. This truth it behooves us to remember in simple terms: there is not and there cannot be a debate about the existence of the gas chambers.

About fifty years ago the great Dutch historian Johan Huizinga remarked that the critical historical faculty required three elements: "Common sense, practice, and above all a historical sense, a high form of that discrimination by which a connoisseur knows a true work of art from a false one." Huizinga believed that a higher level of historical discrimination now prevailed among educated persons than had in the past, and that trained historians had acquired greater sophistication in using historical evidence. Consequently, he concluded, "only the untrained are inclined now to accept flagrantly false versions." On the record presented here, his optimism about the historical profession was premature.

6

THE TRUE HISTORY OF
BABI YAR

Barely four miles from the center of Kiev, the Ukraine's ancient and beautiful capital, is a place called Babi Yar. Once a deep, wooded ravine through which a small stream ran, Babi Yar is now filled in, an open space with brambly growth and a few lonely trees.

There, on September 29 and 30, 1941, the invading and occupying forces of Hitler's Third Reich murdered 33,771 Jewish men, women, and children. But the eeriness at Babi Yar is not just that of a vast necropolis. Babi Yar is haunted. The ghosts of its Jewish dead hover over the desolate field in a perpetual purgatory of historical denial. For the Soviet government has ordered that the memory of their murder be erased from the records and the minds of the Russian people. *

---

*The present essay, marking the fortieth anniversary of the massacre at Babi Yar, was first published on September 27, 1981, long before the upheavals and disintegrations of the post-Brezhnev period. For the fiftieth anniversary, in September 1991, a bronze menorah was set up at the site of the mass murder, and the Ukrainian government, which had in the meantime declared independence from Moscow, held commemorative ceremonies that included delegations from the United States, Europe, and Israel.—Ed.

Yet the remembrance of Babi Yar persists. In the outside world, it symbolizes the fate of the Soviet Jews at the hands of the German invaders, just as the Warsaw ghetto uprising of April 1943 stands for the fate of the Polish Jews. Inside the Soviet Union itself, however, Babi Yar has come to represent more than the site of a Nazi massacre, one among dozens. It speaks as well to a whole range of Jewish experience in Russia, an often harsh and sometimes bloodstained history that reaches back to pogroms under the tsars and on to the arrests and virulent propaganda attacks of the last decade.

In the Ukraine, as in other parts of the Soviet nation occupied by the Germans, many people welcomed the invaders and some actively collaborated in the wholesale slaughter. After the war, such grass-roots anti-Semitic attitudes were frequently reflected in official Soviet policies, which were adapted to meet changing political needs at home and overseas. Thus, for example, the increasingly anti-Israel stance of recent years, which has served Soviet aims in the Arab world.

At Babi Yar, these policies prevented Jews from holding memorial services—part of the government program to deny the facts of the massacre. What we know of Babi Yar today comes from accounts in official German documents and from Soviet eyewitnesses. But for those sources, the government might have succeeded in its intent.

George Orwell in 1984 described the process of rewriting history: "Day by day and almost minute by minute the past was brought up to date. . . . All history was a palimpsest, scraped clean and rein-scribed exactly as often as was necessary." The Soviet government has fulfilled the Orwellian fiction—to the extent of charging that Zionists had been in league with Hitler and were in part responsible for Babi Yar.

The anti-Semitic policies of the Soviet government have had an effect that Moscow may not have anticipated. Not for the first time in history, adversity has led many previously assimilated Soviet Jews to affirm their religion. The struggle to confirm the massacre at Babi Yar, to commemorate the dead there, has been part of that process. For Jewish dissidents, Babi Yar has become a powerful symbol of their Jewish identity.

* * *

The story of what happened at Babi Yar begins with the German invasion of the Soviet Union on June 22, 1941. Attached to each of the advancing German armies was an armed motorized company of from 800 to 1,200 men and officers drawn from the SS, the SD (security police), the Gestapo, and other police forces in the Nazi state. These companies were called *Einsatzgruppen*, "special-duty troops." Their special duty was to murder the Jews and anyone they suspected of being Soviet "commissars." Their chief was Reinhard Heydrich, second only to Heinrich Himmler in the dread SS. The *Einsatzgruppen* were trained in military tactics and mass-murder techniques and indoctrinated in Nazi racism. "Judaism in the East," Heydrich told them, "is the source of Bolshevism and must therefore be wiped out in accordance with the Führer's aims."

German troops reached Kiev on September 19, 1941. With them was *Sonderkommando* ("special commando") 4A, an advance unit of *Einsatzgruppe* C that had been assigned to the Ukraine. Soon other units arrived; by September 25, the full *Einsatzgruppe* C was in Kiev. The special unit immediately recruited a network of informers from among Kiev's ethnic Germans and formed a militia from among those Ukrainians who had welcomed the Germans as liberators.

Before they fled, the Soviet troops had planted mines and delayed-action bombs in Kiev's downtown area. On September 24, the bombs started to go off. Soon Kiev's whole center city went up in flames. People thought that Moscow must have looked like that in 1812. Many buildings burned to the ground; others, no longer safe, had to be evacuated. About 25,000 people were made homeless.

But the conflagration had its uses. The *Einsatzgruppe* officers, conferring with the German army commandant, decided to blame the Jews for setting Kiev afire. On September 27, the army's propaganda company printed 2,000 placards, which the newly recruited Ukrainian militia posted all around the city the following day.

The placards ordered all Jews in Kiev to assemble near the Russian and Jewish cemeteries at 8 A.M. on September 29. (On the Jewish calendar, that was 8 Tishri, the eighth of ten penitential days between

Rosh ha-Shana and Yom Kippur, the most solemn of Jewish holy days.) The Jews were furthermore told to bring with them such things as documents, money, valuables, and warm clothing. Those who disobeyed would be shot. Almost everyone thought that the Germans were going to send the Jews away, and "resettle" them. Since the assembly place was near a railroad siding, rumors spread that the Germans were moving them to Palestine.

The Jews of Kiev, like Jews elsewhere in the Soviet Union, knew little or nothing about the anti-Jewish policies of the Third Reich, Stalin's erstwhile ally. Early in the occupation, a German intelligence officer reported to his superiors that the Russian Jews were "shockingly ill-informed about our attitude toward them." The Soviet Jews knew nothing of the anti-Jewish legislation enacted in Germany and in the countries that Germany had taken over. They knew nothing about Kristallnacht, "the Night of Broken Glass," November 9–10, 1938, when the Nazis, in savage reprisal for a Jewish boy's assassination of a German diplomat in Paris, set the torch to synagogues and Jewish institutions all through Germany. They knew nothing about the Jews in German-occupied Poland who were incarcerated in ghettos, forced to be slave laborers, starved, humiliated, terrorized. They knew nothing of Adolf Hitler's vow to annihilate the Jews of Europe.

Some 175,000 Jews lived in Kiev in 1939. When the Germans invaded Russia, the Soviet authorities ordered the factories and their workers evacuated eastward. Many Jews probably left Kiev then. Most able-bodied men had been in the Red Army and were by September either prisoners of war or hiding in the countryside. On September 22, the German Army commander in Kiev ordered that all adult Jewish males be rounded up and placed in labor camps to perform "dangerous cleanup work." That left probably some 100,000 Jews in Kiev. They were mainly women and children, old people and sick people.

However ignorant they were about the Nazi record, the Jews of Kiev were filled with foreboding as they prepared to obey the Nazi order to report to the assembly area on September 29. They had no idea of their ultimate destination. At dawn, they started their doomed procession from Podol, the rundown, overcrowded slum that was Kiev's Jewish neighborhood. A few well-to-do Jews managed to get cars or carts to move their possessions. Others used baby carriages and barrows. But most simply carried their things in suitcases, bags, baskets, and bundles. Bent under the burden of their baggage and the weight of their worries, they trudged and straggled toward the assembly place, the little ones toddling, the elderly limping, staggering. Some were impassive, stoical; others wailed and cursed.

There were Ukrainians who came to help their Jewish friends, to accompany the old and the sick, though most watched the mournful procession with indifference. And some Ukrainians even rejoiced in the misfortune of the Jews—people who had been neighbors, schoolmates, shop mates, even friends, jeered. The Jews were unprepared for abandonment and betrayal by those among whom they had lived in peace for two decades. They were unprepared for the ease and speed with which some Ukrainians slipped back into the anti-Semitism that had tainted Ukrainian history for centuries.

In Ukrainian history, Bogdan Chmielnicki, who led an uprising against the Poles in 1648, is a national hero, but in Jewish history he is remembered for inspiring the bloodbath of pogroms that decimated the Jews in 1648–49. Two centuries later, the fury of anti-Semitism recurred in the pogroms of 1881 and then again in those of 1905.

In 1913, the Western world was riveted by the trial in Kiev of one Mendel Beilis, an obscure Jewish clerk who was accused of killing a Christian child to use his blood for a Passover ceremony. Thus, in the twilight of tsarist rule, the reactionary regime tried to divert a superstitious people from their real grievances. After an international uproar, the Kiev jury acquitted Beilis of murder, but the blood accusation against the Jewish people was left standing.

The memory of the Beilis trial was eclipsed in 1914 by the Great War and then by the February and October revolutions of 1917. In the civil war that followed the Bolshevik seizure of power, the Whites and the Reds fought mostly on Ukrainian terrain. The Jews were the chief casualties. The late Simon Dubnow, the premier historian of Russian Jewry, calculated that, between 1918 and 1921, some 530

Jewish communities in the Ukraine endured more than 1,200 pogroms. About 60,000 Jews were murdered; many more were injured and crippled. Some Jewish communities were completely obliterated, leaving no living survivors or standing houses.

The Soviet dictatorship at first tried to restrain Ukrainian anti-Semitism, though not out of love for the Jews. The government sought to discredit counterrevolutionary opponents by labeling them anti-Semites. But after the German occupation in 1941, ancient prejudices were unloosed. Thus, as soon as the Jews of Kiev had left their homes for the assembly place on September 29, some Ukrainians began to plunder the abandoned houses. Others were quick to betray Jews in hiding—even children—and to hand them over to the Germans.

Thousands upon thousands of Jews jammed into the assembly area. Germans, assisted by Ukrainian militia, directed them past the Jewish cemetery, through a passage bounded by barbed wire. "It was like a mass migration," according to the testimony of an officer of *Sonderkommando* 4A at his war-crimes trial in 1967. "The Jews sang religious songs on the way." They thought they were going to the railway siding, but there were no trains at their next stopping point—only mountains of baggage and clothing in one place, mountains of foodstuffs in another. The sound of machine-gun fire seemed near and the Jews thought the front was close by.

As their food and belongings were taken from them and heaped on the piles, the Jews' sense of foreboding grew to terror and panic. The lines seemed to stop moving, and people were crushed together, exhausted, terrified. The children were crying. Disorder, despair, nightmare.

Then the Germans began shoving the Jews into new, narrower lines. They moved very slowly. After a long walk, they came to a passageway formed by German soldiers with truncheons and police dogs. The Jews were whipped through. The dogs went at those who fell. But the pressure of the surging lines behind was irresistible, and the weak and injured were trod underfoot.

Bruised and bloodied, numbed by the incomprehensibility of their fate, the Jews emerged onto a grassy clearing. They had arrived at Babi Yar; ahead of them lay the ravine. The ground was strewn with clothing. Ukrainian militiamen, supervised by Germans, ordered the Jews to undress. Those who balked, who resisted, were assaulted, their clothes ripped off. Naked bleeding people were everywhere. Screams and hysterical laughter filled the air. Some people's hair turned gray on the spot. Others went mad in moments.

The Germans led small groups away from the clearing toward a narrow ledge along the ravine. At a sand quarry behind the ledge, hidden from the view of the Jews, the Germans had mounted machine guns. When the ledge contained as many Jews as it could hold, the Germans gunned them down. The bodies toppled into the ravine, piling up layer upon layer. Where once a clear stream flowed, now blood ran.

The machine-gunners worked for an hour at a time and then were relieved by another crew. From time to time, German soldiers and Ukrainian militiamen descended into the ravine, trampling over the bodies to make sure they were dead, tamping them down to make more room, shoveling sand from the quarry over them. According to an official report, *Sonderkommando* 4A—assisted by the staff of *Einsatzgruppe* C, two units of the Police Regiment South and the Ukrainian militia—"executed" a total of 33,771 Jews in two days.

Those statistics set a record in the annals of mass murder. At Birkenau—Auschwitz's killing center—the total capacity of the four gassing and cremating plants was a maximum of 6,000 persons daily. Paul Blobel, the head of *Sonderkommando* 4A, received an Iron Cross from the führer.

The killing at Babi Yar continued for many months, but never again on that scale. By November 3, 1941, the commandant of *Einsatzgruppe* C reported, about 75,000 Jews had been shot at Babi Yar. Nonetheless, he complained that the "Jewish problem" was still not "solved." There were still Jews to be killed, and the Germans scoured Kiev and the nearby countryside for them.

Meanwhile, *Einsatzgruppe* C was also pursuing its "mopping-up" operations among the non-Jewish population. The Nazis shot so-called political commissars, saboteurs, and partisans. They shot Ukrainian nationalists, whom they had at first encouraged. They shot a party of sailors from the Dnieper river fleet and they shot the Kiev soccer team, which had defeated the German Army soccer team. They shot Gypsies and they shot curfew violators. They shot the patients at a mental hospital and they shot people who queued up twice for the same meal. Yet, always and above all, they shot Jews. No one knows the precise figures, but of about 100,000 people murdered at Babi Yar within the next twelve months, some 90,000 were Jews.

Babi Yar was a Jewish gravesite, but the Soviet regime never acknowledged it. The "Final Solution of the Jewish Problem"—the German code name for the murder of the European Jews—became a nonsubject in Soviet history. Virtually no Soviet account of the war has ever recorded the fundamental information that the Germans singled out the Jews for annihilation. All Soviet wartime losses, on the battlefield as well as behind the lines, are merged into the category of "Soviet citizens," and no distinctions are made about the particular fate of any group.

Rewriting history is a continuing and commonplace process in the Soviet Union. As the Communist party changes its political line to fit the strategic interests of the Soviet Union, so history is changed retroactively to make the past harmonize with the present. In 1954, for example, the publishers of the *Great Soviet Encyclopedia* advised their subscribers to remove "carefully" the pages about Lavrenti Beria, former head of the security police, who was purged in July 1953. As a replacement for those pages, they supplied a new article on the Bering Strait.

Why was it necessary to erase from Soviet history the record of the Jews in World War II, including the horror of Babi Yar? The decision was part of a dramatic change in the direction of postwar Soviet domestic affairs and foreign relations, which soon turned anti-Semitism into a major instrument of policy.

Throughout the Soviet Union, there had been varying levels of collaboration with the German invaders. Some ethnic groups were punished severely. But in the Ukraine, the wartime defection had been so widespread that the central government felt compelled to adopt a policy of pacification and reconciliation. Historians believe that the regime sought to appease these former collaborators by demonstrating that it shared their hatred of the Jews.

Anti-Semitism as a government policy also served the postwar foreign-policy goals of the Soviet Union. The wartime Grand Alliance gave way to the cold war. Everything Western was now condemned. Russian nationalism took precedence over all other regional and ethnic loyalties; a kind of jingoist patriotism became the watchword. Because so many Soviet Jews were preoccupied with the experience of their sufferings as Jews, because they were traumatized by the murder of six million European Jews, because they sought the comfort of association with Jews elsewhere in the world, they were now accused of being unpatriotic, of being "rootless," of being "cosmopolitans." Though the Soviet Union had favored the establishment of the State of Israel, by the summer of 1948 there had been a dramatic policy change. Any expression of love or admiration for the new Jewish state of Israel was condemned as "bourgeois nationalism," and the regime severely clamped down on contacts with overseas Jews.

For all the peoples of the Soviet Union, the postwar years were an era of awesome terror. No one knows how many tens of millions were deported to the infernal region of the labor camps or how many millions died there. No group of the Soviet population was safe from the reach of Stalin's tyranny. Yet from all the evidence available, it seems clear that, as a group, the Soviet Jews suffered even more under Stalin than did others. They were the objects of official hate, publicly abused and denounced. Their committees and publications were liquidated, and many of their writers and intellectuals arrested and murdered. Their admission to universities, medical schools, scientific institutes was rigidly restricted. Moreover, anti-Semitism at the grass roots became loud-mouthed and ugly. Western visitors noted its ubiquity.

Soviet anti-Semitism of the 1950s was orchestrated with anti-Semitism in the satellite countries. Elaborate show trials were put on in Czechoslovakia, Rumania, and Hungary, as top Communists were accused of participating in "Zionist" conspiracies against their own countries. The charges were reminiscent of the hoary canards of the *Protocols of the Elders of Zion*, the classic anti-Semitic work concocted by the tsarist secret police half a century earlier.

The climax came in January 1953, when Pravda announced the discovery of a "terrorist group of doctors," publicly identified as Jews, who had allegedly murdered Soviet officials and who were plotting to murder more. Official Soviet anti-Semitism grew more shrill—until it came to a sudden and dramatic halt on March 5 of that year, the day of Stalin's death. In *The Gulag Archipelago*, Aleksandr Solzhenitsyn, whose intense nationalism had not made him a particular friend of the Jews, wrote of the regime's plans for the Jews of Russia had Stalin not died:

> According to Moscow rumors, Stalin's plan was this: At the beginning of March the "doctor-murderers" were to be hanged on Red Square. The aroused patriots, spurred on, naturally by instructors, were to rush into an anti-Jewish pogrom. At this point the government—and here Stalin's character can be divined, can it not?—would intervene generously to save the Jews from the wrath of the people, and that same night would remove them from Moscow to the Far East and Siberia—where barracks had already been prepared for them.

Three years later, in February 1956, Nikita Khrushchev, the new Soviet boss, delivered his famous secret speech at the Communist party's 20th Congress, denouncing Stalin for having fostered a "cult of personality" and for having committed those very crimes of which the West had long accused him. A thaw in Soviet political life set in. Millions of survivors of every ethnic and religious group began to be released from the gulag.

Soviet authorities even publicly admitted that Stalin had pursued an anti-Jewish policy. They relented on his use of terror though they continued to seek popular support by restricting the number of Jews

110

in education and government. But the memory of Babi Yar and of what they called Stalin's "black years" had made many Soviet Jews aware of their Jewishness, even though few of the younger people knew anything of Jewish history or culture. And the existence of a sovereign Jewish state thrilled them. They took courage from the thaw.

An early public expression of Jewish solidarity came in 1958 on the festival of Simhat Torah ("Rejoicing in the Law"), when dozens of youths congregated around the synagogue in Leningrad, singing and dancing in the street to celebrate their Jewishness—in violation of Soviet law. It was one of the earliest and most dramatic instances of Jewish dissidence. Clandestine groups were organized to study Hebrew, to read Jewish history, to distribute Jewish literature.

In Kiev, too, Jews sought to express their identity. In keeping with Jewish tradition, their first concern was to sanctify the mass graves at Babi Yar and to hold memorial services for their murdered relatives.

By this time, Babi Yar had become a pasture for cattle. When Khrushchev had been Communist party boss in the Ukraine, right after the war, he had turned down proposals for a memorial to the murdered Jews. In 1957, the idea for a monument came up again. But when the authorities studied the statistics of those who had died there and saw that any memorial would have to recognize the preponderance of Jewish victims, they once again vetoed the suggestion. Instead, they undertook to fill in the ravine and build a sports stadium there.

In the process, engineers constructed a dam that turned the ravine into a huge lake. As the operation continued, from year to year, the level of the dam was raised until, by the beginning of 1961, the dam had reached the height of a six-story building. Then, on March 13 of that year, torrential spring rains caused the dam to overflow. Moments later, a thirty-foot tidal wave of mud poured into Kiev. Anatoly Kuznetsov, in his book *Babi Yar,* described the disaster:

Whole crowds of people were swallowed up instantly in the wave of mud. People sitting in trams and in cars perished. . . . Houses which stood in the way of the wave were swept away as if made of cardboard.

111

The media in the Soviet Union seldom report accidents or disasters that happen in their country. The *New York Times* correspondent put the number of deaths at 145 and estimated the injuries at about the same number.

In Kiev, people said: "Babi Yar takes its revenge." Peasants went to church to light candles and pray for the souls of the murdered Jews. Orthodox priests conducted memorial services for the victims of the tidal wave and for the Jews killed twenty years earlier. Soviet officialdom might deny the statistics and rewrite history, but everyone in Kiev knew that most of the dead of Babi Yar were Jews.

More than a million Jews had been killed by Germans at dozens of Babi Yars throughout the Soviet Union, and these Jewish dead continued to haunt the population. In the gulag, it was often said that when a man screamed in his sleep, he was "dreaming of Yids," of those whom he had once helped to murder and who now returned in his dreams.

It was in the year of the mud disaster that a young Ukrainian poet, Yevgeny Yevtushenko, wrote "Babi Yar." Perhaps, like the peasants and priests of Kiev, he wished to propitiate the dead. Published in the USSR's leading literary journal, *Literaturnaya Gazeta,* on September 19, 1961, the poem was read and admired across the nation. It began:

> There are no memorials at Babi Yar—
> The steep slope is the only gravestone.
> I am afraid.
> Today I am as old as the Jewish people.
> It seems to me now that I am a Jew.

Yevtushenko tempered his courage with discretion. While condemning the contemporary "pogrom thugs" who followed in the tradition of the tsarist Black Hundreds—the anti-Semitic groups whose slogan had been "Beat the Yids and Save Russia"—he absolved the Communist party and the Soviet Union of anti-Semitism:

112

Let the "Internationale" ring out
When the last anti-Semite on earth is buried.
There is no Jewish blood in mine,
But I am hated by every anti-Semite as a Jew,
And for this reason,
I am a true Russian

Even so, Yevtushenko's "Babi Yar" raised a storm of official criticism. Khrushchev himself condemned the poem because it presented "things as if only the Jews were the victims," whereas "of course many Russians, Ukrainians, and Soviet people of other nationalities were murdered by the Hitlerite butchers."

Meanwhile, undaunted, the Kiev authorities in 1962 resumed work at Babi Yar. The plan for a sports stadium on the site was abandoned; instead, the area was simply to be filled in and leveled off. The bulldozers were dispatched. They kept turning up bones tangled in barbed wire. After four years, the project was done: Babi Yar was erased. The old Jewish cemetery nearby was also leveled and a television center erected on its grounds. Apartment houses were built near the site. The rest of the area remained desolate.

Each year thereafter, on September 29, the Jews of Kiev came to commemorate the murdered dead and to recite *kaddish*, the mourner's prayer, for their relatives. Each year, the local police dispersed the mourners. Once, in 1968, to preempt the Jewish commemoration, the local authorities organized an official memorial at which the party speaker eulogized the dead as "Soviet citizens, Russians, Ukrainians, and others." In 1972, twenty-seven Jews were arrested for putting flowers on the ground at Babi Yar. They were sentenced to fifteen days in jail. A year later, about a thousand Jews turned up on the anniversary, but the police prohibited any religious services and banned even the lighting of memorial candles. The gathering was dispersed, and five persons were arrested for unlawful assembly.

The murmuring protests that there was no monument at Babi Yar grew louder as the dissidents grew bolder. To still their voices, the

authorities finally erected a monument in 1976. It was a huge, mul-
tifigured sculpture with all the trite sentimentality characteristic of
Socialist Realism. At its foot was a bronze tablet inscribed as follows:
"Here in 1941–43 German Fascist invaders executed more than
100,000 citizens of the city of Kiev and prisoners of war."

In October 1964, Khrushchev was ousted from power. Within a short
time he was replaced by Leonid Brezhnev, another native Ukrainian. Before long, Brezhnev turned de-Stalinization back toward re-
Stalinization. The regime began to censor writers more rigidly, to
harass the dissidents more cruelly, to arrest the troublemakers more
frequently, and to put the recalcitrant cases in psychiatric wards.

In 1968, Brezhnev sent troops into Czechoslovakia to depose the
new government, which had been moving toward greater intellectual
and economic freedom. He became preoccupied with China, moving
more and more army divisions to the Russian-Chinese border. He
undertook the largest military buildup in the history of the Soviet
Union. He also stepped up his pursuit of allies in Latin America and
among the countries of the Third World. He particularly wooed Arab
nations, with ardor and with military equipment.

These new policies, in the view of many students of contemporary
history, brought about a shift in the Soviet attitude toward the Jews.
Under Khrushchev, official anti-Semitism had been intended to serve
domestic political goals and most propaganda was directed against
Judaism rather than against Israel and the Zionist movement. Under
Brezhnev, anti-Semitism was to a much greater extent synchronized
with Soviet foreign policy, and Soviet anti-Semitic propaganda concentrated almost exclusively on Zionism and the state of Israel as
central to the alleged Jewish plot to seize control of the world. The
objects of attack now included not only the Jews in the Soviet Union
but Jews the world over, and particularly those in Israel. Moreover,
while official Soviet anti-Semitism had, under Khrushchev, been intended solely for the consumption of the home market, now Soviet
anti-Semitism was designed for export as well—for worldwide dissem-
ination to the Arabs, to the third world, to all disaffected peoples.

114

A hint of things to come surfaced at the United Nations in 1965 in a committee of the General Assembly. In a ploy to defeat a resolution specifically condemning anti-Semitism, the Soviet delegate introduced a motion against "anti-Semitism, Nazism and all other forms . . . of colonialism, national and race hatred, and exclusiveness." The motion never came to a vote, but it served its purpose: no resolution against anti-Semitism was adopted. Ten years later, the Soviet Union, supported by its satellites, by Arab and Third World countries, engineered the passage in the General Assembly of a resolution that condemned "zionism"—the small "z" was an added insult—as "a form of racism and racial discrimination."

After the Six-Day War of June 1967, when Israel defeated the Arab states, which had been armed by the Soviet Union, there was an outpouring of anti-Semitic propaganda from the Soviet media. Bibliographies compiled by recent Soviet émigrés show the escalation of books and pamphlets exclusively devoted to anti-Jewish material. Between 1960 and 1966, five of these publications appeared. Over the next four years, the number increased to twelve. Between 1971 and 1974, the figure rose to forty-seven, and between 1975 and 1978, it reached fifty.

The fevered pace of anti-Semitic publications was matched by their bizarre content: Zionism was actually presented as being in the service of Nazism. Articles in propaganda publications and in the national and regional press claimed that the "Zionists" had "collaborated" with reactionaries, progromists, and anti-Semites all through their history. They had entered, as one publication put it, into "a dirty alliance with the Hitlerites."

Even Babi Yar was not exempt. An article in *Pravda*, March 16, 1971, said that "the tragedy of Babi Yar" would "forever remain the embodiment not only of the cannibalism of the Hitlerites but also the indelible shame of their accomplices and followers—the Zionists."

The flood of anti-Semitic propaganda stiffened the determination of the Jewish dissidents. The story of Boris Kochubiyevsky is a dramatic case in point. Born in Kiev in 1936, son of a Babi Yar victim, Kochubiyevsky was an engineer at a radio factory in Kiev. Though he

115

had no Jewish education, he grew up, by his own account, in a milieu that never let him forget he was Jewish. After the Six-Day War, the workers in his factory—as in thousands of factories across the Soviet Union—were assembled to hear an agitprop tirade against Israel and to adopt a "unanimous" resolution condemning Israel's "aggression."

It's easy to picture what happened. The open anti-Semitism at the meeting released Kochubiyevsky's long-festering rage over the hurts and humiliations he had suffered for being Jewish. Courage welled up in him. He spoke out against the resolution and insisted that the record show his opposition.

The factory's union committee insisted that Kochubiyevsky resign. He held out stubbornly for a year but finally had to give in to their pressure. During that year, he wrote an essay entitled "Why I Am a Zionist." In it, he asked how it happened that young Russian Jews, raised as atheists, knowing nothing of Jewish culture or tradition, could become proud and passionate Jews. The simple answer, he said, was that anti-Semitism had turned them into Jews—the anti-Semitism that the Soviets now labeled anti-Zionism and the conventional anti-Semitism of the Black Hundreds, which still flourished in Russia.

In the summer of 1968, Kochubiyevsky and his wife applied for exit permits to leave for Israel. Small numbers of Jews were then allowed to leave for Israel to be reunited with their families. But the Kochubiyevskys were refused exit papers. They reapplied. Meanwhile, on September 29, 1968, Kochubiyevsky attended that official commemoration at Babi Yar where the murdered Jews were not mentioned. When the official program was over, the Jews remained to mourn their dead. Kochubiyevsky spoke up with passion: "Here lies a part of the Jewish people."

He was arrested two months later and charged with slandering the Soviet Union. He was tried in May 1969 in the same courthouse in Kiev where Mendel Beilis had been tried some fifty years earlier. Past and present coalesced. According to the accounts of Jewish dissidents, friends and supporters of Kochubiyevsky were barred from his trial and the courtroom was filled with hostile observers; the evidence was rigged; the witnesses had been suborned. Kochubiyevsky was found guilty of slandering the Soviet Union. He served three years in a labor camp before he was at last allowed to emigrate.

At the beginning of the 1970s, in part because of pressure from the United States, the Soviet regime significantly increased the number of Jews who were allowed to leave the country for Israel. During the last decade, more than 250,000 Jews have left the Soviet Union using exit permits for Israel, though recently many of them have opted for the United States. However, during this time, the Soviet regime has arbitrarily accelerated or restricted the flow of Jewish emigration.

But in one regard, at least, the immigration policy has been consistent. Those Jews who apply for exit permits are turned into pariahs overnight. They lose their jobs—even if they must wait months or years for their exit papers. They are subject to police surveillance and harassment. Their friends and neighbors shun them. Sometimes they are arrested.

Yet the overwhelming majority of the Jews in the Soviet Union choose to remain there. They feel the whiplash of official anti-Semitism in the ubiquitous propaganda against Israel and the "Zionists." They suffer restrictions in access to higher education and to the professions. They feel grassroots hostility from the playground to the army camp.

Any sudden change in the top leadership, any extraordinary shift in Soviet foreign policy, could transform the present climate. No one can predict the future course of the Soviet regime with regard to the Jews. But for the time being, this much is sure: so long as the demons of anti-Semitism still haunt the Soviet Union, the Jews there will have no peace—and neither will the Jewish ghosts of Babi Yar.

POSTSCRIPT

For historians—and novelists—the sources about Babi Yar are Nazi records and eyewitnesses accounts.

As World War II came to an end, enormous quantities of Nazi records fell into Allied hands. These documents were used as evidence at the trials of major war criminals at Nuremberg. The records were then sorted and microfilmed and, by now, most of them have been returned to the Federal Republic of Germany. A full set is in the National Archives in Washington.

Among these records are the many reports prepared by the *Einsatzgruppen* for their Berlin headquarters. These documents, amplified and explicated by the testimony offered at the Nuremberg trial of the *Einsatzgruppen* leaders in 1947–48, contain the most important data about the murder of the Jews at Babi Yar. Further corroborative evidence was elicited at the trial held in Darmstadt, West Germany, in 1967–68 of the men and officers of *Sonderkommando* 4A, who were directly responsible for the Babi Yar killings.

Accounts by survivors are few. The Soviet journalist and novelist Ilya Ehrenburg collected eyewitness accounts of the experiences of Soviet Jews under the German occupation. These were to be published in an accusatory Black Book, but the Soviet authorities suppressed it. A highly abbreviated English version of this book, published in New York in 1946, contained two eyewitness accounts of what happened at Babi Yar. Ehrenburg's novel *The Storm* also deals with the events of Babi Yar.

The major Russian source is *Babi Yar,* a documentary book by the Kiev-born writer A. Anatoly (Anatoly Kuznetsov). A censored version first was published in the Soviet Union in 1966. Kuznetsov fled to the West in 1969 and expanded the original text. The book's most gripping chapter is the first-person account of Dina Mironovna Pronicheva, a Jewish woman who was at Babi Yar but who managed to escape. She testified at the Darmstadt trial. For my summary of what happened at Babi Yar, I drew extensively from her account and from other sections of Kuznetsov's book. I am not the only one to have done so. D. M. Thomas has appropriated Dina Pronicheva's testimony as the experience of his central character in his novel, *The White Hotel.*

There are few official Soviet sources that document the murders at Babi Yar. One is the note of Soviet Foreign Minister Vyacheslav M. Molotov, dated January 6, 1942, addressed to the ambassadors of all countries with which Moscow maintained diplomatic relations, headed

"Regarding the Wholesale Looting, Ruin of the Population and Monstrous Atrocities Perpetrated by the German Authorities on Soviet Territories Seized by Them." He specifically refers to Jews as the primary victims of the *Einsatzgruppen* at Kiev.

7

HISTORY
AS IDEOLOGY

Nearly half a century has passed since the murder of the European Jews during World War II, and it might be thought that at this late date we understand fully how and why the German state under Hitler committed its terrible crimes. Yet scholars are still producing monographs and books with new explanations of how it all came about. To be sure, every new generation of scholars revises the work of its predecessors and rewrites history according to its own lights. Today, however, a number of professional historians are propounding interpretations of the murder of the European Jews so implausible and so perverse that, even as they strain credulity, they undermine the credibility of the historical enterprise itself.

The origin of these bizarre explanations can be traced to West Germany, where, indeed, most scholarly work on the subject has been produced. In the wake of the student riots in the late 1960s, leftist historians, searching for a more sophisticated social theory than that provided by Marxism, reached out to other disciplines for theoretical concepts of "system, structure, and function." These "structuralist" historians began to transform the writing of history from an account of the deeds and ideas of men into a record of the workings of impersonal institutions.

In studying the Nazi past, the new generation of historians concluded that the Nazi state had functioned not in accordance with its leaders' intentions and policies but largely through the near-autonomous workings of its bureaucracies. Thus, these historians became tagged as "functionalists," in contrast to "intentionalists," who held, and hold, that Hitler's ideas and intentions were what determined the course of Germany's history. The structuralists/functionalists furthermore believed that Hitler's Germany, far from being a dictatorship operating under the führer principle, was more like a bureaucratic jungle, in which officials scrambled to establish their own jurisdictions and to exercise authority independently of Hitler.

As against the universally held view that Hitler's will and intentions had set Germany's agenda and shaped its policies, and that the state's institutions—notably the infamous SS—had been dedicated to executing that will, the structuralists/functionalists claimed that Hitler was a weak leader. They also minimized or altogether dismissed the view that the racial anti-Semitism which obsessed Hitler (and which afflicted German society as a whole after World War I) had succeeded in penetrating into all aspects of policy-making in the German dictatorship. One leading functionalist went so far as to claim that the "Jewish question" in the Nazi state was merely a matter of tactics, not a fundamental aspect of state policy.

Actually, few functionalists were familiar with all the sources and documents relevant to the murder of the European Jews, which was not the area of their specialization. But lack of competence did not inhibit them from imposing their dogmas on the historical evidence. They focused on one particular issue, for which, as in many crucial junctures in history, the documents are not as precise and explicit as historians would like: when, if at all, and by whom, if anyone, was a decision made to murder the Jews? Much functionalist writing concentrated on the absence among the Nazi records of unambiguous written instructions to murder the Jews.

One functionalist, Uwe Dietrich Adam, claiming from the start that Germany's anti-Jewish policies had not been planned in advance and that "Hitler merely reacted to existing circumstances and did not create them himself," went on to argue from the absence of a written

121

order to kill the Jews that Hitler had not decided on a systematic program of murder even when the *Einsatzgruppen*, the SS special-duty forces, began shooting Jews *en masse* in the summer of 1941, in Soviet-held territory. From the fact that by November 1941 the *Einsatzgruppen*, operating in four specially trained armed divisions, had already murdered about a million Jews, Adam did concede that Hitler *might* have made such a decision late in 1941, but not before then. [*]

A spate of functionalist articles appearing in the wake of Adam's book spawned a series of academic conferences, and from these conferences, in turn, emerged book-length collections of papers. [†] Still, notwithstanding their energy and industry, the functionalists have succeeded in persuading only a coterie of those who share their articles of faith. Their views, being profoundly at variance with the knowledge accumulated over decades, have remained outside the historical consensus and have so far failed to alter public consciousness of the Nazi period.

Yet functionalist theory still plays a role, and is sometimes used as a gambit to undermine long-established historical judgments. Thus, Arno J. Mayer, who holds an endowed chair in European history at Princeton, in his book *Why Did the Heavens Not Darken?: The "Final Solution" in History*, [‡] presents the thesis that Hitler was embarked on a premeditated, holy crusade to crush the Soviet Union and liquidate international communism, but that he never intended to murder the Jews. Echoing Uwe Dietrich Adam, Mayer argues that only in the fall of 1941, when they came to believe that their anti-Bolshevik crusade was faltering, did Hitler and his generals turn against the Jews, convenient scapegoats on whom the Germans now discharged their frus-

---

[*] *Judenpolitik im dritten Reich* (1972). Adam's is the only full-length functionalist book dealing with Nazi Germany's anti-Jewish policies. For more on his thesis, see the introduction to the Tenth Anniversary Edition of my *The War Against the Jews 1933–1945* (Bantam, 1986).

[†] One such volume, edited by François Furet, the historian of the French Revolution, has been published as *Unanswered Questions: Nazi Germany and the Genocide of the Jews* (Schocken Books, 1989).

[‡] Pantheon Books, 1989.

122

tration and rage at having been thwarted in their holy war against the Soviet Union.

Mayer's revisionist agenda is an ambitious one, which he presents without any inhibiting footnotes to document his questionable assertions and debatable interpretations. (In a recent interview, Mayer ridiculed footnotes as "a fetish [that] very often interferes with careful intellection and rumination.") He undertakes to show (1) that racial anti-Semitism was never a significant factor in the Nazi party or in the governance of the Nazi state; (2) that the Nazis intended only to deport the Jews, not to murder them; (3) that the murder squads of the *Einsatzgruppen* had no orders to kill Jews; and (4) that at Auschwitz more Jews died of "natural causes" than in the gas chambers.

Anti-Semitism as the fueling energy of Nazi ideology gets short shrift from Mayer. "Just as anti-Semitism was not the core of Hitler's presumption," he claims, "it did not have precedence over his other dogmas, particularly anti-Marxism and anti-Bolshevism." Though he concedes that "inwardly anti-Semitism may have been Hitler's core idea and all-consuming passion," in the very next sentence he also asserts that "before 1933 neither [Hitler's] public discourse nor the creed and ritual of the Nazi movement put [anti-Semitism] first, or were perceived as doing so." So much for *Mein Kampf,* the thick dossiers of Hitler's anti-Semitic speeches before he came to power, and the twenty-five-point program the fledgling Nazi party adopted in 1920, which stated that no Jew could ever belong to the German *Volk* and that only persons of German blood could be citizens of the German state.

Even when Mayer does acknowledge the presence of anti-Semitism in Hitler's mind and in the Nazi movement, he does not define it as an irrational hatred of the Jews or as fanatical racism, but as a screen for other resentments. Thus, he turns the Jews into "*surrogate* victims of [Hitler's] counterattack against polymorphous modernity, which was his ultimate *target*" (emphasis in the original). According to Mayer, "if Hitler's world-view had an epicenter, it was his deep-seated animosity toward contemporary civilization, and not his hatred for Jews, which was grafted onto it."

123

Given this upside-down account of Hitler's anti-Semitism, it is not surprising that Mayer scants the role played by racial ideas in Nazi political thinking and in the plans for war. Only now and then does he acknowledge that the goal of *Lebensraum*, "living space" for the master Aryan race in its quest for empire, was the motivating idea for the war and for the invasion of Russia. Nor does he associate the murder of the Jews with the aim of racial empire, despite convincing evidence that Hitler and his associates planned the two in synchronization, with the elimination of the Jews being necessary in order to ensure the purity and supremacy of the Aryan race.

In laying the groundwork for his thesis that the Germans never intended to murder the Jews, Mayer redefines the term "Judeobolshevism," which in Nazi jargon was an epithet for the so-called Jewish conspiracy that already controlled Russia and aspired to control the world. Mayer gives this lunatic fantasy a more rational meaning than it ever had in the Nazi lexicon, suggesting that "bolshevism" referred simply to the Soviet regime, and the modifying "Judeo" to a Jewish presence in that regime. In this way he derives warrant to conclude that when the Nazis invoked the term "Judeobolshevism" they were referring to the Soviet Union and not to the Jews. The war against Russia was therefore, according to Mayer, a crusade to extirpate Bolshevism, not to acquire *Lebensraum*, create an Aryan empire, or murder the Jews.

Yet Mayer also cites texts which contradict his definition of "Judeobolshevism." One, for example, is Hitler's proclamation to his troops in October 1941, explaining that poverty in Russia was

the result of nearly twenty-five years of Jewish rule, with a Bolshevik system that is essentially similar to the capitalist system, the carriers of both systems being the same, namely Jews and only Jews.

This compelling illustration of the Nazis' irrational understanding of capitalism and Bolshevism makes not the slightest dent in Mayer's reasoning.

*　　*　　*

Mayer's next step is to dust off a long-discredited hypothesis—namely, that once they had crushed Russia, the Nazis originally intended not to kill the Jews but to deport and resettle them "in a Lublin-like reservation beyond the Volga or the Urals." Mayer likely borrowed this idea from Adam, who holds that as late as mid-1941 "the final solution of the Jewish question" meant only resettling the Jews in Madagascar.

The notion of shipping the Jews to Madagascar originated in Germany in the early 1930s. In 1939, the German Foreign Office appropriated the idea as a proposed "solution" to the "Jewish problem," but dropped it after the invasion of the Soviet Union. An alternative plan was conceived in November 1939 to establish a reservation in the area of Lublin as a dumping ground for Jewish and non-Jewish "destructive elements." German Jews were then being shipped to Poland, presumably to be incarcerated there. Early in 1940 the plan for a Lublin reservation was approved at the highest level, but no practical steps were ever taken to implement it. In April 1940 the plan was abandoned.

Still, the idea of resettlement, whether to Madagascar, a Lublin reservation, or beyond the Urals, remained in the repertory of Nazi propaganda, a tactic of deception to conceal the mass killings of Jews. Even Hitler, on July 22, 1941, when he knew that the Madagascar plan had already been dropped and that the *Einsatzgruppen* had already been given their instructions, told Marshal Kvaternik, head of the Croatian armed forces, that it was a matter of indifference to him where the Jews were sent, whether to Siberia or to Madagascar. Soon thereafter, the SS routinely used the deceptive promise of resettlement "in the East" to lull the persecuted and terrorized Jews who were in fact being deported to killing camps. Today we are being asked once again to believe the propaganda about resettlement, this time by a university professor.

To support his scenario that the Germans never intended to murder the Jews, Mayer must somehow account for the massive operations of the four *Einsatzgruppen* on Soviet territory. He begins by claiming that "when they set forth on their mission, the *Einsatzgruppen* and the RSHA [Reich Central Security Office] were not given the extermination of Jews as their principal, let alone their only, assignment." That statement contradicts what has been known and documented for over forty years. License for the *Einsatzgruppen* to kill was written into the military orders for "Barbarossa," the code name for the invasion of Russia, issued March 13, 1941, and explicit orders were later given orally to murder Jews, Gypsies, and "commissars." The Roundup Report of *Einsatzgruppe* A for the period ending October 15, 1941, unambiguously states: ". . . in accordance with the basic orders, the mopping-up work of the Security Police had as its goal the annihilation, as comprehensive as possible, of the Jews."*

How does Mayer explain the fact that Jews began to be murdered as soon as the *Einsatzgruppen* entered Soviet territory? He has a ready answer: "Some of the first and for a time the worst outrages against the Jews were committed not by the new-model *Einsatzgruppen*, but by latter-day local progromists in . . . Lithuania, Latvia, Estonia." And, "[i]n the early triumphant days of Barbarossa the Jewish massacres were the product of random pogroms rather than of an official plan or warrant for systematic genocide." In fact, however, those "random pogroms" were planned and instigated by the *Einsatzgruppen*. The evidence, which Mayer either does not know or chooses to ignore, is in the Round-up Report of *Einsatzgruppe* A quoted above:

> . . . in the first hours after our entry [Kovno June 25, 1941], even under considerable hardships, native anti-Semitic elements were induced to start pogroms against Jews. In conformity with orders, the Security Police was determined to solve the Jewish

---

*Extracts from these field reports are in my book *A Holocaust Reader* (Behrman, 1976), pp. 89–96. No document has even been found containing the "basic orders" referred to here. According to oral testimony given at the *Einsatzgruppen* trial in Nuremberg in 1945–46 by Otto Ohlendorf, commander of *Einsatzgruppe* D, and by others in postwar trials in West Germany, those orders were issued orally at the *Einsatzgruppen* training centers, in preparation for the invasion of the Soviet Union.

question with all means and full decisiveness. It was, however, desirable that the Security Police should not be visible, at least in the beginning, since the extraordinarily harsh measures would attract attention even in German circles. It had to be demonstrated to the world that the native population itself took the first measures by way of natural reaction against decades-long suppression by the Jews and against the terror exercised by the Communists in the preceding period.

We now come to the crux of Mayer's thesis—that only after "the breakdown of Barbarossa" did the Jews become, as he puts it, "the chosen martyrs of [Germany's] fiery crusade against Bolshevism." To prove this thesis, Mayer postdates the *Einsatzgruppen* killings and antedates the collapse of the German campaign in Russia. Following Adam's lead, Mayer settles on the fall of 1941 as his great divide. Until then, he insists, "the Nazi drive against the Jews remained indeterminate and erratic."

The real sequence of events was quite different. (Even a few of Mayer's functionalist colleagues have disputed his rigged timetable.) The Germans began the actual killing of the Jews in the summer of 1941. By September, *Einsatzgruppe* C, operating in the Ukraine, had already slaughtered tens of thousands, including some 34,000 in Kiev, shot *en masse* in two days at Babi Yar. By mid-October, *Einsatzgruppe* A had completed the first cycle of its killings in the Baltic and White Russia and had started a second cycle. According to the report cited above, the number of "executed persons" during the period from June to October 15, 1941, in Lithuania, Latvia, Estonia, and White Russia, reached a total of 118,430 Jews and 3,387 Communists—hardly the result of an "indeterminate and erratic" drive. The disproportionate number of "executed" Jews (as against Bolsheviks) indicates well the priorities of the *Einsatzgruppen*. [*]

[*] For more on Mayer's falsification of *Einsatzgruppen* operations, see Daniel Jonah Goldhagen's informative review, "False Witness," *New Republic*, April 17, 1989.

Nor does the evidence support Mayer's premature date for the break-down of Barbarossa. He claims that Hitler and his generals knew they had failed to crush Russia as early as December 6, 1941, when Zhukov's counterassault relieved the siege of Moscow. But though the German generals may have been ready to quit during that perilous winter of 1941–42, Hitler refused to let them retreat. And his strategy worked—at least for another year. Though the Russians did manage to recapture a little territory in White Russia and the Ukraine in the spring of 1942, in a powerful counteroffensive the Germans retook those areas in July and then swept through the Ukraine and the Caucasus, pen-etrating as far east as Stalingrad by September. This German advance catastrophically reduced Russian agricultural supplies and threatened widespread famine, relieved only by the massive United States food shipments. Leningrad, meanwhile, under siege since September 1941, remained unrelieved until January 1943.

On account of Hitler's persistence, in other words, Barbarossa did not break down in December 1941, but a year later. By that time, the *Einsatzgruppen* had already murdered about two-thirds of the Jews in the area of their operations. The killing of the Jews was carried out as an operation parallel with the invasion of Russia; it was not a consequence of the failure of that invasion.

In a farfetched historical analogy, Mayer compares the operations of the *Einsatzgruppen* to the First Crusade of 1095–99. (The title of his book is taken from a medieval Jewish chronicle about Jewish martyrdom in the Rhineland during that crusade.) Pope Urban II launched the crusade to liberate the holy land from the Muslim in-fidels. Marching across Europe, the Crusaders massacred the Jews en route, even though the pope had not intended or ordered them to do so.

The analogy is absurd on several counts. For one thing, haphazard extemporaneous pogroms committed by the soldiers of Christ and by undisciplined hordes of peasants are not in any way comparable to a bureacratically organized mass murder carried out by tightly structured and trained battalions which, when they completed their work, had killed about two million Jews. Nor, by any stretch of the historical imagination, can the Crusades be compared to the death camps, where millions of people—mostly Jews—were gassed and their corpses burned.

But this brings us to Auschwitz. How, if he insists that the Germans had no intention to murder the Jews, does Mayer deal with it? Ingeniously, he transforms the very nature of Auschwitz from a place whose name has become a byword for unspeakable evil and horror into a place where "more Jews were killed by so-called 'natural' causes then by 'unnatural ones.' " "Indeed," he adds, "ultimately the execrable living, sanitary, and working conditions in the concentration camps and ghettos took a greater toll of life than the willful executions and gassings in the extermination centers." To this breathtaking assertion, no comment would be adequate.

Mayer, who is in general cavalier about documentation, turns singularly scrupulous when it comes to the sources concerning Auschwitz, about which, he writes, "there is no denying the many contradictions, ambiguities, and errors." And further:

> Sources for the study of the gas chambers are at once rare and unreliable. . . . Most of what is known is based on the depositions of Nazi officials and executioners at postwar trials and on the memory of survivors and bystanders. This testimony must be screened carefully, since it can be influenced by subjective factors of great complexity.

But the sources for the "study of the gas chambers," consisting of official and personal documents by perpetrators and victims, are not any rarer or less reliable than for other historical events and periods. They are assuredly more numerous, more detailed, and more trustworthy than the sources for the history of the First Crusade, on which Mayer relies with total confidence. As for "subjective factors," the first lesson every graduate student learns about historical method is that *all* documentary sources have to be screened carefully for such factors.

"Both radical skepticism and rigid dogmatism about the exact processes of extermination and the exact number of victims, are the bane of sound historical interpretation," Mayer pontificates. Against whom is he taking aim in this enigmatic reference? Clues may be found both in his text and in his bibliography. Omitted, conspicuously, are two of the most authoritative eyewitness accounts of the death camps. One is the detailed report of operations at Auschwitz, complete with diagrams and statistics, compiled in the spring of 1944 by Alfred Weczler and Rudolf Vrba, two Slovakian Jews who had managed to escape and whose documented account, the first to reach the West, was published by the United States War Refugee Board late in 1944. The second is the testimony of Kurt Gerstein, an SS officer whose task was to deliver to Bełżec and Treblinka the cyanide gas known as Zyklon B. Captured by the Allies after the war, Gerstein wrote two depositions of his activities, including his witnessing of actual gassings. Before he came to trial, he was found hanged in his cell.

There are those who have tried to discredit these documents, particularly Gerstein's, along with the rest of the substantial body of evidence of mass shootings and mass killings. Such persons come from the ranks of the deniers of the Holocaust, those who claim that the Germans never murdered any Jews or gassed human beings at Auschwitz. How extraordinary to find that Mayer's bibliography, innocent of reference to Gerstein or Weczler and Vrba, includes works by two of the most rabid deniers. One is *The Hoax of the Twentieth Century*, by Arthur Butz, and the other is a 1979 reprint of a book originally published in 1949 by Paul Rassinier, entitled *Le Mensonge d'Ulysse*. Rassinier, a former French Communist interned in Buchenwald during the war, turned rabidly anti-Semitic after liberation. He died in 1967, but his book, which denies that the Germans committed any atrocities against the Jews in the camps, was reprinted in 1979 by La Vieille Taupe, a leftist French publishing house. A year earlier, Robert Faurisson, then an associate professor of literature at a French university in Lyon, also began to publish essays about the "alleged gas chambers" and the "alleged genocide." An international scandal ensued, fueled by the efforts of some leftists connected with La Vieille Taupe, and

seconded by Noam Chomsky, to defend Faurisson's rights to dissem-
inate his ideas from the protected precincts of a university position. *

Is it possible that Mayer has these crackpots and other neo-Nazis
in mind when, with Olympian detachment, he admonishes against
"radical skepticism" as a bane "of sound historical interpretation"? If
so, does his second bane, "rigid dogmatism," then apply to those
survivors and historians who stick to their conviction that six million
is a realistic estimate of the number of Jews murdered by the Germans?
This would be historical evenhandedness with a vengeance.

In setting out to interpret the murder of European Jews as the fortuitous
by-product of the Nazi state's crusade against international communism, Mayer excises the unique complex of racial ideas that fueled
Hitler and his Germany, dedemonizes Hitler and normalizes his dictatorship, and substitutes rational political goals for the Nazis' fanatically racist agenda. Though he has taken a different political route
to get there, Mayer ends up with much the same view of the Nazi
regime as that held by right-wing German scholars like Ernst Nolte,
who try to justify the Nazi regime by arguing the necessity of crushing
Communist Russia.

In declaring early in his book that it is time to revise, reappraise,
and historicize the European "Judeocide," Mayer calls upon historians
to "abandon the vantage point of the cold war" and discard "residual
cold-war blinders." By the cold war, however, Mayer does not mean
what we commonly define as the struggle for power and influence
between the Soviet Union and the Western democracies after World
War II, when the Soviet Union established its hegemony over Eastern
Europe. Rather, Mayer's cold war dates back to the Bolshevik Revolution and is a war "between change and resistance to change, between optimism and pessimism, dawn and dusk." What Bolshevism
represents to Mayer is clearly stated in the opening pages of his earlier
book, *The Persistence of the Old Regime:*

---

*See chapter 5 in this volume, "Lies About the Holocaust."—ED.

Historians . . . will also keep trying to penetrate the agony and ferocity of the Bolshevik Revolution and regime, *which were the main ray of hope during one of Europe's darkest nights.* Russia was fatally caught up in this colossal turbulence, sacrificing more blood and patrimony than any other nation. Paradoxically, though peripheral to Western civilization, Russia was nevertheless among its greatest destabilizers and *ultimate saviors.* [Emphasis added]

Mayer further insists that the "Judeocide" be placed "in its pertinent historical setting." As we have seen, however, he does not locate that setting within the framework of German history or in a matrix of German nationalism and racist anti-Semitism. Mayer has in mind a grander design, already drawn in his previous book as "the Thirty Years War of the general crisis of the twentieth century." In his new book, too, Mayer compares the thirty-year period of 1914–45 to the religious conflicts of the Thirty Years War of 1618–48, but now he defines the modern period as "the climacteric of the ideological struggle between fascism and Bolshevism."

Finally, Mayer insists on "an overarching interpretative construct" to explain both "the Jewish catastrophe and the historical circumstances in which it occurred." Stripped of its intellectual pretension, this "construct" turns out to be, once again, the ideological struggle between fascism and Bolshevism. And an integral element in that construct is what can only be called apologetics for the Stalinist regime and *its* treatment of the Jews.

Thus, Mayer describes the Jewish communities of interwar Europe in Marxist terms of class differentiation and occupational structure, while neglecting all the other complex social elements and institutions which those communities had created to preserve their Jewish heritage and ensure their continuity. Waxing lyrical, he tells us how the Soviet Union modernized and acculturated the Russian Jews—glossing over the Bolsheviks' utter destruction of the religious, cultural, communal, and political institutions which, for decades and centuries, had embodied the Russian Jews' commitment to tradition and their aspirations for the future.

Thus, too, Mayer repeatedly justifies the Hitler-Stalin pact, not only as "Moscow's strategy of gaining time and space for the inevitable Nazi-Soviet showdown"—this could more appropriately be said of Hitler's strategy than of Stalin's—but also for its "fortuitously redeeming features" where the Jews were concerned. How so? Because by "securing"—i.e., annexing—eastern Poland, Stalin "momentarily kept 300,000 Jews from falling under the Nazi heel." Elsewhere, Mayer writes that the Nazi-Soviet pact was "a partial and disguised blessing" to the Jews as it kept them "temporarily" out of German hands, and that "Stalin inadvertently saved large numbers of not only Polish but also, later, Soviet Jews." The index to this book even contains an entry—"Jews, salvation of"—referring to the material cited here.

Now, it has long been shown that the Soviet regime made no effort to evacuate endangered Jews. Moreover, by suppressing the grim truth about Nazi anti-Jewish policies, the Soviets rendered the Russian Jews even more vulnerable to the Nazi onslaught. But to bring up such facts would no doubt be to betray one's commitment to the "vantage point of the cold war," just as to insist on the cardinal element of murderous intentionality in the Nazi war against the Jews would be to overlook or slight what to Mayer is the greater tragedy by far, the fascist war against "optimism" and "dawn."

A contemporary German scholar recently extolled the practice of history as a means of tearing down the walls of self-deception that people erect around themselves. History, he wrote, confronts us with the truth about the past, thus saving us from the distortions of personal prejudice and political ideology. Arno Mayer has done the reverse, conscripting history into the service of ideology, reinforcing the walls of self-deception. That his book has met with a generally cordial reception is a sign of the casual, or, worse, ignorant and indulgent standards prevailing these days in the historical profession.

133

8

POLES, JEWS,
AND HISTORY

In 1983, the Polish authorities, planning an official observance of the fortieth anniversary of the Warsaw ghetto uprising, invited Marek Edelman to join the honorary sponsoring committee. Edelman, a member of the Jewish Socialist Bund since his youth, had been the deputy commandant in the Warsaw ghetto uprising. The only one of his comrades, Bundists and Zionists, still remaining in Poland—for the last thirty years he has been a physician in Lodz—he had never joined the Communist party and never lent his name in support of the regime. Nor was he daunted, in 1983, by the government's effort to co-opt him for its official observance. He rejected the invitation and distributed his statement as an open letter:

> Forty years ago we fought not only for our lives, but for life in dignity and freedom. To observe our anniversary here, where enslavement and humiliation are now the lot of the entire society, where words and gestures have become nothing but lies, would betray the spirit of our struggle. It would mean participating in something totally the opposite. It would be an act of cynicism and contempt.
>
> I shall not be a party to this, nor can I condone the partici-

pation of others, regardless of where they come from and whom they speak for.

The true memory of the victims and heroes, of the eternal human striving for truth and freedom, will be preserved in the silence of graves and hearts—far from manipulated commemorations.

Thus did Edelman once again exhibit the defiant heroism that had distinguished his actions forty years earlier.

This was not the first interruption of the privacy of Edelman's life as a doctor. In 1976 the journalist Hanna Krall published in a Polish literary journal a series of interviews with him, focusing on his two lives—first as a young man in the Warsaw ghetto where, under the German occupation, human life had no value, and later as a cardiologist dedicated to saving human life. Miss Krall's interviews appeared in book form in 1977, and the first edition of 10,000 copies sold out swiftly, as did a second edition of 30,000. The book catapulted Edelman into celebrity; more significantly, it reportedly sparked considerable interest among the younger generation of Polish readers and was said to have launched intense discussions, especially in dissident circles, about the need to improve understanding between Poles and Jews.

In its English translation, Hanna Krall's book* is unlikely to have the kind of impact it had in Poland. For one thing, its readers here, whether Jews or non-Jews, hardly need Miss Krall's instruction on the exemplary nature of the life-and-death struggle of Warsaw Jewry during World War II. Another obstacle is Miss Krall's style, which Timothy Garton Ash in his introduction to the English translation characterizes as a kind of "Polish New Journalism." By shuttling back and forth between chunks of transcribed conversations with Edelman and

---

*Shielding the Flame: An Intimate Conversation with Dr. Marek Edelman, the Last Surviving Leader of the Warsaw Ghetto Uprising, translated and with an afterword by Joanna Stasinska and Lawrence Weschler (Holt, 1986).

chunks of interviews with his heart patients, Miss Krall manages to create a maximum of confusion; it is not always clear who is speaking or when the conversation has taken place. As for Edelman, he talks as though in the privacy of his home, perhaps after a drink or two. Some of his remarks are smartalecky; others leave themselves open to misinterpretation. Matters of importance are eclipsed by trivialities.

The matters of importance center on the harrowing deportation of Warsaw Jews to Treblinka in mid-1942, which Edelman witnessed at first hand while working as a messenger for the ghetto hospital. He had been assigned by the underground the task of rescuing, from among the tens of thousands assembled at the railroad siding to board the trains to Treblinka, as many as he could remove on the pretext that they had to be hospitalized. Another subject of importance concerns his comrades in the Bund underground and the desperate courage that motivated them to build their resistance organization. Edelman recounts how they fought their unequal battle with the German SS and, finally, how he and members of his combat group managed to escape from the burning ghetto through sewer passages into "Aryan" Warsaw.

These subjects compose a story of historical magnitude, but Miss Krall has reduced it to mere chatter. The chatterers themselves play a game of tag with memory, a commodity which in Poland seems to be even more elusive than it is in the West. (Perhaps remembrance has been outlawed there.) It is extraordinary, for instance, that neither Miss Krall nor Edelman ever mentions that Edelman himself wrote a short account of his ghetto experiences when the past was, as it were, still present. The Polish text of *The Ghetto Fights*—just about as long as Edelman's ghetto reminiscences here—was published by the Bund in Warsaw in 1945; an English translation appeared in New York a year later. It is precisely the same story that Edelman tells in this book, except that then he told it with greater coherence and dignity, and with a deeper appreciation of its historical import. But the pamphlet and the very remembrance of it have disappeared down Poland's memory hole.

Since Edelman wrote that account forty years ago, he has changed his view of the past in only one respect. He no longer believes that fighting was the only way to "die with honor," as he said in 1945 and as his comrades, Bundists and Zionists alike, used to assert in the familiar rhetoric of the Left. Edelman has come to the view that the millions of Jews who walked quietly into the trains taking them to Treblinka and Auschwitz were no less courageous, no less honorable, no less heroic than those who died wielding weapons and homemade Molotov cocktails.

Yet he cannot find appropriate words to express these thoughts. He comes across as tough, unsentimental, and crude. He speaks almost contemptuously of the resistance itself. Referring to the relatively small number of people—some two hundred—in the Jewish Combat Organization, Edelman asks: "Can you even call that an uprising?" Has he become a *Nestbeschmutzer*, befouling the nest he was raised in? Or is he just swaggering, heedless of the implications of his unthinking words? Emerson was right when he said that "every hero becomes a bore at last."

One of the hazards of oral history is that people do not always remember things quite the way they happened. That is why reminiscences need to be checked, corroborated by documents or other witnesses. Miss Krall's evidence of the past consists only of imperfect remembrance combined with hearsay, some of which is just plain wrong. For instance, she states that Henryk Grabowski, a Pole, was ordered by the Polish Scout movement to go from Warsaw to Vilna to "organize Jews for the struggle." This statement is as preposterous as it is false. Grabowski was a brave and good man, but never had such a task. He served as a liaison for some Jewish youth groups, because as a Pole he could move about more freely than Jewish couriers. He brought information from Vilna back to Warsaw and later helped a member of the Jewish Combat Organization in Warsaw.

Even more egregious are the two references in the book to the Communists as arms suppliers to the ghetto. Neither the Communist Armia Ludowa, nor the People's Army (mistranslated in the book as "Popular Army"), nor the Polish Workers party, the wartime version of the Polish Communist party, delivered any arms at all to the be-leaguered Jewish ghetto fighters. Only the rightist Armia Krajowa—the Home Army, the resistance arm of the Polish government-in-exile—gave weapons to the Jewish Combat Organization. But they gave far too little and delivered much too late.

Amid the chatter of Miss Krall's book there are also silences. No-where does Edelman speak of his feelings toward Poland, or explain why he alone of all his comrades chose to remain there. Nowhere does he mention Polish anti-Semitism, except for an Aesopian ref-erence to the anti-Semitism campaign which the regime launched in 1968, driving all but the last few thousand Jews and crypto-Jews from the country.

To be sure, when Miss Krall interviewed Edelman in 1976, gov-ernment repression was the order of the day and journalists exercised caution in discussing politics and touchy issues like Polish anti-Sem-itism. But that was also the year when the first important dissident organization, KOR (Workers' Defense Committee), came into being. The rise of Solidarity in 1980 breathed fresh air into Poland's polluted political atmosphere and people began to speak out more freely. Edel-man himself became one of Solidarity's ardent supporters. He was awarded an honorary membership in the organization, and in Sep-tember 1981 he was elected a regional delegate to Solidarity's first—and only—annual congress in Gdansk. Even after Jaruzelski's military dictatorship crushed Solidarity and imposed martial law in December 1981, Polish dissidents continued to speak their minds and express their contempt for the regime. Edelman was arrested at that time, but was released after six days.

As his defiant statement of 1983 demonstrates, Edelman has not ceased to speak out—or to suffer the consequences (he was put under house arrest and police surveillance for his 1983 statement). In 1985 *Czas*, a Solidarity journal, published an interview with him in which he speaks with fierce honesty about his personal history as well as about Polish-Jewish relations.

In this interview Edelman describes his orphaned childhood. His father, of whom he can scarcely summon a memory, died when he was about four, his mother when he was twelve. It is his mother whom he remembers and to whose legacy he has remained faithful all his life. She gave him a secular and socialist Jewish upbringing and inducted him into the Bund. It is she to whom he owes his identity as a person and as a Jew.

As a youngster Edelman internalized the Bund's ideology and held fast to it the rest of his life. Bundist ideology, a combination of socialism and Diaspora Jewish nationalism of a militantly secular variety, was the source of his anti-Zionism and his fixed belief in the unviability of a Jewish state, a belief which even the reality of the forty-year existence of Israel has been unable to shake. Bundist ideology gave him his doctrinaire anticlericalism, which he now vents evenhandedly against both Hasidism and the Catholic Church, though neither possesses the social or political authority it once exercised. In the Bund, too, he learned to hate communism and the Soviet system. Finally, through the Bund he made his covenant with the Jewish people, though after the murder of European Jewry the form of Jewishness to which the Bund committed him—secular Yiddish culture—came to an end. Edelman now believes, like Freud in his day, that being Jewish means identifying oneself with the opposition.

In the *Czas* interview, Edelman talks also of Polish anti-Semitism, especially before the war—the pogroms, the anti-Semitic political parties, the role of the Catholic Church in fomenting anti-Jewish prejudice. He describes his own experiences with anti-Semites before, during, and afer the war. As he relates an incident involving anti-Semites in the Armia Krajowa who wanted to have him shot, he breaks off impatiently and says:

Don't pay attention to my telling you such disgusting stories. They're not fit to print in any newspaper. Because as you know, the Poles are a tolerant people. Nothing bad ever happened here to national minorities, to religious groups. No. The Poles are exceptional people. Casimir the Great took the Jews in, honored

139

them, and loves them to this day. But that's enough. Why bother talking about it?*

Why, then, if he feels this way, did Edelman stay in Poland? He has never explained, even to the *Czas* interviewer. Certainly he has never displayed any Polonist passion, not for the language of Poland, its culture, its history, or (especially) its politics. On the contrary, in the *Czas* interview he shows his loathing for the Polish anti-Semites he has encountered in every decade of his life.

Yet at each opportunity he had to leave, Edelman chose to stay. When the war ended, his closest friends in the Bund and in the Jewish Combat Organization decided to emigrate. Poland had become the graveyard of the Polish Jews, of the European Jews. Besides, the Poles, far from welcoming back the Jewish survivors, refused to restore Jewish property to its rightful owners. They even indulged in a few pogroms to make sure the Jews got the message. Some of Edelman's friends went to Palestine. Most went to the United States. They pleaded with him to join them. American Jews had papers for him and made him job offers. But he turned them all down.

He married a Jewish girl he had met after the Warsaw uprising of August 1944. Despite a deep depression, he began to study medicine, as did his wife. They had two children. Then his wife, convinced that Poland was no place for Jews, no place to raise her children, decided to leave. Once again Edelman stubbornly insisted on staying. She took their children and settled in Paris, where she still lives. The Edelmans are not divorced; whenever he is allowed to travel abroad, he visits his family in Paris.

What was it, then, that kept him in Poland, especially during those early years when he was constantly harassed by the police? Was it really the Bund's commitment to *do-ikeyt*, a Yiddish coinage denoting "hereness," the obligation of Jews to maintain their presence in the

---

*An English translation of the *Czas* interview appears in *Across Frontiers*, Winter 1986–87 (Berkeley, California), a quarterly devoted to East European matters.

country where they were born and where they felt they belonged? This was something that Edelman's friends in the Bund had also once believed in. But after the war they realized it was no longer a viable ideal. They left Poland without feeling that they were betraying their Bundist principles.

In the *Czas* interview Edelman drops a clue to his anomalous behavior. The interviewer asks what made him the person he became. Edelman hedges, then says:

> Well, you must admit that every person has a particular upbringing. My mother thought, and brought me up to think, that things would be fine here, that all are equal, all are good, etc.

Here, I believe, is the morbid, perhaps even the macabre, reason Edelman has stayed behind in Poland, why he has relinquished the love and companionship of wife, children, friends. The key to the enigma resides not in a rigid adherence to ideology or political loyalty, but in the pathology of orphanhood, a disease from which he has never recovered. His tormented commitment to his mother and to her charge to him has kept him chained to Poland. She, the one person in the world he truly loved and the only person with whom he has retained an unbroken relationship, even long after her death, is the reason why Marek Edelman is the last surviving leader of the Warsaw ghetto uprising in Poland.

All this, fascinating in itself, takes on an added twist of interest in the light of the current debate over Polish-Jewish relations, both historical and contemporary, that is now going on in Poland and the West. (See Ruth R. Wisse's article "Poland's Jewish Ghosts" in the January 1987 *Commentary*.) Edelman, in his *Czas* interview, is certainly right in saying that the Poles do not like to hear about their anti-Semitism, and neither do their apologists. Norman Davies, for instance, a British professor of Polish history who is noted for his virtuosity in erasing Polish anti-Semitism from the history books he writes, asserts in a review of the Krall book (in the *New York Review*

141

of Books, November 20, 1986) that Edelman "calls the Poles, among whom he has lived all his life, 'a tolerant people.' " Just for that sentence alone Davies could be sued for historical malpractice.

But this transformation of Edelman's bitter sarcasm on the Polish-Jewish question into benign praise for Polish tolerance is only one instance of how Davies has manipulated historical evidence over the years. His chief work, *God's Playground,* a two-volume history of Poland which, *faute de mieux,* is used widely as a college text, contains a chapter on the Polish Jews that is replete with errors, misconceptions, misrepresentations, and prejudices.

According to Davies, anti-Semitism in interwar Poland was an invention of the Zionists, who "sought to persuade the Jews to leave their homes in Poland," and therefore painted "Polish life in the most unfavorable colors." That is not quite the way it was. The Polish Jews did not need to be brainwashed by Zionist propaganda. They knew from the bitter experience of their own lives, day in, day out, that they were being starved, economically strangled, pressured to leave the country. They were excluded from whole areas of business and industry, discriminated against in higher education and the professions, subjected to physical violence and even pogroms. Their schools and religious and communal institutions were shortchanged by the government, which had reneged on the minority-rights treaty it had signed after the Versailles peace conference, obligating itself to respect the political and cultural rights of its minorities. Davies does not mention such unpleasant matters in *God's Playground.*

The farthest Davies is willing to go toward acknowledging the existence of Polish anti-Semitism is to suggest a kind of moral equivalence. "Polish hostility toward the Jews," he writes, is "complemented by Jewish hostility toward the Poles." He does not, unfortunately, offer any convincing examples of such equivalence (maybe a pogrom perpetrated by the Orthodox Agudah, or an instance of Hasidim picketing Polish stores?). Instead, on the Polish side he proceeds to assert repeatedly that there was good reason to dislike the Jews, who, being Communists, "did much to launch the popular stereotype of the *Zydokomuna*"—the "Jew-Communist."

142

*   *   *

Davies's piece in the *New York Review* offers a sampling of the same prejudices that abound in his book. Here, to discredit the "Zionists" who created the "myth" of Polish anti-Semitism, Davies uses Edelman and the Bund as his foils. According to him, the "most noble element" in the makeup of the Bund was "its staunch opposition to nationalism." This he writes of a movement defined, as we have seen, by its commitment, precisely, to its own form of Jewish nationalism! Bundists believed that Jews would continue to live collectively as Jews, even in a socialist society, enjoying autonomy in the internal affairs— schools, communal services, and cultural activities, all of which would be conducted in Yiddish, which Bundists regarded as the Jewish national language. Even in its earliest days, when the Bund was an autonomous party within the Russian Social Democratic Labor party, it was recognized as a nationalist party, and was so denounced by Bolsheviks like Plekhanov, who used to quip that Bundists were "Zionists who were afraid of seasickness."

In interwar Poland, the Bund put up the most aggressive defense among the Jewish parties against Polish anti-Semitism and in behalf of Jewish interests. At election time, it deployed its party militia to guard voting places and battle the anti-Semitic hoodlums who terrorized Jews to prevent them from exercising their right to vote.

Besides getting the Bund all wrong, Davies peppers his review with anti-Semitic tidbits which his editors at the *New York Review* astonishingly left undisturbed. Thus, he compares the Betar (Zionist-Revisionist) youth movement with the viciously anti-Semitic prewar Polish party ONR, which patterned itself on the Nazi party. He refers to American professors of Jewish studies as "professors of anti-Semitic studies, whose courses proliferate on American campuses"; apparently he thinks of Jewish professors as an academic franchise of the Elders of Zion.

This last notion may, incidentally, lurk behind a legal controversy between Davies and Stanford University. It seems that Davies had applied for an opening in East European history, but the Stanford department turned him down on the plentifully sufficient grounds that his scholarship did not meet their professional standards. Davies has since filed suit against individual professors in that department, and has widely bruited it about that "Zionist cells" in Stanford were responsible for his rejection.

This is the man who has attached himself to Marek Edelman on the ludicrously mistaken assumption that Edelman is something of a Polish patriot—a point about which Davies is as wrong as he has been about everything else in the history of the Polish Jews. The whole episode serves only to remind us that the proper reconstruction of that history is as treacherous—and urgent—a task as any now facing us.

144

9

VISUALIZING
THE WARSAW GHETTO

T he explosion of interest in the Holocaust has increased the
demand for audiovisual materials that can be used in the classroom and for adult education. A film enjoying some currency
is *The Warsaw Ghetto*, produced in 1968 by BBC Television as a
"documentary" film. But this film, purporting to depict conditions in
the Warsaw ghetto from November 1940, when the Germans forced
the Jews into the ghetto, until the ghetto uprising in April 1943,
gravely distorts historical reality. For it has been assembled from photographs and film footage produced by Nazi propaganda teams for Nazi
propaganda purposes. *

The footage of the Warsaw ghetto which the BBC utilized in this
film derives from three German sources: (1) film shot by a Nazi team

---

*The film was coproduced with one Alexander Bernfes, who supplied the BBC with
photographic materials. Mr. Bernfes, a Polish Jew who states that he fled Warsaw in
1941, eventually came to England where he settled. During the postwar years he
amassed a collection of German photographs and films, as well as other documentary
or pseudodocumentary materials on the Warsaw ghetto, about whose provenance he
has made unsubstantiated claims. Some of these photographs were published also in
Günther Deschner, *Menschen im Ghetto* (Bertelsmann Sachbuchverlag, 1969). Deschner disputes some of Bernfes's claims, but does not substantiate his own with regard
to either the identity of the photographers or the purposes of their photography.

in the Warsaw ghetto in May 1941; (2) film shot by an SS team in the Warsaw ghetto in May–June 1942, just before the deportation of 350,000 Jews to the death camp at Treblinka; and finally (3) film shot at the order of SS General Jürgen Stroop in April–May 1943 during the uprising of the Warsaw ghetto.* The footage taken during the uprising is straightforward photographic reportage, showing German military operations against the ghetto—the destruction of buildings and of the people in them and the taking of prisoners. This collection of photographs includes several well-known pictures, the most familiar that of the small boy, his hands up, as the SS men train their guns on him and the other frightened prisoners. But the SS footage made in 1941 and 1942 is of an altogether different character. Most of those sequences were elaborately staged fakeries, intended to serve the purposes of Nazi propaganda.

A few words first about Nazi propaganda.

The Nazis were masters at producing it. They learned from Adolf Hitler, the party's first propaganda chief, who instructed his followers in the primacy of concentrating on the essential message of propaganda. When the Nazis came to power, Hitler elevated the status of propaganda to cabinet level, appointing as Reich minister of public enlightment and propaganda Joseph Goebbels, a man of no small talents.

Under Goebbels's direction, the propaganda agencies of the Third Reich became adept in using photography and film to influence public opinion at home and abroad in favor of Nazi Germany. Taking his cue from his führer, Goebbels made anti-Semitism—that is, the racist view of the Jews—a central subject of Germany's domestic and foreign propaganda. He doubtless also spurred the propaganda agencies of the SS and other Nazi formations to more "creative" efforts in this area. Thus, when the SS's *Einsatzgruppen*, the mobile killing squads, began

---

*There is no foundation to the surmise that some footage was filmed by members of the Jewish resistance in the Warsaw ghetto (they had no camera) or by members of the Polish underground who had gotten inside the ghetto.

to carry out their instructions to round up and murder the Jews, they first arranged—that is, staged—pogroms against the Jews by the local population of Lithuanians, Letts, Estonians, Ukrainians. The Germans then photographed and filmed these anti-Jewish acts of violence, later using the pictures to "prove" that all peoples and nations, not the Germans alone, hated the Jews and wanted them killed.

When the Germans undertook to photograph the Warsaw ghetto in 1941 and 1942, they intended to use the film to justify their anti-Jewish policies and atrocities. From the records left by the Jewish diarists in the Warsaw ghetto (Adam Czerniakow, Emanuel Ringelblum, and Chaim Kaplan) showing how the Nazis staged the scenes to be filmed,* the propaganda objectives of the Nazis become quite transparent. The film would graphically illustrate how generous the Germans were in providing the Jews with a place of their own in which to live.† The ghetto would then be shown as a place of pleasure and plenty, where the Jews, looking like the hook-nosed monsters of racist stereotypes and the bloated capitalists of Julius Streicher's Stürmer caricatures, gorged themselves on food and drink and reveled in vulgar, even depraved, entertainments. Indeed, the faces of the Jews we see during most of the film definitely conform to those racist stereotypes. It comes almost as a relief, near the end of the film, to see the real faces of real Jews in the Stroop sequences.

An altogether different presentation of German magnanimity toward the Jews is evident in the scenes of Jews at religious services. The Germans no doubt filmed these sequences to show how much freedom they gave the Jews to pursue their own activites. But until March 1941, religious worship in the Warsaw ghetto was forbidden upon penalty of death; Jews then prayed in secret minyanim. Thereafter public and private worship was permitted on the Sabbath and designated festivals. (The sequence of Jews during services shown in the

---

*See the Appendix at the end of the chapter for extracts from these diaries.
†A similar objective was intended with the film Der Führer schenkt den Juden eine Stadt, made in the ghetto of Theresienstadt, the so-called model ghetto.

147

BBC film is mistakenly identified as footage of "clandestine" services. Can one seriously suppose that Jews, risking their lives to pray in an illegal *minyan*, would give German photographers an opportunity to film them in this "criminal" act?)

Besides showing German indulgence or liberality toward the Jews, the filming was to document "Jewish degeneracy," to depict the Jews as lewd, immoral, debauched, and decadent. Furthermore, the footage would concentrate on the most persuasive element of racist anti-Semitism: the image of the Jew as filthy, literally lousy, the deadly parasite, the bearer of disease and death, impervious to human feeling, without care and compassion even for his own kind. The sources quoted in the Appendix disclose how the German photographers staged their scenes. Practically every sequence was deliberately and diabolically fabricated to produce a photographic forgery of reality.

The film that the BBC produced out of this German footage (plus additional footage, also presumably German, which was shot in places other than the Warsaw ghetto), had an unobjectionable intention: to show the terrible fate which the Germans brought upon the Jews in the Warsaw ghetto, to direct the viewer's horror toward those criminal German acts, and to evoke the viewer's pity for the Jewish victims. Both the narration and the background music—a dramatic rendition of the *El Mole Rahamin*, the traditional Jewish prayer for the dead— make clear beyond any doubt that the BBC objective is to condemn the German treatment of the Jews, even though the visual material is sometimes at variance with the narration. The film does indeed elicit horror and revulsion in response to the German cruelties and, to a much lesser extent, it arouses pity for the Jewish victims. Viewers who have not already been rendered insensitive by overexposure to presentations of horror and violence and who are not susceptible to the implicit sadomasochistic character of much of this footage will come away with feelings of disgust for the Germans.

Many viewers will come away also with unpleasant feelings with regard to the Jewish victims. For the images of the Jews which persist in our minds long after the spoken words of the BBC narrator have been forgotten are the very images which the Nazi propagandists originally wished to impress on the minds of *their* viewers. Consider, for instance, the sickening sequence of a Jew in tattered rags, the camera moving slowly up and down his lice-infested body, photographing the scratching hands, the visible pruritus. Consider the still more repellent sequence of the handling of the ghetto corpses by the Jews, their brutish callousness toward the dead. These were the images of Jews which the Nazis wanted to convey to their audiences. Even though the BBC film has taken these sequences out of their original anti-Semitic context, even though these and many other sequences have been embellished with a narrative text sympathetic to the plight of the Jews, the photographic images remain what they were intended to be—pictures that elicit disgust and revulsion. Indeed, Goebbels understood the effectiveness of pictures over captions or narration far better than does the BBC. At one of his ministerial conferences in 1942, he severely criticized a Nazi publishing house for a brochure it had issued that was intended to be anti-American but whose effect was pro-American. The photographs themselves, Goebbels said, produced a favorable impression, despite their unfavorable captions: "Captions, generally speaking, could never undo the publicity value of a picture."

The BBC, lacking authentic photographic documentation of the Warsaw ghetto, edited these spurious Nazi films and tried to impose upon them a straightforward documentary character. The result is often a garbled misrepresentation of fact. One example will serve as illustration. Czerniakow and Kaplan both describe how the SS film staged a sequence in a ritual bath (see Appendix). The BBC film used bits of this footage, edited and pruned to avoid the mendacity of the original film. The BBC film shows some naked men entering the ritual bath and, in what appears to be a separate scene, some naked women entering the ritual bath. (The Germans forced men and women into the pool together.) But the BBC does not use these film bits to depict Jews in a ritual bath (a religious purification), but to depict Jews bathing to keep clean of lice and vermin. Though few viewers will know the difference, the ritual bath, though public, was not a public bath, that is, a place in which to bathe. Consequently, the BBC film, in this instance as in others, lies. The fakery in this film is not intended to deceive; it is a forgery "in a good cause," an attempt to right the wrongs of the German footage. But ultimately the BBC sequences do not portray the factuality of life in the Warsaw ghetto any more authentically than did the SS film.

To be sure, the fundamental condition of Jewish existence in the Warsaw ghetto, as indeed everywhere under German rule, was compounded of hunger, disease, and death. The ghetto was a place of suffering, particularly for the thousands of friendless refugees from towns and cities all over Poland. Expelled from their homes, forced into the swollen tenements of the Warsaw ghetto, the refugees endured the worst lot of all Jews, thrust as they were upon the mercy of a community without resources even for its own residents. Class differences persisted in the ghetto. In fact, the Germans encouraged the rise of a Jewish semiunderworld that thrived on the misery of the poor. But the ghetto as a whole, in its struggle for survival, transcended class differences and regional differences. A community of subcommunities, it was, besides a site of suffering, also a place of Jewish solidarity and self-help, of succor and self-sacrifice.

In his diary Czerniakow noted that he asked SS Obersturmführer Brandt why the photographers did not take pictures of the schools, why they were not filming "positive subjects." Though he understood the objectives of German propaganda, he nonetheless made what remonstration he could. Czerniakow knew, as we do, that the Germans had no intentions of filming "positive subjects." The massive efforts at self-help of the Warsaw ghetto's Jewish population would never appear in German propaganda. The public kitchens which the Jewish political parties and social organization maintained were not filmed. No photographs were made of the schools which the Jews operated for their children, sometimes legally, more often as clandestine institutions. The Germans made no films of the children's day-care centers, where social workers and young volunteers fed, washed, warmed, and played with the little ones, giving them shelter against the brutality of German rule. The Germans made no films of Jewish cultural activities, of the secret lending libraries, the choral groups, the mandolin orchestras. They made no films of the tenement committees whose self-help activities in each overcrowded building created islands of responsibility and refuge from a world gone mad. They made no films of the political parties and their youth organizations, of the valiant men and women, boys and girls, who conceived, planned, and carried out the ghetto uprising.

Nowadays we live in an era of photomania, where photographs are regarded as the magic key to unlock the doors of the past, which only the more effortful study of history had previously been able to open. Nowadays people regard pictures as the essence of truth, forgetting that, like written documents, pictures too can lie, can distort the truth. Even more effectively than written documents, the camera falsifies objective reality because it creates its own illusion of reality.

Too often pictures have been made to serve the uses of propaganda. Selective photography, posed or staged subject matter, technical tricks of the trade which bring into existence nonexistent subjects—these are the standard ways the camera is made to lie. Too often the camera serves ends that contribute neither to the truth of art nor to the truth of history.

APPENDIX

Jewish diarists in the Warsaw ghetto describe SS filming.

I. From the diary of Adam Czerniakow, head of the Judenrat of the Warsaw ghetto.

May 2, 1941
8 A.M. the photographers of Aussendienst came and photographed the workshops near the Kehilla.

May 4, 1941
In the morning the photographers came.

May 6, 1941
The corpses from the isolation chamber were viewed by Dr. [Wilhelm] Hagen [Medical Officer of the Health Department of the Civil Administration of Warsaw] and the German photographers.

May 2, 1942

The German propaganda [team] came to the Kehilla. Went to the prison on Tlomackie Street, to the deportees, and took films.

May 3, 1942

The propaganda cameramen arrived at 10 o'clock. They filmed my work room, staged a crowd arriving to see me: rabbis, etc. Then they photographed the pictures and charts. They placed a menorah on my desk, with all the candles lit.

May 5, 1942

The photographers keep filming: extreme poverty and luxury [cafés]. They do not film positive subjects.

May 6, 1942

The Commissar ordered some arrangement with the photographers about making civilian clothes for them, which, it seems, will make it easier for them to do their filming.

May 12, 1942

[SS Hauptsturmführer Franz] Avril [of the Sicherheitsdienst—SD—in Warsaw] appeared with the cameramen and demanded to film a scene in the ritual bath on Dzielna Street. For this purpose 20 pious men with side locks were needed as well as 20 women of good family. There is also a circumcision scene. Dr. [Israel] Milejkowski [head of the public-health department of the Judenrat] was ordered to arrange it. The candidate, unfortunately, weighs only 2 kg. There is reason to worry that he will not live that long.

May 13, 1942

Yesterday they took pictures in the ritual bath. The women they brought had to be replaced, because one of them refused to undress.

They demanded that the circumcision not take place in a clinic, but in a private home. I questioned [SS Obersturmführer Karl Georg] Brandt, assistant to the head of the Warsaw branch of the Reich Security Main Office] and the Commissar about the subjects being filmed. I asked why no pictures were taken of the school, etc.

May 14, 1942

At 4 o'clock when I returned home, I found the photographers dressed in uniforms, etc. They decided to film my apartment.

May 15, 1942

At home the film crew is expected at 8:30. I asked that a man and some women be hired to act the roles for the camera.

They arrived at 8:45 and filmed until 12:30. They hung a sign on the door

152

with an address. They brought two women and a "lover" to the apartment. Also an old Jew. They filmed a scene.

In the afternoon the photographers took pictures in the bedroom of neighbors, the Zabludowskis. They brought a woman who put makeup on her face before the mirror. The photographers admired a carving of Confucius in my home and a sculpture *Motherhood* by Ostrzega. One asked if the Watteau on the wall was the original and I replied that the original was in the Berlin Museum and that this was only a poor reproduction.

May 19, 1942

The photographers visited the Jewish restaurant. They ordered that food from the kitchen be brought to the tables. With great appetite the Jewish guests devoured all the courses, worth several thousand zlotys. The Council was informed that it would have to pay the restaurant owner the standard price. The ball is scheduled for tomorrow. In accordance with the photographer's demand, the prisoners were in a separate room. The "ladies" are to be dressed in evening gowns.

May 21, 1942

Avril came to the Kehilla and was greatly enraged at [Israel] First [of the Judenrat's Economics Department and presumably a go-between of the Judenrat and the Gestapo], for the blunders that were apparently made during the filming.

In the afternoon a hall was made ready for the cameramen. A dance is to take place there tomorrow at 8:30 with champagne, etc.

Someone appeared from the Jewish police and announced that Avril was expecting me to serve as the host at the dance the following day. I answered that at 8:30 I was due, together with Lejkin, at Brandt's. He answered that he would try to release me from the appointment with Brandt so I could present myself for the filming.

I phoned Auerswald who told me: I forbid you to appear. He ordered me to be at the Kehilla at 7:30. Maybe, still and all, something will change. The matter was, obviously, not settled. Will I have the strength to maintain myself on a level of honor?

Toward evening I see flowers being carted from the cemetery on a hearse, for the dance.

May 22, 1942

It is 5:30 A.M. At 7 I must be at the Kehilla to wait for a telephone call from Auerswald about the matter of filming.

June 2, 1942

In the morning at the Kehilla. At 10 o'clock, I was once again photographed in my study.

II. From the diary of Emanuel Ringelblum, historian, founder and head of Oneg Shabbat, underground documentation project of ghetto life under the Germans.

May 7, 1942

They are now filming the ghetto. Two days ago they filmed the Jewish prison and the Kehilla. On Smocza Street they rounded up a Jewish crowd and then ordered the Jewish police to disperse them. In another place they filmed a sequence in which a Jewish policeman wants to beat up a Jew and a German comes to help the assaulted Jew and doesn't let him be beaten.

May 12, 1942

They're still filming the ghetto. Every scene is staged. Yesterday they instructed a child to leap over the other side of the ghetto wall and buy potatoes there. A Polish policeman caught the boy and raised a hand to beat him. At that moment a German hastened up, stopped the Pole's arm: one shouldn't beat a child. Today they called for a *shohet* [ritual meat slaughterer] and instructed him to kill a fowl.

III. From the diary of Chaim Kaplan, a Hebrew teacher in the Warsaw ghetto.

May 4, 1942

This week they have invented a new torture. Whoever hears of it doubts its veracity, yet this has happened—

First they seized a few dozen young and beautiful women and transported them to a certain Jewish ritual bathhouse; afterward they seized some strong, powerful, virile men and brought them to the same bathhouse. Both sexes were forced by means of intimidation and whiplashes to remove their clothes and remain naked; afterward they were made to get into one bath together and were forced into lewd and obscene acts imitating the sexual behavior of animals. The captives who underwent this ordeal are ashamed to relate the details of the abominable acts. Any sensitive person would be nauseated not only at seeing them, but even at hearing of them.

And all of this was done for a purpose. While one Nazi cracked his whip over the heads of the captives, his partner set himself up in a corner with a camera. Henceforth all the world will know how low the Jews have fallen in their morals, how the modesty between the sexes has ceased among them, and that they practice sexual immorality in public. Such acts, which offend the moral sensibilities of man and which are intolerable to the pure soul, are the customs of a lewd and degenerate people that is not worthy of being let alone. There is no place for them in civilized Europe, and by implication their property must be confiscated and taken possession of. And don't think this is a libel: "Here you have a living photograph!"

154

May 19, 1942

This is a basic rule: Every Nazi is a killer by nature, and when he is in Jewish surroundings he spreads death and destruction.

But today—wonder of wonders—at ten in the morning three trucks full of Nazis, laughing, friendly, with complete photographic equipment, stopped near Schultz's famous restaurant on the corner of Karmelicka-Nowolipki. It was evident that they hadn't come for murder and larceny this time. They behaved in a friendly manner toward whomever they met, and entered into personal conversations with the ghetto dwellers.

Why the difference today? Today they came to take photographs of the ghetto and its inhabitants, and the pictures must mirror the abundance and good fortune in the ghetto. And since in the ghetto there is poverty and famine, there is nothing to stop them from creating a temporary, artificial abundance and good fortune, made by the Nazis themselves. First they detained every beautiful young girl and every well-dressed woman, and even some who were not beautiful or well-dressed, but who were made up and somewhat elegant. The women were ordered to move around gaily and to look and sound animated. This was recorded on the film, so that the mouths of the liars and propagandists against Nazi cruelty will be stopped up. Behold life in the ghetto! How lighthearted and joyous it is!

Starving people are incapable of showing the laughter and lightheartedness that come from the zest of life and great good fortune. The Nazis detained every fat Jew and everyone with a potbelly which had not yet had a chance to cave in. Jews overloaded with flesh are almost nonexistent in the ghetto, but among tens of thousands of passersby even this kind may be found. Even plutocrats, those serious men so hated by the führer, were good material for the film. On order, they crowd up and push their way into Schultz's while at the same time a waiter shoves them back because of lack of room. All the tables are taken and other plutocrats sit around them eating rich meals and enjoying sweets and dainties. The Nazis are footing the bill because it is worth their while.

Thus nothing is lacking in the ghetto. On the contrary, every delight is enjoyed, for the Jews of the ghetto have attained paradise in this life.

Why did the Nazis do this? No one knows, but one can guess that it is for propaganda abroad. Before the Cracow ghetto was created, they showed us how the happy Jews were running to the ghetto with gladness. Whoever saw them in the newspaper picture would say: These are people who are contented with their lot. And the same will be true this time. This is the way of the deceit, lies, and falsehoods of Nazism. Nazis distort the truths of life, and the unfortunate Jews are forced to help them.

A few days ago the Nazis came to the cemetery and ordered the Jews to make a circle and do a Hasidic dance around a basket full of naked corpses. This too they recorded on film. All of these are segments of some anti-

Semitic movie, which upon being spliced together will emerge as a gross falsification of the life of the Jews in the Warsaw ghetto. Just as Nazism itself is a lie and distortion, so everything it produces is a lie and a distortion. All of Europe is fighting against England! Hasidic Jews dance around their dead!

10

COULD AMERICA HAVE RESCUED EUROPE'S JEWS?

T he murder of the six million European Jews during World War II by National Socialist Germany and its partners continues to preoccupy us, but as the years pass, public attention is diverted to ever more grotesque interpretations of those events and to ever more bizarre attributions of responsibility for that mass murder. In the Soviet Union and its satellite countries, the official propaganda relentlessly slanders the Jews (code name: Zionists) as allies and accomplices of the Nazis, even in the murder of their own people. Meanwhile, the ragtag remnants of the fascist Right in Europe, the neo-Nazis, and lunatic anti-Semites everywhere claim that the European Jews were never murdered at all, that the idea of the Final Solution was a hoax perpetrated by the Jews—to what purpose, they have never made clear.

In the United States, where the Puritan ethic has made moralism something of a national trait and moralizing a national posture, Americans have been more inclined to make universal moral judgments than to draw political conclusions from history. They have preferred to address themselves to the eternal verities, the large questions of good and evil, rather than to understanding how Nazi ideology and racist prejudice were embodied in the state's institutions and how the Nazi state enlisted those institutions in the murder of the Jews. During the Eichmann trial in the early 1960s, for instance, the American press, secular and religious, moralized a lot about man's capacity to sin and his propensity for evil, but did not give much thought to Eichmann himself, the deeds he did, and the system that created him. Blaming themselves for harboring racist prejudices and for being sinful creatures, the editorialists intoned as one: "We are all guilty."

American Jews, too, have succumbed to self-castigation. Haunted by feelings of guilt for not having moved heaven and earth to have averted the murder of their fellow Jews, they blame themselves for their practical and political failures as well as their moral ones. They keep asking if they could not have done more. In the last two decades many books and articles have probed the historical record to determine what American Jews did or failed to do and also what United States government agencies, pressed by American Jews, did or failed to do to help the European Jews. The story has by now been told many times.

Arthur Morse's best-selling *While Six Million Died: A Chronicle of American Apathy* first appeared in 1967. Three years later came Henry Feingold's more scholarly account, *The Politics of Rescue: The Roosevelt Administration and the Holocaust, 1938–1945.* In 1983 Monty Noam Penkower's densely documented book *The Jews Were Expendable: Free World Diplomacy and the Holocaust* was published by the University of Illinois Press. The most notable of all has been Martin Gilbert's scrupulously researched *Auschwitz and the Allies* (1981).

From the welter of historical memory and record, two distinct issues have emerged, though they have seldom been considered apart. The first concerns America's immigration and refugee policy in the years before and during the war. The second concerns the possibility of rescuing sizable numbers of European Jews from the murderous grasp of the Nazis.

The dismal facts about America's immigration and refugee policy are familiar by now. During the Great Depression, Americans, worried about their daily bread and what tomorrow would bring, afraid that foreigners would compete with them for jobs that weren't there, were unwilling to relax the country's restrictionist immigration laws in those years when exit from Europe was still possible. Americans may have been touched by the plight of persecuted people in Europe, but in those days they had more immediate cares.

It was a time also when pro-Nazi, anti-Semitic groups mushroomed in this country, reflecting the ascendancy of fascism and Nazism in Europe. Precisely then, against logic and likelihood, American Jewish organizations persisted in trying to open the immigration gates. They enlisted liberal political groups and leading non-Jews in their efforts, but none of those strategies worked. Anti-Semites may believe that the Jews rule the world, but why should anyone else have expected that American Jews, 3 percent of the population, could have changed the immigration laws whose enactment the whole country had supported? Yet even today people continue to fault the Jews for not having turned this country's refugee policy around.

All through the 1930s and even into the war years, government officials in charge of refugee matters wholeheartedly endorsed the restrictionist policies they were empowered to carry out. Furthermore, they did so in a more mean-spirited manner than the law required. Breckinridge Long, assistant secretary of state in charge of refugee affairs, the chief architect of the government's obstructionist policy on refugees, especially Jewish ones, harbored pro-Fascist sympathies from the days when Mussolini first made the trains run on time. Long's sympathies eventually congealed into vicious anti-Semitism and his private prejudices, which he amply confided to his diary, shaped his policies as a public official.

The State Department's Visa Division and its consular service too were determined to exclude refugees, especially Jewish ones, from the United States. Consequently, they never even used up the small complement of available visas under the quota system. Had those regulations been more generously interpreted, it is now generally agreed, some additional tens of thousands of refugees could have been admitted to the United States even under the then existing laws. They would have been lives saved, lives subtracted from the awesome statistic of six million murdered Jews.

Besides obstructing the admission of refugees to the United States,

159

the officials running the State Department's European Affairs and Refugee Affairs divisions, operating in large measure autonomously, sabotaged other undertakings designed to help European Jews. They blocked the channels of communication and suppressed information coming from European listening posts about the terrible fate of the Jews. They bottlenecked attempts to transmit financial aid when such aid was possible and desperately needed. They even caviled at language in an Allied declaration threatening the Germans with retribution for their crimes against the Jewish people in Europe.

Everyone who has written on this subject has criticized those government policies and actions. The historicial record has amply documented the selfishness, narrow-mindedness, prejudice, and xenophobia which animated many members of Congress and many officials in government agencies, especially those in the State Department who oversaw matters of immigration and refugees. For the most part, historians have concluded that those politicians and officials allowed their personal prejudices to shape their public policies and their idea of what was in America's best interest.

Nor has Franklin Delano Roosevelt escaped the censure of the historians. He has been faulted for not standing up to Congress in the struggle to liberalize the immigration laws, for not pressing the State Department on matters affecting the admission of refugees or helping Jews, for not speaking out more often, more loudly, and more effectively to mold public opinion on behalf of the European Jews.

But no one, until now, ever charged the United States and its people with complicity in the murder of the European Jews. This is David S. Wyman's contribution in his book *The Abandonment of the Jews* (Pantheon, 1984). The grandson of two Protestant ministers, Wyman is a natural heir to the Christian moralist tradition and he presents a moralist interpretation about the responsibility for the murder of the Jews that is as eccentric as the interpretations by the extremists of the Left and the Right. He accuses the United States not only of "abandonment of the Jews" but of complicity in their murder: "The Nazis were the murderers, but we"—Wyman, in a broad sweep, includes the American government, its president and its people, Christians and Jews indiscriminately—"were the all too passive accomplices." This book is but another variation on the theme that "we are all guilty."

Much of Wyman's book retreads familiar ground—the inhospitality to refugees and the obstructionist immigration policy, the inadequate coverage by the national media of news about the European Jews, and the widespread lack of interest in the fate of the Jews among Christians and their spiritual leaders. But in three areas Wyman gives us new readings of the past.

First, with Christian forbearance, he absolves Breckinridge Long of anti-Semitism, though he never supplies any evidence to justify his indulgence. Second is his partisan treatment of the American Jewish organizations, Zionist and non-Zionist, and their activities on behalf of the European Jews. Wyman understates their efforts and belittles their accomplishments.

On the other hand, he puffs up the so-called Bergson group, a coterie of European and Palestinian Jews associated with the Irgun Zevai Leumi, a terrorist group in conflict with the Zionist movement and with most of the organized Jewish community. Stranded in the United States during the war, the Irgunists organized a series of front organizations, one of which was called, with appropriate modesty, the Emergency Committee to Save the Jewish People of Europe. They did not succeed in rescuing the Jewish people of Europe, but they effectively dramatized their fate in the media. Since then, they have made exaggerated claims to a place in history that is not rightfully theirs. *

Here we are concerned with the third area in which Wyman gives us a new version of the past. Wyman believes that opportunities for rescuing European Jews existed, but that the United States made no effort to rescue them. According to him, Roosevelt and the War Department were unconcerned with the terrible fate of the Jews and unwilling to help them. Consequently, he concludes that the Americans were "the all too passive accomplices" of the Nazis.

This extraordinary insight has been embraced by book reviewers,

*See chapter 11 in this volume, "Indicting American Jews."—ED.

even by some who profess to be historians, and by a large reading public, including many Jews. I have yet to learn of any challenge to Wyman's analysis or conclusion, yet to see if anyone has noticed what is surely a most remarkable historical anomaly. For if the Americans were "the all too passive accomplices" of the Nazis in the murder of the Jews, how did it happen that these very same Americans were at the same time fighting the Nazis? How can one reconcile Wyman's charge with the plain evidence—which, even in our unhistorical era, no one has yet had the temerity to deny—that the United States had mobilized all its industrial, military, and, yes, human resources to defeat and destroy National Socialist Germany?

Wyman accuses Roosevelt repeatedly of indifference to the murder of the European Jews, characterizing it "as the worst failure of his presidency." Yet he never once tells us that Roosevelt, surrounded as he was by Jewish friends and advisers with whom he talked about the terrible plight of the European Jews, believed the only way to rescue the European Jews was to win the war against Hitler as fast as possible.

Nowhere does Wyman adduce any specific evidence to support his charge of Roosevelt's hardheartedness toward the Jews. Instead he resorts to circular logic: Roosevelt's alleged indifference is proven by Roosevelt's failure "to act." But other, more probable, explanations can be hypothesized for these alleged failures to act. Is it not likely that some proposals for rescue might have been rejected because they were considered unfeasible or because their costs in human life outweighed their possible benefits? Some proposals might have been rejected because they would have impeded or interfered with military operations and the speedy prosecution of the war.

But much of this is mere speculation about Roosevelt's views, for he left scarcely any record of his feelings and ideas. Even Wyman, notwithstanding his relentlessly repeated accusations of Roosevelt's indifference and lack of interest in the fate of the Jews, concedes at the end of his book that "Roosevelt's personal feelings about the Holocaust cannot be determined" and that Roosevelt "seldom committed his inner thoughts to paper."

162

Still, the lack of evidence has not inhibited Wyman from indulging his historical imagination. Having "established" Roosevelt's lack of interest in the fate of the European Jews by reference to his lack of action, Wyman then vouchsafes us a clairvoyant glimpse into Roosevelt's motives: "Roosevelt's overall response to the Holocaust was deeply affected by political expediency." Wyman surmises that Roosevelt, knowing he already had the Jewish vote in his pocket, felt he did not have to respond to Jewish pressure, whereas the pursuit of "an active rescue policy" would lose him other, less firmly committed votes. But this is merely a hypothesis for which no reliable documentary source exists.

By isolating Roosevelt's response to the murder of the European Jews from the ongoing history of the time and by considering his motives in this regard apart from his other responsibilities, notably the prosecution of the war, Wyman does a disservice to the historical Roosevelt and to the history of that period. To understand Roosevelt's behavior on any one question, one must understand his overall behavior. Even Roosevelt's admirers have faulted him for the way he ran his administration. His administrative operations have been described as "wasted effort, faulty coordination, disorder, delays, muddle." When he was dissatisfied with a particular agency, he created a new one by executive order, reshuffling his staff, making them divide or share power that was circumscribed and at times uncertain. His associates grumbled that he always waited for a crisis before acting, that he did things piecemeal, that he had no list of priorities, no timetables, no grand strategy.

The complaints are justified, but in Roosevelt's defense one must adduce the burden of his responsibilities. He was faced with the economic collapse of the United States, the political collapse of Europe, the military collapse of China. No president before or after him ever had to confront responsibilities of such urgency and gravity, whose range and complexity, domestic and foreign, often put them beyond one man's capacity to resolve and, impinging as they did upon one another, beyond any man's capacity to reconcile.

In dealing with that tangled web of responsibilities, Roosevelt had

163

to cope with entrenched bureaucracies which operated with a large measure of autonomy. For all his power, he could not impose his ideas or his policies upon the legislative or judicial branches of the government, and not even upon all of his subordinate executive agencies. He had constantly to weigh the cost and benefit of yielding on one issue in order to win on another as he tried to maneuver his policies through Congress. Roosevelt once told a young visitor: "If you ever sit here, you will learn that you cannot, just by shouting from the housetops, get what you want all the time." Another time, when the chairman of the Federal Reserve Board complained about the Treasury Department, Roosevelt replied: "The Treasury is not to be compared with the State Department. You should go through the experience of trying to get any changes in the thinking, policy and action of the career diplomats and then you'd know what a real problem was."

Nevertheless, in the face of all obstacles, Roosevelt succeeded in bringing the American people out of their moral despair and in rescuing the country from economic and social collapse. In foreign affairs, he was the architect of Allied victory. With Winston Churchill, he brought about the defeat of Hitler's military forces and the destruction of National Socialist Germany. To rally the American people behind him in his effort to bring America into the war, Roosevelt undid the public image that the isolationists had projected of themselves as peace-loving patriots. His persistent attacks on them turned the tide of public opinion and they came to be seen, according to Wayne S. Cole, the historian of isolationism, "as narrow, self-serving, partisan, conservative, antidemocratic, anti-Semitic, pro-Nazi, fifth columnist, and even treasonous." No wonder the Jews loved Roosevelt.

American Jews were the most interventionist of all Americans and Roosevelt's most ardent supporters. They knew that he, more than any other American political leader, understood the threat that National Socialist Germany posed to Jews and to the civilized world. In November 1938, after the pogroms of *Kristallnacht* throughout Germany, Roosevelt ordered the American ambassador in Berlin "to return at once for report and consultation." For the first time since World War I an American president had summoned home an am-

164

bassador to a major power under such circumstances. At his press conference then, Roosevelt said: "I myself could scarcely believe that such things could occur in a twentieth-century civilization." Is it likely that later, when even worse disasters befell the Jews, Roosevelt's heart would have hardened like Pharaoh's, that he would have turned indifferent to their murder, passive toward their murderers? Wyman's charges seem especially paradoxical, for in Roosevelt's lifetime American anti-Semites caricatured him as a Jew or a tool of the Jews and the war as the "Jew war," a view which was shared by Adolf Hitler and propagated by Joseph Goebbels.

American Jews were not deluded in their fierce devotion to Roosevelt. Before the Nazi state began to carry out the "Final Solution of the Jewish Question," most American Jews agreed with him that the surest way to help the European Jews was to defeat Hitler on the battlefield and Franklin Delano Roosevelt was Doctor Win-the-War. He remained committed to the priority and primacy of the war against Germany, despite the urgings of some of his military advisers to redirect America's major military effort toward the war in the East against Japan.

Before September 1942, the agenda which American Jewish organizations pursued on behalf of their beleaguered fellow Jews under German occupation had consisted essentially in providing relief and assistance in immigration. But after receiving the famous cable from Gerhart Riegner of the World Jewish Congress in Switzerland, which informed them that Hitler planned to murder all the European Jews, the Jewish leaders revised their agenda and made the rescue of the European Jews their top priority. They tried to persuade the United States to undertake to rescue the European Jews.

Until then any suggestion of a mass evacuation of Jews from the European continent would have been regarded as fantastic. How could over three million Polish Jews or a community of some 650,000 Hungarian Jews be uprooted? Where would they go? How would they be transported? Who would pay the costs?

Whether or not rescue of massive numbers of Jews was at all possible or practicable, the American Jewish organizations, acting in concert, developed an ambitious and comprehensive program to do just that— to remove the European Jews from the grasp of their murderers. In March 1943, American Jewish leaders presented their program to top American and British officials. They proposed that the Allied powers approach the German government, its allies and satellites, through the Vatican or neutral governments, to secure the release of the Jews and to allow their emigration to havens of refuge. In effect, they proposed that the Allies beg Hitler to let the Jews go by appealing to his moral sense. They did not have a single bargaining chip to put on the negotiating table. That proposal, conceived in hopelessness and helplessness, was as naive politically as it was unrealizable logistically.

By that time millions of Jews had already been murdered. Could the rest still be saved? The bitter truth was that it hinged on Hitler's wishes. So long as he commanded the European continent from the Atlantic Wall to the gates of Moscow and Leningrad, the fate of the Jews in his grip depended on his, Hitler's, will. The Allies had, after all, in a formal declaration issued in December 1942, threatened the Germans with retribution for the murder of the Jews, but that had not stayed Hitler from his course.

We now know that Hitler would never have let the Jews go, though no one knew it then. We now know that Hitler never abandoned his goal of destroying the European Jews, not even until his dying day, when six million Jews had already been murdered on his orders. But Wyman still does not know that. After reprimanding United States for its failure to save the Jews, he argues that one of the steps this country could have taken was precisely this. The American government, he says, "could have pressed Germany to release the Jews."

It was to be expected that the Allied leaders would declare the appeal to Hitler as "fantastically impossible." Still, however disheartened, the American Jewish organizations did not give up their efforts for government intervention on behalf of the European Jews. It took over a year for their efforts to produce any result. Finally, in January

1944, President Roosevelt established the War Refugee Board. Proposals for such an agency had been afloat in the Jewish community for about a year. This particular plan originated in the Treasury Department and the Treasury secretary, Henry Morgenthau, Jr., was the one who brought it to Roosevelt for his approval.

Wyman thinks that the War Refugee Board could have been established earlier, if only Roosevelt would have cared to do so. But the creation of the War Refugee Board in 1944 was clearly facilitated by the then more hopeful military situation. A year before, the Germans were still at Stalingrad and the Allies did not yet have a toehold on the European mainland. By January 1944 the Russians had regained the military offensive in the East. The Anglo-American forces were fighting their way, bitterly to be sure, up the boot of Italy. Operation Overlord, the cross-channel invasion of Europe, was being prepared. Since the Allies expected that their forces would soon be advancing on the European plains, the humanitarian goal of helping refugees must have seemed less quixotic than it had appeared a year before.

Besides negotiating with Hitler for a mass evacuation of the Jews from Europe, what real possibilities for rescue existed which Wyman believes the United States neglected to pursue, shelved, or sabotaged?

He mentions ransom, for instance. The particular case at issue involved an unconfirmed report—perhaps a trial balloon—that Rumania would release 70,000 Jews then languishing in Transnistria and allow them to emigrate to Palestine in exchange for transportation costs. But the Rumanians never put the offer on the table. It was said that the Arabs pressured the German Foreign Office and that Eichmann pressured the Rumanians to call it off. But Wyman is not to be diverted by mere facts. "The main issue," he says, "is not whether the plan might have worked" [sic], but that the British and Americans "*almost* cursorily dismissed this first major *potential* rescue opportunity" (my emphasis). In Yiddish we would say to this: "If grandma had wheels, she'd be a streetcar."

But suppose the Rumanians meant business. Could their offer have been accepted? At just that time, Rumanian troops were fighting alongside the Germans at Stalingrad. Would Stalin have permitted such a deal even if Roosevelt would have approved paying a huge ransom to an enemy country? The Americans were to confront a similar dilemma just before the war's end, when Eichmann, presumably acting for Himmler, proposed to exchange Hungarian Jews for trucks to be used by the Germans on the Eastern front. Could such a morally entangling bargain ever have been struck?

The absence of real opportunities to rescue the Jews from Hitler's murder machine has not deterred Wyman from denouncing the United States for failing to rescue the Jews. He often confuses the issue of rescue with that of refugees. Refugees were those unfortunates stranded on the outer perimeters of Hitler's Europe, beyond his grasp, but in desperate need of safe haven. Wyman accuses American military authorities of callousness because they did not, during the war, arrange transport to the United States for Jewish refugees then living in abysmal conditions in makeshift transit camps in Spain, Portugal, and North Africa. It could have been done, Wyman says, had the military wanted to do so. To make his case, he cites the instance of military assistance to Yugoslavs.

The American military helped, over a six-month period, to transfer some 35,000 wounded partisan fighters and refugees from Yugoslavia into southern Italy, then under Allied control. If they were willing to help the Yugoslavs, Wyman argues, why not the Jews? But Wyman does not tell his readers that transporting the Yugoslavs had nothing to do with preference or prejudice. It served a military objective. The Yugoslav partisans under Tito were military allies. At the Teheran Conference, November 1943, Churchill convinced Roosevelt and Stalin that they should give Tito's forces whatever support they could spare from land operations elsewhere, because the Yugoslav guerrillas were keeping twenty-one German and nine Bulgarian divisions pinned down on the Balkan peninsula. After Italy capitulated in September 1943, the partisans controlled the Dalmatian coast. They could then transfer their wounded by boat and air across the Adriatic.

The care of the wounded had become a major factor in Tito's guerrilla operations. Small hospitals had been set up wherever regional guerrilla units existed. When the guerrillas had to move, the hospitals moved with them. F. W. D. Deakin, Churchill's emissary to Tito, wrote that at times "the shape of the battle ahead would now be conditioned, and at moments dictated, by the protection of long columns of the hospitals." The evacuation of the wounded Yugoslav guerrillas was intended to restore greater mobility to the partisan fighters and to free them from the responsibility of caring for their wounded and helpless.

In 1944 a new proposal emerged which, it was hoped, might save Jews from the gas chambers. At first the proposal entailed bombing the railway lines leading to Auschwitz. Later it was extended to include bombing also the gas chambers and the crematoria. The idea had originated with Slovakian Jews late in May 1944. Just weeks before, two Slovakian Jews who had escaped from Auschwitz arrived at Bratislava, where they told their story to Jewish underground leaders. Their written report, with a chronology and statistics of mass murder and diagrams of Auschwitz's layout and installations, reached the West in mid-June.

Meanwhile, that May, Eichmann had begun to organize the deportation of the Hungarian Jews to Auschwitz. The Slovakian Jewish underground, knowing what would be the fate of the Hungarian Jews, sent urgent letters to Jewish leaders in the West, demanding the destruction of the rail lines to Auschwitz.

Those requests were transmitted to British and American military authorities, but they were turned down. The official U.S. reply read:

> The War Department is of the opinion that the suggested air operation is impracticable for the reason that it could be executed only by diversion of considerable air support essential to the success of our forces now engaged in decisive operations.
>
> The War Department fully appreciates the humanitarian importance of the suggested operation. However, after due consideration of the problem, it is considered that the most effective

169

relief to victims of enemy persecution is the early defeat of the Axis, an undertaking to which we must devote every resource at our disposal.

The War Department's rejection of this proposal on the ground that it would divert air support from the war effort was, according to Wyman, merely an excuse. "The real reason," he confides to us, again without proof for this insight into the collective mentality of the whole War Department—was that "to the American military, Europe's Jews represented an extraneous problem and an unwanted burden." A more objective historian might have concluded that the War Department and its air staff regarded such operations as costly and hopeless, a view readily documented, since the War Department turned down a number of similar proposals in which Jews were not at all involved.

A more responsible historian would surely have looked into the War Department's reason for turning down the Jewish proposal, but Wyman never even explains what were the "decisive operations" to which the War Department referred and from which it refused to divert its air resources. Did he think that such an explanation would have undercut his denunciation of the military? Those "decisive operations" were nothing less than the Allied landings on Normandy and the Allied invasion of Europe. Wyman never mentions these military engagements at all. Indeed, his only reference in this chapter to D-Day lies buried in a footnote at the back of the book.

Those "decisive operations," it may be argued, were at least as urgent as the proposed mission to bomb Auschwitz and its railway lines. Those "decisive operations" involved the lives of millions of people, Jews and non-Jews, Americans and Europeans. Alas, that Hitler's wars against the Allies and against the Jews posed such irreconcilable alternatives and demanded such desperate choices.

Wyman believes that had Auschwitz been bombed and the railway tracks to it, many Jewish lives would have been saved. Yet by now everyone knows that bombing railway tracks was of little avail in impeding the Germans in their conduct of war. According to Craven and Cate's standard history, *The Army Air Forces in World War II*, the Germans repaired their tracks "with admirable efficiency" and were "fairly successful" in redistributing their traffic flow. In some cases, they reestablished through traffic within a few hours after the bombing.

Would the destruction of Auschwitz's gas chambers have impeded the German's mass-murder operations? No one can know for sure. One obstacle which even advocates of bombing Auschwitz had to reckon with was the fact that the masses of Jews, herded together by the SS, waiting their turn at the gas chambers, would become victims of the Allied bombing. Wyman dismisses that argument: those Jews were doomed to die anyway, whereas the bombing might save those not yet rounded up.

In defense of precision bombing, he cites the rescue mission at Amiens. There the Germans held 258 French resisters imprisoned. It was said they would soon be executed. Since those resistance fighters were militarily helpful to the Allies and because the Free French had pressured them, the RAF undertook a rescue at Amiens. The bombers flew so low and dropped their bombs with such precision that they blew up the walls of the prison and the prisoners ran out.

Would a similar bombing operation have succeeded at Auschwitz? There is further instruction in the Amiens experience. Despite the precision of the bombing, about one hundred prisoners were killed in the raid. The installations at Auschwitz were spread over a considerably larger area than the Amiens prison and would therefore require heavier bombing. As the pleas for bombing Auschwitz continued in the ensuing months, the dilemma of killing the assembled prisoners in order to save others troubled Jewish leaders. Some opposed the bombing; others held that the risk should be taken to gain the possible benefit. The War Department thought otherwise. It often had to make hard choices in such matters of life and death, as for instance during the preparations for D-Day.

Since March 1944, the Allied air forces had been carpet-bombing the railroad marshalling yards in France and Belgium in preparation for the landings in Normandy. That kind of wide-area bombing en-

171

tailed killing thousands, even tens of thousands, of innocent and friendly civilians in France and Belgium. It became a matter of profound concern to Churchill, who discussed it in his cabinet and wrote about it to General Eisenhower and President Roosevelt. He finally set a limit of 10,000 French civilian casualties for that operation.

In balancing the costs in civilian deaths against the military costs and gains, the purely humanitarian consideration—that is, concern for the lives of innocent civilians—did not always prevail. Nevertheless, that consideration often determined military decisions. Walt W. Rostow told me that when he had been a member of the Enemy Objectives Unit (EOU) of the Economic Warfare Division of the U.S. Embassy in London, the staff considered bombing factories at Dachau and Nordhausen which were employing slave laborers to produce armaments. From information supplied by escaped prisoners, the EOU knew the exact layout of the factory at Dachau. After serious study, they turned the plan down, concluding that there was no way to destroy the armaments factory without killing the slave laborers.

The decision not to bomb Nordhausen was reached under more dramatic circumstances. The Allies knew that the Germans operated an underground aircraft factory at St. Astier, near Bordeaux, whose structure was similar to that at Nordhausen. Rostow went with a colleague to Bordeaux, as the Germans were withdrawing in October 1944, in order to examine that site and to evaluate the possibility for bombing Nordhausen and other underground installations in Germany. But the idea of a Nordhausen mission was also dropped because the costs in human life were judged to outweigh the benefits.

Advocates of bombing Auschwitz believed that such bombing would have created the chance for hundreds, perhaps thousands, of the inmates to escape from Auschwitz during the ensuing chaos. Once again Amiens is instructive. There most of the Free French prisoners who escaped were speedily recaptured by the Germans. In the inhospitable environs of Auschwitz, from which few prisoners had ever managed successful escapes, it was hardly likely that large numbers of

Jews in flight could have found hiding places in the countryside or shelter in an "Aryan" household willing to take that risk.

Still, it is argued, the damage done to Auschwitz by bombing might have slowed down or halted the murder of the Jews. Possibly, though not probably. The bombing might not have damaged the installations beyond repair. We know, for instance, that Allied saturation bombing of the German ball-bearing industry did not appreciably retard German ball-bearing production.

But even if Auschwitz had been bombed beyond repair, would the Jews have been saved? The answer is provided by the grim facts of history. In November 1944 the Germans themselves began to dismantle Auschwitz, lest the advancing Allied armies find evidence of the murder operations. On Himmler's orders the gassings ceased on November 2 and the gas chambers and crematoria began to be destroyed on November 26. Nevertheless, Jews kept arriving at Auschwitz until January 1945. The SS was not deterred and sent them into Germany and Austria, first in open freight cars, later on foot, on the so-called death marches. Jews who survived became slave laborers, but not many survived.

Albert Speer, in an interview in July 1972, is reported to have said that Allied bombing of German cities in retaliation for the murder of the Jews and Allied bombing of Auschwitz would have prompted Hitler to divert more of his manpower and material resources to speed up the murder of the Jews. Three hundred "little Auschwitzes," he said, would have been established or the SS would have reverted to the system of shooting-commandos which the *Einsatzgruppen* (special-duty SS/SD troops) had used in Russia. *

The very title of Wyman's book premises an obligation on the part of the United States toward the European Jews. "Abandonment" means desertion of an allegiance, duty, or responsibility. The impli-

---

*Shlomo Aronson, "Die Dreifache Falle: Hitler, Judenpolitik, die Alliierten und die Juden," *Vierteljahreshefte für Zeitgeschichte*, January 1984. Dr. Aronson interviewed Speer in July 1972; the filmed interview is in his possession.

cation, then, is that the United States had a commitment to the European Jews which it failed to live up to. A parallel comes to mind, though Wyman never mentions it—the American relationship to Great Britain.

Early in 1941, nearly a year before the United States became a belligerent in the war, American military authorities, with the approval of the president and the State Department, conferred for two months in secret with British military officials. Those talks were held because the highest authorities in the United States believed that the future of the West depended on the early defeat of Germany and that they had an obligation to Britain, then standing alone against the Nazis.

The United States was not yet in the war, but it had already—by way of Lend-Lease and other forms of aid—made its firm commitment to Britain. Could the United States have made such a commitment to the European Jews? One calls to mind the Anglo-French guarantee to Poland in the event of aggression. To put that question is to demonstrate its implausibility. The European Jews had no corporate identity, no government to represent them, no agency to negotiate on their behalf. The European Jews were individuals, citizens or residents of different countries. How could the United States extend its legal protection to Jews who were being persecuted by the government within whose borders they lived and which in fact was obliged to protect them?

Even today, despite the high rhetoric of the United Nations, no country permits another to intervene in its internal affairs, especially not in matters of human rights. One need only point to the impotence of international public protest, even when exercised on the highest diplomatic levels, as in the case of Andrei Sakharov.

One might argue that the United States had a military obligation toward the Jews, who were after all not mere bystanders to the war but the primary, indeed the primal, foe of the Nazis. In *The War Against the Jews 1933–1945*, I concluded that the Nazis launched two wars at the same time: a conventional war for empire and political supremacy which they conducted against the Allied nations and an ideological war which they fought against the Jews. But in 1942, when news of the mass murder of the Jews first reached the West, no one entertained such an outlandish concept. The war was viewed in familiar military and political terms as a war of aggression by Germany against the sovereign nations of Poland, Britain, France, Belgium, the Netherlands, Luxembourg, Czechoslovakia, Norway, Denmark, Greece, and later the Soviet Union.

Jews fought in the armed forces of the Soviet Union, Great Britain, and the Free French, or in the resistance movements in occupied Europe as nationals of their countries. Except for a few ghettos, foremost among them the Warsaw ghetto, the Jews had no military apparatus of their own, no supplies of weapons. Locked as they were in ghettos and slave-labor camps, without freedom of movement, they had no military or strategic value to the Allies.

What, then, of America's moral obligation toward the Jews who were being murdered? The formal declarations which the United States issued threatening the Germans with retribution for their crimes against the Jewish people and President Roosevelt's warnings to the Hungarians in 1944 were surely an acknowledgment of moral obligation. Yet these acts proved to be futile. Would retaliatory bombing of German cities for crimes against the Jews have stopped the Germans from murdering the Jews? Besides Speer's testimony, we have also the testimony of history. The bombing of German cities by the British in retaliation for the German bombing of English cities did not halt the Germans from launching over one thousand V-2 rockets against London in 1944.

How, practically speaking, could the United States have fulfilled its moral obligation beyond its commitment to destroy National Socialist Germany and to await Germany's unconditional surrender? An implicit answer can be found in the case of the Soviet prisoners of war, to whom the USSR had legal, military, and moral obligations. Yet the Soviet Union was unable to rescue some 3.5 million of its Red Army soldiers and officers whom the Germans murdered, most of them the same way they murdered the Jews.

Yes, the European Jews were abandoned—by the governments that were obliged to protect them. Some, to be sure—the Czech Protectorate, Poland, and that part of the Soviet Union which the Germans occupied—could no longer protect the Jews, even if they would have wanted to. Occupied by the Germans and ruled from Berlin, deprived of their sovereignty, they could no longer shelter their Jewish subjects from the murderous reach of the SS.

As for the German satellites (Hungary, Rumania, Bulgaria) or German-occupied countries which retained some degree of self-government (Denmark, Belgium, Vichy France), the fate of the Jews depended on whether those governments were willing to resist German demands to deport the Jews. Whether Jews lived or died depended also on whether the people of those countries were prepared to risk their own security, even their lives, to save the Jews. In Denmark, both the government and the people did just that. They protected all Jews, citizens and refugees alike.

Bulgaria resisted German demands to deport its Jews, but agreed to deport Jews living in territories which it had newly annexed from Rumania, Greece, and Yugoslavia. Vichy France protected only those Jews who were French nationals, but not "foreign" Jews, though many of them had lived in France for decades. Throughout Italy after 1943, when the Germans occupied the northern half of the country, many Italians conspired against both the German and Italian police to conceal and protect Jews. In contrast, the Slovaks and the Croats were among those who gave their Jews no protection.

Preaching history turns the record of the past from the reality of what it was into a record of what it should have been. Historians do, to be sure, make moral judgments, but they do so on the basis of the historical evidence, on the *is* of history, not its *ought*. No doubt that a more humane refugee policy on this country's part would have saved tens of thousands of lives. But even a liberal U.S. immigration policy would not have diverted Hitler and National Socialist Germany from their will to annihilate the Jews of Europe.

We study the history of the murder of the European Jews, not just to mourn and commemorate them, but to try to understand the past

176

and, if possible, to learn from it. But history can instruct only if we know what to ask of it. If we are to learn any lessons from this terrible past, the question "Could the United States have rescued the European Jews?" will lead us astray. Instead, the question to ask is: How could one country—National Socialist Germany—have gained dominion so rapidly over Europe and enlisted so many different peoples into the commission of mass murder? The answers to that question suggest the lessons to be learned.

The first is about anti-Semitism. National Socialist Germany demonstrated anti-Semitism's terrifying power when harnessed to the apparatus of the state. In converting racist ideology into practical politics, the Nazis made the passage of anti-Semitism from prejudice to mass murder appear not only easy but irresistible, as the behavior of many European nations attested. Here is a lesson to be learned about the dynamics of anti-Semitism and racist thinking.

The second is about military power. That was the only way the United States could have saved the European Jews, not by negotiating with Hitler or by bribing his satellites. Had the United States maintained a strong defense capacity, Hitler might not have succeeded in dominating the European continent as swiftly and easily as he did. Had the Western powers been better prepared for war, they might have defeated Hitler's armies on the battlefield sooner than they did. Had the German military machine been stopped in 1941, not only would there have been fewer Jewish dead, but today there would be a vibrant Jewish presence in Europe, with Jewish communities flourishing across the continent.

The third lesson, and one which every Jewish child now knows, is about political power. Without political power Jews had no chance for survival. Had a Jewish state existed in 1939, even one as small as Israel today, but militarily as competent, the terrible story of six million dead might have had another outcome. As a member of the Allied nations, contributing its manpower and military resources to the conduct of the war, a Jewish state could have exercised some leverage with the great powers in the alliance. Even though it would not have diverted Hitler from his determination to murder the Jews, a Jewish

177

state might have been able to wield sufficient military and political clout to have inhibited Slovakia, Rumania, and Croatia from collaborating with the Germans in that murder. A Jewish state could have persuaded neutral countries to give Jewish refugees safe passage. A Jewish state would have ensured a safe haven. A Jewish state would have made a difference.

In war and politics, it is only power that counts. Power counts when it is exercised by governments of moral responsibility. Power counts even more—in diplomacy and in war—in confrontation with governments that operate without morality and without acknowledgment of their moral obligations.

11

INDICTING
AMERICAN JEWS

The rabbis of the Talmud blamed the Roman destruction of the Temple in 70 C.E. on "groundless hatred" among the Jews. The enigmatic phrase presumably refers to political and religious differences that split the Jewish community at that time and set one faction against another. In the nearly two thousand years since then, the penchant for self-castigation has remained as constant among Jews as the divisions the rabbis alluded to.

Among American Jews, the latest example of groundless hatred born of divisiveness has been the exploitation of the Holocaust by some with old political scores to settle within the Jewish community. Charging that American Jews could have rescued the European Jews during the Holocaust, these accusers have created a new staple of propaganda which has already been seized upon by enemies of the Jews, especially on the Left. The present agitation has been sparked mainly by the so-called American Jewish Commission on the Holocaust, whose birth, death, and resurrection have been chronicled on the front pages of the *New York Times*. It has been sustained by the release of a self-styled documentary film, *Who Shall Live and Who Shall Die?*, which deals with the role of American Jews during World War II. Both the commission and the film have much in common besides subject matter.

The public life of the American Jewish Commission on the Holo-

caust began in August 1981, when Arthur J. Goldberg, former justice
of the Supreme Court and former U.S. permanent representative to
the United Nations, wrote to several dozen persons, including me,
inviting them to join this body of which he had accepted the chair-
manship. He did not say from whom he had received his appointment.

The commission, wrote Goldberg, was to consist of "outstanding
American Jews"; once again he did not say by whom they were chosen,
or by what criteria. The commission's task was to "embark on a searching inquiry into the actions and attitudes of American Jews and others
in our country during the Holocaust." The purpose of the inquiry was
"to learn and publicize the lessons to be learned from what occurred,"
with the hope that the commission's findings would "perhaps" help
to ensure that "such a Holocaust" would never happen again.

Goldberg advised the prospective members that the working papers
for the commission would be prepared by a research team at the Jack
P. Eisner Institute for Holocaust Studies at the Graduate Center of
the City University of New York (CUNY). The research team was to
be headed by Professor S. M. Finger, who had been in the U.S. foreign
service and had also once been Goldberg's deputy at the UN. Finger,
a political scientist, directs CUNY's Ralph Bunche Institute; he has
no connection with CUNY's Institute for Holocaust Studies, or any
record of research into any aspect of the Holocaust.

Goldberg's letter arrived just as I was going abroad and I had no
time to respond. Had I done so, I would have focused on the list of
ten questions included with the invitation, concerning the "actions
and attitudes of American Jews" to which the commission inquiry
would address itself. Question number 4 read: "Why were so many
American Jews passive or relatively unconcerned about the plight of
European Jews?" In other words, even though the commission was
not yet constituted, it had already found American Jews guilty. By
what authority, I would have asked, had Goldberg and Finger undertaken to sit in judgment on American Jews, and what competence
did they or CUNY's Graduate Center have to conduct such a pseudo-
judicial proceeding?

Commonly a government creates a commission, authorizing it to

180

inquire into a specific event or situation, with a view to some remedial action, usually in the form of legislation, or, in an investigation of wrongdoing, to determine responsibility for that wrongdoing. For example, in 1980 the United States Congress established the Commission on Wartime Relocation and Internment of Civilians to review the facts about how American government agencies, civilian and military, handled Japanese Americans during World War II and to recommend appropriate remedies. It consisted of nine members (Goldberg was one), a special counsel, and thirty-three staff members.

Another example is the Commission of Inquiry into the Events at the Refugee Camps in Beirut 1982, which the government of Israel established on September 28, 1982, to inquire into "the atrocity carried out by a unit of the Lebanese forces against the civilian population in the Shatilla and Sabra camps." The three-man commission—the president of Israel's Supreme Court, a justice of that court, and a major-general—had the full authority of the government behind it to gather information and conduct hearings. *

In terms of empowerment, authority, purpose, and personnel, these commissions contrast sharply with the American Jewish Commission on the Holocaust, which, despite its grandiose title, had no mandate from any responsible institution.

Upon my return home two months later, I found that even though I had not replied to the invitation I was listed as a commission member and was getting its mail. I wrote a note to Finger asking that my name be removed from his list. But the commission materials in my mail absorbed my attention like a sore, and the sore was aggravated by a memorandum prepared for the first meeting, September 23, 1981, stating to the members that "much of the background research has already been done, notably by scholars at the Jack P. Eisner Institute for Holocaust Studies and at other institutes in the U.S. and Israel."

---

*The official findings are available in English translation, with an introduction by Abba Eban and supplementary materials, in *The Beirut Massacre: The Complete Kahan Commission Report* (Karz-Cohl, 1983).

This was surely a record for speedy research unsurpassed in the annals of historical scholarship. Then, four days after the meeting itself, a front-page story about the commission appeared in the *New York Times* (September 27, 1981), in which the reporter faithfully transmitted hints and innuendos about "potentially embarrassing" findings and referred darkly to "neglected opportunities" which American Jews had failed to seize, thereby dooming their European brothers.

On November 2, however, Finger sent out another communication, which indicated that something had gone wrong, though he did not say what. He did say that, at the suggestion of some commission members, an academic-review committee would be set up "to screen the work of the research staff." What had happened?

Here we must revert to the prehistory of the commission, which I have had (without other corroboration) from Finger himself. The idea had originated with Jack Eisner, a Holocaust survivor who has prospered in the United States and who largely funds the institute at CUNY that bears his name. Eisner had proposed to underwrite an inquiry into the role of American Jews during the years of the Holocaust, and the president of CUNY's Graduate Center asked Finger to develop this proposal. Finger turned the task over to an old friend, not associated with CUNY; in due course the friend's proposal was presented to Eisner, who endorsed it enthusiastically and agreed to fund it. That is how the American Jewish Commission on the Holocaust came into existence.

Finger's friend, who prepared the proposal and who was subsequently entrusted with the commission's central and most sensitive task—the preparation of its report—was Samuel Merlin, himself a key actor in events on the American Jewish scene in the 1940s. In those days Merlin was an ardent member of the militant Irgun (about which more below). Although he no longer has the same politics he did then, having apparently moved leftward on questions concerning Israel and the Arabs, he still retains undiminished a forty-year-old hostility to the mainstream Zionist movement and to American Jewish communal institutions.

That Merlin accepted the commission's assignment was extraordinary. Usually a person who has been personally or institutionally involved in events under investigation is expected to disqualify himself as a judge. Yet here Merlin was not only judge but had become the chief architect of the commission's inquiry. Small wonder, then, that from the day the commission first met until its dissolution in August 1982, a year later, the attention of the members was occupied by the Merlin question.

2

Born in Kishenev in 1910, Samuel Merlin lived there until 1931, when he moved to Paris. There he studied modern history at the Sorbonne, though without receiving a degree. He joined the militant Revisionist wing of the Zionist movement led by Zev Jabotinsky and moved up fast, becoming secretary of the Revisionist World Executive in 1934. In 1935 he and the Executive moved to Warsaw.

In those years differences over goals, tactics, and strategies created ugly strife between the Revisionists and mainstream Zionists in Palestine and in Jewish communities abroad. A major issue of conflict centered on the military posture of the Palestinian Jewish settlement. The Haganah, an arm of the Jewish Agency for Palestine, whose objective was to protect Jews from Arab assault, was committed to a mainly defensive policy. A group within the Haganah advocating a more aggressive posture, including the use of terror in resonse to Arab terror, broke away and formed the Irgun Zevai Leumi (National Military Organization). Thenceforth, until Israel was established, the Haganah and the Irgun were bitter antagonists (though also sometimes joining under unified commands).

In mid-1938 Merlin became an Irgunist and an editor of the Irgun's Yiddish newspaper. He managed to leave Warsaw just before the German invasion of Poland and early in 1940 arrived in New York, where he stayed through the war years. There, together with other comrades whom the war had stranded in New York, Merlin began anew to work for the Irgun cause.

Since the Irgun was a military organization, the group's leadership fell to whoever held the highest military rank. In New York that was Hillel Kook, who operated under the assumed name of Peter Bergson so as to spare his family in Palestine (which in the previous generation had included the chief rabbi, Abraham Isaac Kook) embarrassment over his politicial activities. A few years younger than Merlin, he had migrated with his parents from Lithuania to Palestine. In 1930 he joined the Haganah and then left it for the Irgun. By 1937 he was a member of the Irgun's high command.

A handful of young men, these Irgunists in New York were without a constituency, and in the conduct of their operations free of institutional constraint. (Jabotinsky, the charismatic Revisionist leader, had died in August 1940.) Their charm and the aura of glamour and mystery attached to their undertakings won them access to circles on Park Avenue and in the entertainment world.

In their first incarnation, 1941–42, the Irgunists emerged as the Committee for a Jewish Army (also known as the Committee for an Army of Stateless and Palestinian Jews), which so dissembled its connections that to most people it appeared indistinguishable from the general Zionist campaign for a Palestinian Jewish brigade to fight in the war. In their next incarnation, which lasted only from late 1942 until early 1944, they changed their letterhead to the Emergency Committee to Save the Jewish People of Europe, but kept the names of the celebrated supporters they had attracted to their first cause. Now they collided with the larger Zionist movement and also with all the American Jewish organizations, into whose work the Irgunists abruptly jumped—without, for the most part, identifying themselves for what they were. In their final incarnation in 1944, the Irgunists represented themselves as the Hebrew Committee of National Liberation. The Jewish Agency for Palestine branded this committee "an unscrupulous piece of political charlatanism."

After the war, the Irgun cohort in New York continued to compete with the Haganah in efforts to raise funds for the defense of the Palestinian Jewish settlement. Finally, when the new state of Israel was proclaimed, the Irgun agreed to halt its independent arms purchases and to integrate its members into the army of the new state.

But in June 1948, during a short cease-fire in the War of Independence, the *Altalena,* an Irgun ship in whose outfitting Bergson and Merlin had played a major role, arrived on Israel's shores carrying immigrants, machine guns, rifles, and ammunition. (Merlin was said to have been on the ship.) In the battle that ensued the ship was sunk by government artillery. It was an ugly incident, but it established the authority of the state and the national army.

In 1948 Merlin and Bergson were among the founders of the Herut party, which (under the leadership of the Irgun's commander, Menachem Begin) merged the military organization of the Irgun and the political organization of the Revisionists. They were both elected to Israel's first Knesset, but within a few years, each broke with Begin. Bergson returned to New York in 1951, became a commodity broker and then an investment banker. He retired from business in 1968. As for Merlin, he returned to New York in 1956 and the following year established the Institute for Mediterranean Affairs, which he describes as an independent educational institution (and which, when I visited it in 1982, consisted of two rooms with a kitchen in a rundown Manhattan tenement). Merlin has been its executive director and Peter Bergson a trustee, vice-chairman of the board, and presumed underwriter. S. M. Finger has been its president since 1971. In its quarter-century existence, Merlin's institute has had a meager record of accomplishment: a short-lived journal, and one small book on the Palestine refugee problem (1958) and another on Cyprus (1967), and two colloquia on the Middle East (1967 and 1973), the proceedings of the latter edited by Finger.

It was this institute which was being used as a research arm for the American Jewish Commission on the Holocaust. To compound the indiscretion of assigning Merlin to write the report, the commission had also hired as its principal researcher a young Israeli then studying for his doctorate at CUNY's Graduate Center. He happened to be a disciple of Merlin. Like his mentor, the young man had already found American Jews guilty of failure to rescue the European Jews, and had even published a few articles to that effect. As for CUNY's Institute for Holocaust Studies, at no point did it prepare any research for the commission.

When it became clear to the commission members that Merlin could not or would not produce a balanced report, the academic review committee mentioned above was formed to screen the document Merlin was to prepare. The review committee consisted of some four or five professors, nearly all of whom had written on one or another aspect of the Holocaust, though only one—a non-Jew—had ever dealt with the role of American Jews. (I was invited to join the academic review committee, but declined.)

The review committee studied Merlin's first draft and at a meeting in March 1982, with Merlin present, picked it apart. Some changes were consequently made. On May 17, 1982, the edited version, a seventy-six-page typescript entitled "Introduction and (Preliminary) Overview," was sent out to the commission members. The report's preface declared that the draft had been prepared by a "research group," not further identified but consisting presumably of Finger, Merlin, and the Israeli graduate student (who in the meantime had withdrawn from CUNY's doctoral program and whose contract with the commission had been terminated).

Despite the editing, the report was in essence a reiteration of the old Irgun attacks on the mainstream Zionist movement and American Jewish organizations, and an effort to ensure the Irgun's place in history as the sole defender of the Jewish people in its darkest hour. The thesis, in brief, was that the European Jews could have been saved, had not the "Jewish establishment" interfered with the efforts of the Irgunists to do so. Thus on page 25, to take one illustration, the report stated that "the leadership of major Jewish organizations . . . knew enough to act or rather counteract, had there been enough compassion and a will." (By "counteract" Merlin perhaps meant that Jewish organizations could have outfitted ships, as he and Bergson did in 1948, and sent them out against the armed forces of the Third Reich.) The report contained no new documents, no new data, no analyses, no historical evaluation of evidence.

*   *   *

186

On June 2, 1982, the commission met to consider Merlin's typescript. It was reportedly a stormy meeting, with members vehemently protesting the undocumented charges against the Jewish community. In the wake of the uproar, during which he complained he was insulted, Merlin resigned.

As a consequence, Eisner (who, it turned out, was a strong Merlin partisan) stopped the flow of money. On August 19, 1982, using the letterhead of CUNY's Ralph Bunche Institute, Goldberg informed the commission members that since the necessary funds had not been remitted, he had no alternative but to terminate the commission's work.

There seemed to have been few mourners after the commission's demise. But Merlin was not yet done. Months later, he leaked the story of the commission's dissolution to a *New York Times* reporter, and it was his version of the events in question that appeared in yet another front-page story in the *Times* (January 4, 1983), complete with spicy accusations against the American Jewish leadership taken from Merlin's original text.

Eisner, for his part, denied that his failure to provide the funds was what brought on the commission's dissolution. He charged that "the vestiges of the old establishment were fighting to protect its name" and that Goldberg had given in to the "pressure" of "old-timers of established groups," who "were determined to hold back the truth." With the help of the *Times*, Eisner and Merlin thus managed to salvage something from the wreckage of the commission. If they could not convict the Jewish organizations by commission, at least they had succeeded in broadcasting their accusations to a large audience.

Goldberg rose to the challenge. To demonstrate his independence, he announced that he would resuscitate the commission and personally provide or raise the funds necessary for its operations. Finger was quoted as saying that Goldberg resented "any implication that he gave way to anybody's pressure." On January 20, 1983, the *Times* accorded the same front-page treatment which it had lavished upon Merlin's account of the commission's demise to the story of its resurrection.

Only two voices, neither of them reported in the *Times*, spoke to the real issue. One was that of Martin Peretz, editor-in-chief of the *New Republic* and a member of the commission, who said that the selection of Merlin to write the report was "appalling," and that Merlin, as someone with "a lifelong grudge against the Zionist leadership," was using the commission "to wreak vengeance on the established Jewish leadership." The other voice was that of Gerhart Riegner of the World Jewish Congress in Switzerland. Riegner was the man who, in August 1942, had provided the British Foreign Office and the United States Department of State with the information that Hitler planned the total destruction of European Jews, and who was a central mover in the efforts of the American and world Jewish organizations to succor the European Jews. He branded Merlin's charges "absurd." In an interview in the *Washington Post* (February 5, 1983), Riegner asserted that the commission was "ideologically fueled by people determined to rewrite history."

On February 1, again on the letterhead of CUNY's Ralph Bunche Institute, Finger sent the commission members a lengthy recapitulation of events since the previous June. He also informed them that, with his assistance, Goldberg had prepared a draft report to be considered at a meeting on February 9. Yet on that very morning commission members, some of whom had not yet received their copies of this draft, were astonished to read in the *New York Times* a story about the report and extensive citations from it. Merlin, though he too had not seen the document, volunteered an opinion: he "knew," he told the *Times* reporter, that its purpose was to "whitewash the responsibility and guilt of the Jewish leadership of that time."

Finger's report was, in fact, little more than a sanitizied version of Merlin's draft. Most of the accusations against American Jews had been excised, but the tendentiousness remained. Some material was added, consisting mostly of photocopied pages from books published long before. The rush for publicity was never explained.

The CUNY Graduate Center has now severed its tenuous connection with the commission. Finger was informed that his own association with it thenceforth was to be only in a personal capacity. As for the commission itself, now that it has been cut off from its original source, it is like the debris of a misguided missile, adrift in space, its mission aborted, beyond recall.

3

Though Merlin lost the battle with the commission, he and Peter Bergson are the stars of the ninety-minute "documentary" film entitled *Who Shall Live and Who Shall Die?*, produced and directed by Laurence Jarvik, a former graduate student in philosophy at Berkeley, now in his mid-twenties. Purporting to be "the story of what happened in the United States during the extermination of the Jews in Europe," the film is a pastiche of news clips and interviews. Interviewed are thirteen persons who participated in events of that time and an unidentified group of Jewish survivors now living in the United States. The subject matter of the film is divided into three main parts: a critique of America's restrictive immigration policy before the outbreak of the war; an indictment of the Roosevelt administration, the Zionist movement, and the American Jewish organizations for their alleged indifference to the fate of the European Jews and their reluctance to rescue them; and an account of the origin and activities of the War Refugee Board.

Bergson and Merlin are identified in the film with the Emergency Committee to Save the Jewish People of Europe, but the viewer is never told exactly what that committee was. Nor is there a clue that Bergson and Merlin have been adversaries of the organized Jewish community for forty years.

As spokesmen for the "Jewish establishment," Jarvik presents Nahum Goldmann and Gerhart Riegner. They are not given nearly as much time as is allotted to Bergson and Merlin, and it is curious, to say the least, that "the story of what happened in the United States" with regard to the Jewish organizations should be told by non-Americans. Goldmann and Riegner, both with the World Jewish Congress, were refugees from Germany who in the 1930s moved to Switerland. Goldmann came to the United States shortly after the outbreak of the war to establish an office of the Jewish Agency for Palestine in Washington. Riegner was never in the United States in those days.

189

There is no one at all in the film who speaks out of his own direct experience about the work of the American Jewish organizations during the war. Failing that, there is no one even to read the heartrending letters that Rabbi Stephen Wise, the president of both the American and the World Jewish Congress, wrote to Roosevelt, Frankfurter, and other people in high places. To be sure, Jarvik presents former congressman Emanuel Celler, who in his day vigorously fought for a more liberal immigration policy and for programs to rescue European Jews. Celler could have said a great deal about the persistent efforts which the American Jewish organizations made all though the 1930s to get Congress to enact special or emergency legislation to admit Jewish refugees, so as to bypass the restrictions of the quota system. But nothing of this sort appears in the film.

Jarvik claims to have spent three years in research and in interviewing. Yet not only did he fail to come up with any authentic participant-witness to speak for American Jews, he failed utterly to offer a trustworthy account of the subject he undertook to document. There is nothing in this film of the public activities in which the American Jewish organizations engaged during the war years—nothing of the mass meetings (with one distorted exception), nothing of the demonstrations, fast days, radio programs, nothing of the formal appeals to the United States government, to other governments, to international organizations, to the Red Cross. There is nothing of the masses of information about the fate of the European Jews with which Jewish organizations deluged America's newspapers and news agencies, its periodicals and radio stations, and which was distributed to private agencies across the country. Nothing of the work done among Catholic and Protestant church leaders, in the labor movement, and among America's ethnic and racial groups to rally public opinion against the Third Reich and its treatment of the Jews long before America's entry into the war. Nothing of the efforts to cultivate allies in educational institutions and civic agencies to come to the aid of the Jews.

Nor does Jarvik even give his viewers any hint of the private, off-the-record activities of American Jewish organizations and their leaders. His narrative tells nothing of the countless intercessions with dozens and dozens of government officials in the White House entourage, in the State Department, in Treasury, in Commerce. Nothing of the meetings with congressmen and senators. Nothing of the money and supplies sent via direct and indirect channels to the beleaguered Jews of Europe. Nothing of the endless stream of letters, memoranda, documents which American Jewish organizations produced. Nothing of the meetings at which Jewish leaders sat day and night.

Jarvik has accused the Jewish organizations of refusing to give him access to their files. But at the American Jewish Congress, a staff member spent several days briefing him. The library of the American Jewish Committee, which keeps records of its visitors and requests for information, has none to indicate that he ever wrote, called, or came. Nor did he visit the National Archives in Washington or the Roosevelt Library at Hyde Park, both indispensable sources for documenting the activities of the Jewish organizations.

When one sees the film, one understands why: Jarvik had the answers before he even knew what questions to ask. In the film's leading roles, Bergson and Merlin expatiate on the perfidy of their fellow Jews, while puffing themselves. Thus the one reference in the film to a mass meeting—which took place at Madison Square Garden in March 1943 under the sponsorship of all the Jewish organizations— is alleged by Merlin to have come about only under pressure from the Irgun. There is no one in the film to challenge this falsehood.

Two undertakings indisputably organized by the Irgun are, however, shown in the film. One is the Ben Hecht pageant, *We Will Never Die*, put on in 1943; the other is the "pilgrimage" of five hundred Orthodox rabbis to Washington later in the same year. The rabbis' march was an impressively stage-managed event. These venerable gentlemen were to present President Roosevelt with a petition containing a seven-point plan to rescue the European Jews. The plan had originated at a rally of the Emergency Committee to Save the Jewish People of Europe in July; it was an Irgunist counterpart of an earlier and more substantial rescue program which the American Jewish organizations in concert had worked out early in 1943 and which they had submitted to top American and British officials in advance of the Bermuda Conference on refugees in April 1943. (Not the slightest inkling of that feverish activity appears in the film.) But the rabbis had no appointment with Roosevelt, because the White House staff had learned that the group behind the petition was "not representative of the most thoughtful elements in Jewry." And in truth, this was not an ungenerous way of describing them.

In one of the film's sequences, Peter Bergson tells how he first learned about the mass murder of the Jews. "It changed my life," he says. The story goes like this: in November 1942, Bergson read in the *Washington Post* of Hitler's plan to murder all the European Jews (this was the Riegner report, whose release the State Department had finally permitted). In shock and sorrow, Bergson canceled his appointments and went to the State Department to see if the news were really true. When it was confirmed, he understood that the only thing to do was to start a rescue operation. That is when he decided to revamp the Committee for a Jewish Army into an Emergency Committee to Save the Jewish People of Europe.

Bergson told me the same story two years ago when I interviewed him in connection with an article I was preparing on American Jews and the Holocaust. I believed then, and I still believe, that he and Merlin both cared about the Jews and were motivated to act by the terrible plight of their people, even if they could not, and still do not, believe that Chaim Weizmann and David Ben-Gurion cared at least as much as they did. Yet a big question remains.

After June 1942, when the first reports gave a figure of 700,000 European Jews murdered, the estimates of the mass Nazi killings kept skyrocketing. In July, the American Jewish organizations called a mass meeting in New York's Madison Square Garden. President Roosevelt sent a message declaring that the American people would "hold the perpetrators of these crimes to strict accountability in a day of reckoning which will surely come." Across the country—more meetings, memorial services, fast days. One might speak of a frenzy of activity despite the shock of the news.

Every Anglo-Jewish journal and Yiddish newspaper—there were three Yiddish dailies then—carried columns of news about the murder of the European Jews. Even the *New York Times,* which did not publish much on this subject, carried reports. Other New York papers were better. How is it that Bergson did not realize the extent of the Jewish catastrophe until November 1942, or had not heard the clamor raised by the Jewish organizations? Where was he?

What the Irgunists were doing in those six months between June and November 1942 I do not know. But I think it is possible that they had decided to abort the Committee for a Jewish Army, whose public-relations work since Pearl Harbor, when the United States entered the war, must have collapsed anyway. Even if the committee had been just a front for gun-running across continents and oceans, the war would have brought that activity to a standstill as well. To fill the vacuum left by the Committee for a Jewish Army, then, they may have decided to launch an operation to rescue the European Jews from the Third Reich.

On screen, Bergson indulges himself in a tirade against American Jews and their leaders. If they had been less cowardly and self-centered, he thunders, it would not have been difficult in those early days for them to convince the American government to make the rescue of the European Jews a primary goal of the war. This absurd claim, delivered histrionically, almost drowns out the more sober assessment of John Pehle, an official in the Treasury Department under Henry Morgenthau, Jr., and later head of the War Refugee Board, who further on in the film tries to explain that winning the war and defeating the Axis were Roosevelt's topmost priority.

Let us recall just a few facts about the progress of the war in November 1942, at the time Peter Bergson had his great revelation. About six million American men and women were then in the U.S. Army, nearly four million in the Navy, and over a half-million in the Marines. At home, defense plants were working three shifts to produce the weaponry which the Americans, the British, the Russians, and the Chinese desperately needed. Everywhere the war was going badly. In the Pacific the United States had just launched its offensive against

193

the Japanese, and had finally succeeded in retaking the Solomon Islands, the westernmost outpost of the Japanese advance. (Earlier that year, after the Japanese had scored a series of striking victories in the Pacific, Secretary of War Henry L. Stimson had persuaded Roosevelt to sign the executive order which removed Japanese Americans to the notorious relocation centers.) On the European front, the situation was touch-and-go. The Americans had just landed in North Africa to join the British against Rommel's army. The Germans had meanwhile seized Vichy France, to protect their southern flank against a possible Allied invasion. In the East, Leningrad was still under siege. At Stalingrad the slaughter was estimated in the hundreds of thousands.

Against this background of a desperate global war, Bergson fatuously insists that if American Jews had only had the will, they could have convinced the American public and Roosevelt to make this into what would no doubt have been called a "Jewish war."

"It's garbage," Bergson shouts, "to say that Jews couldn't do anything because of anti-Semitism." As it happens, anti-Semitism did not intimidate the Jewish organizations into silence; they did speak out. But when historians cite the pervasive presence of anti-Semitism during the war, they mean to underscore the relative powerlessness of American Jews, only 3 percent of the American people. Anti-Semites may believe that the Jews rule the world, but the fact is that American Jews were in no position to change national priorities in the war even if they had wanted to. And as a group Jews had the greatest stake in winning the war as fast as possible. For that was the surest way to save the European Jews.

The War Refugee Board occupies a substantial segment in Jarvik's film, and here too we get more propaganda than truth. In addition to John Pehle, we see Josiah DuBois, Jr., who had also worked under Morgenthau in Treasury and who later became the board's general counsel; Ross McClelland, who represented the board in Switzerland; and Ira Hirschmann, who carried out special tasks for it. DuBois summons up old passions as he tells how the State Department sup-

194

pressed the information that it received from its legation in Switzerland about the murder of the European Jews, and how it sabotaged the efforts by Treasury—which was responding to the pressure of the Jewish organizations—to send funds abroad to aid the suffering Jews. This is a story that has been told before. In an article I published on American Jews and the Holocaust (*New York Times Magazine*, April 18, 1982), I was able to add some details not previously known.

When Treasury officials finally obtained incontrovertible evidence of State's obstructionism, they presented Morgenthau with an eighteen-page memorandum entitled "Report to the Secretary on the Acquiescence of This Government in the Murder of the Jews" (January 13, 1944). Morgenthau himself had been profoundly affected by the news of the murder of the European Jews and had persistently prodded the State Department to act more expeditiously. He had even directly accused State's chief obstructionist, Breckinridge Long, of anti-Semitism. Now Morgenthau condensed his staff's report, cooled down its language, retitled it "Personal Report to the President," and took it to Roosevelt on January 16. Morgenthau also had with him a draft for a presidential executive order providing for the creation of a War Refugee Board. Roosevelt did not read the report, but listened while Morgenthau and his staff summarized it. He looked at the executive order, suggested one change, and told Morgenthau to go ahead with it. On January 22, 1944, the White House announced that the War Refugee Board had been established.

Two months earlier, the Irgunists had used their contacts in Congress to introduce a resolution urging the president to create a "commission of diplomatic, economic, and military experts to formulate and effectuate a plan of immediate action designed to save the surviving Jewish people of Europe." Exploiting the coincidence in timing, the Irgunists now falsely claimed credit for the creation of the War Refugee Board. Jarvik in the film follows suit, by splicing his interviews to create the impression that the Irgunists deserve the credit.

I raised this issue with DuBois. He believes (as I do) that the Irgunists succeeded in raising the level of public awareness about the terrible fate of the European Jews. But DuBois was nevertheless quick to say that the sequence of events within Treasury that led to the War Refugee Board was unrelated to the Irgun's public-relations activities. The pressure of conscience within Treasury and the need to respond to the desperate entreaties of the American Jewish organizations were what led to the creation of the War Refugee Board.

Near the film's end, Pehle says that the accomplishments of the board, however important, were late and little. No one will dispute that. Surely more Jews might have been rescued—though none who were in Hitler's vise. Without doubt, the restrictive immigration policies of the United States doomed tens of thousands of Jews who might have found sanctuary in this country before the outbreak of the war. The mean-spiritedness of American consular officials in carrying out their instructions barred other thousands of Jewish refugees stranded in inhospitable places just barely beyond Hitler's reach. Had the American people been more generous, more tolerant, less xenophobic, more Jews could have been saved.

But is the United States to be reviled and repudiated on this account? Better to ponder where American Jews would be today had not America—and Britain too—held back the Nazi tide. Some say that the United States fought "only" to preserve Western civilization. Had it not so fought, and won, no Jews at all would have been left in the world, and no civilization either.

As for American Jews, they too could certainly have done more, tried harder, shouted more loudly. But I am not persuaded that in the end they would have accomplished much more than they did. At one point in the film, Bergson rages: "What would have happened if [American Jews] had stormed the White House?" One knows what would have happened. They would have been seized, removed bodily, booked, jailed, and condemned. Any interference with the country's prosecution of the war or with war production—strikes, race riots, as in Detroit in June 1943—brought out the army. When necessary, the army seized plants and restored order in the streets. Imagine how Americans would have reacted to an attempt to "storm" the White House. And for what? To hold the president hostage for the European Jews?

196

4

One of the supreme ironies in this whole episode has to do with the identity of those making capital out of the accusations of indifference and betrayal which the Irgunists, the American Jewish Commission on the Holocaust, and Laurence Jarvik have entered against the "Jewish establishment." For when one searches the record of the past for those who were *truly* indifferent to the fate of the European Jews, one discovers in many instances the forebears of those who today find retroactive fault with the wartime Jewish record or are detractors of the contemporary American Jewish community for its "uncritical" support of Israel.

Consider the case of the *New York Times*, which has solicitously recorded the pulse rate of the commission, spotlighted Merlin, and treated the Jarvik film as a major cultural event. The *Times* was not very attentive to the fate of the European Jews during World War II. When, for instance, the Polish government-in-exile and five other governments-in-exile submitted a memorandum on the mass murder of the Jews to the Big Three Allied powers and to the pope, the *Times* ran the story (July 2, 1942) in a single column on an inside page. The continuing stream of terrible news about the European Jews was similarly treated.

The scanting coverage may be fairly attributed to the policies and politics of Arthur Hays Sulzberger, then the *Times*'s publisher. Sulzberger's major Jewish passion was anti-Zionism. He was an ardent supporter of the American Council for Judaism, a minuscule dissident group which had been formed at the end of 1942 by Jews who felt their status as Americans threatened by the rising demand for a Jewish state in Palestine. The council's president, Lessing Rosenwald, had been a member of America First, the isolationist organization that harbored anti-Semites like Charles Lindbergh. That was just one measure of the distance that lay between the American Council for Judaism and most American Jews.

Sulzberger was not averse to using six columns of the *Times*, on November 6, 1942, to publish a talk he delivered to a Reform congregation in Baltimore, in which he condemned the "professional agitators" for a Jewish state. In August 1943, when the American Jewish Conference met in New York to consider the problem of Palestine and other questions on the Jewish postwar agenda, the *Times* took the occasion to publish a story about the American Council for Judaism and its anti-Zionist principles. The philosopher Isaiah Berlin, then serving in Washington as an information officer with the British embassy, noted the *Times* attack on the conference in a dispatch of August 28, 1943: "There seems no doubt that Sulzberger, so far as lies in his timorous nature, has generally decided to expose what he regards as a dangerous chauvinist movement."*

But much worse than the *Times's* deficiencies in those days was the failure of the Left in the United States. Hardly any group or party along the Marxist spectrum—from the Socialists of the Second International to the Stalinists of the Third International and the Trotskyites of the Fourth International to the myriads of sectarian splinters—ever gave a passing thought to the fate of the European Jews. As an explanation for the "tardiness" with which he and other leftists responded to the Holocaust, Irving Howe in his memoir *A Margin of Hope* writes that he and his friends "continued to think more or less in Marxist categories." Those categories harbored no rubric for Jews, even as the particular victims of Nazi racism, another concept absent from Marxist thinking.

The Socialists (including their leader, Norman Thomas, who was also a member of America First) and the Trotskyites opposed American entry into the war. In the July–August 1941 issue of *Partisan Review,* which was then loosely connected with Trotskyism, two of the editors argued that "all support of whatever kind must be withheld from Churchill and Roosevelt" on the ground that any such support "clears the road for fascism from within." Then, after *Partisan Review* had

---

Washington Dispatches 1941–1945: Weekly Political Reports from the British Embassy, edited by H. G. Nicholas (University of Chicago Press, 1981), p. 240.

changed its position and decided to support the war, no one on its editorial board, not even the Jews, and with one exception no one among its contributors ever mentioned the European Jews, even if only to illustrate the depth of Nazi/Fascist barbarism. George Orwell alone—whom no one could ever accuse of philo-Semitism—wrote in a "Letter from London" (July–August 1943):

> People dislike the Jews so much that they do not want to re-member their sufferings, and when you mention the horrors that are happening in Germany or Poland, the answer is always "Oh yes, of course that's dreadful, but—"—and out comes the familiar list of grievances. Not all of the intelligentsia are immune from this kind of thing. Here the get-out is usually that the refugees are all "petty bourgeois"; and so the abuse of the Jews can proceed under a respectable disguise.

As for the American Communists, they zigged and zagged in accordance with Soviet foreign policy. During the life of the friendship pact between Nazi Germany and Communist Russia (August 23, 1939–June 22, 1941), American Communists opposed U.S. entry into the war. Their slogan was: "The Yanks Are *Not* Coming." After the Germans invaded the Soviet Union, the line abruptly changed. Nothing must be permitted to impede the prosecution of the war, not even strikes by defense workers for higher wages. A new Communist slogan was adopted to fit the new line: "Open Up the Second Front *Now.*" Millions for defense of the Soviet Union, but nothing for rescue of the European Jews.

Today the Left, heartland of anti-Zionism, bays loudly against the "Jewish establishment" for having "betrayed" the European Jews during the Holocaust. It appropriates the cruel and ill-founded charges of collaboration which Hannah Arendt, in *Eichmann in Jerusalem,* leveled against the Jewish leadership in the Nazi-controlled ghettos in Eastern Europe, and applies them to the Jewish leadership of the United States. In so doing it finds itself, in one more instance of the bizarre political cross-breeding we witness nowadays, in a retrospective

199

alliance with the Irgun whose commander was none other than Menachem Begin.

In its day the Irgun stood on the Right in Jewish political life—in Eastern Europe as in Palestine. Like its ideological progenitor, the Revisionist party, it defended bourgeois capitalism and was the declared enemy of the socialists within the Zionist movement. Yet Irgun veterans like Bergson and Merlin, having cut their ties with Begin and the Herut party, are welcomed by the Left, with its view of Begin as its primal foe.

Lenni Brenner is a good illustration of this hybrid. A self-styled anti-Zionist Jew of the Left, Brenner is the author of *Zionism in the Age of the Dictators,* * a pseudoscholarly book determined to prove that the UN was right: "zionism [sic] is racism." In fact Brenner echoes the Soviet-Arab line about "Zionist collusion with the Fascists and the Nazis." In his preface Brenner asserts that "the Palestinian people are deeply appreciative of the firm support given them by progressive Jews." Among the six he cites are Elmer Berger, longtime executive of the American Council for Judaism, and Felicia Langer, an Israeli Communist lawyer who has represented PLO terrorists. In his text, Brenner has good words for two other Jews—Peter Bergson and Samuel Merlin—and says of them and the Irgun that they "did more than all other Zionists to help the Jews in occupied Europe." (He does not say what it is they did.)

All the characters in this sad and politically grotesque tale were gathered in reunion, as it were, in a column by Alexander Cockburn in the *Village Voice* (March 1, 1983). In that column, Cockburn, who has made a reputation as a particularly virulent opponent of Israel, the Jewish community, and Western values altogether, interviewed Laurence Jarvik, quoted Peter Bergson, reviewed Lenni Brenner's book, and condemned Israel and the American Jewish organizations. Jarvik told Cockburn: "The Holocaust is used to browbeat the Christians and keep them from criticizing anything that Jewish organizations

*London: Croom Helm; Westport, Conn.: Lawrence Hill.

200

do, or anything that Israel does." Here is a textbook example of projection if ever there was one. For it is Jarvik and his compansions on the Left who have turned the Holocaust into a stick with which to beat the Jewish community for its "sin" of supporting Israel.

The murder of the European Jews was the greatest Jewish disaster of our time, perhaps the greatest in all Jewish history. Unlike other disasters that have afflicted the Jews, this one has taken on a particularly ugly afterlife. It is not enough that one-third of the Jewish people were murdered, and that Ashkenzai civilization was destroyed. The Holocaust's bitter history is now being transformed into a vehicle of anti-Semitism. The anti-Semites of the Right, as I have had occasion to point out, deny that there ever was a Holocaust. * The anti-Semites of the Left blame it on the Jews.

*See chapter 5 in this volume, "Lies About the Holocaust."—ED.

3

EXPERIENCING

DEMOCRACY

12

ON EQUAL TERMS:
JEWISH IDENTITY
IN AMERICA

O n March 13, 1881, Russian terrorist revolutionaries in St. Petersburg threw a bomb which killed Tsar Alexander II. That assassination set in motion a chain of events which eventually transformed the destiny not only of the Jews in Eastern Europe but also of the Jews in America. It set off a mass migration without parallel in any people's history, a migration that eventually brought approximately half of the East European Jews to America. As we look back over the span of the century, we realize that even though persecution, poverty, and ceaseless upheaval had driven the Jews forth on their wanderings, the migration to America signified a providential course for the survival of Ashkenazi Jewry.

In the minds of the European Jews, America had long been a symbol of freedom. Indeed, everywhere in Europe America was perceived as a beacon of liberty and equality. It was the "New World," fresh with possibilities that no longer existed in the Old World. Goethe's poem to the United States, written in 1827, affirmed the image that had put generations of immigrants in motion:

> America, you have it better
> Than we on the Old Continent . . .

America offered a vision of a society without the ancient prejudices, freed from the chains of tradition. America was a place without the fixities of established society, without distinctions of caste and class. One of Sholem Aleichem's characters extolled America as "the only land of real freedom and real equality. In America you can sit right here and next to you will sit the president." America, said the same character, was also the land of opportunity: "All the millionaires and billionaires in America worked hard and long when they were young. Some in the shop and some on the street. Ask Rockefeller, Carnegie, Morgan, Vanderbilt, what they once were. Didn't they sweep the streets? Didn't they sell newspapers? Didn't they shine shoes for a nickel?" For America was the "golden land," rich in opportunities to make a better and more comfortable life for oneself than was ever possible in the bleakness of the Old World.

The Jews who came to America were cut of a single cloth. Sons and daughters, young and adventurous, they were eager to depart, ready to seek their independence from parents and also from community. The impulse to emigrate was stimulated by the lack of opportunity and by persecution, but especially by the restless energy of young people discontented with their lot. The discontent was, of course, greatest among the poor and the lowly. Those who owned property, who had solid occupations or who were professionals, who could maintain themselves despite the oppressive restrictions and discrimination, were the least likely to emigrate.

Among the discontented and the distressed, the most avid emigrants were those who wished to break away from the watchful eyes of their elders, who wished to escape the prescribed patterns of behavior set by the traditional community, who were ready to abandon the observance of the 613 commandments of Jewish law, who resented the condescension of Jews with status and the contempt of Jews with learning. These emigrants had confidence in themselves and high hopes. In the New World, they believed, where they would be rid of the age-old heritage of anti-Semitism, where they could jettison the class distinctions of the traditional community, they would be on their way to success and prosperity, to that better life toward which all Jews

206

strove. They were characteristically the new Americans, those for whom the country was conceived and founded.

About such new Americans Hector St. John Crèvecoeur, a French farmer who lived in the colony of New York before the Revolution, had written: "Here individuals of all nations are melted into a new race of men, whose labors and posterity will one day cause great changes in the world." Some 125 years later, observing the teeming immigrant population in America's big cities, Israel Zangwill used the same image, celebrating America as "God's crucible, the great melting pot where all the races of Europe are melting and re-forming."

Nowadays we reject the concept of America as a melting pot which blends the racial and cultural ingredients of all America's immigrants to produce a homogeneous species. For it is a crude and inaccurate description of the more complex processes of acculturation and assimilation. Yet undeniably America transformed the immigrants of foreign tongues and alien cultures into Americans. Within a brief span of time, these people of diverse stocks came to share a greater devotion to their new country than they would ever again feel for their old one.

To be sure, all America's immigrants retained strong ties of kinship with their families and communities back in the Old Country. Immigrants from the same town and country, speaking the same language, clung to each other in the unfamiliarity of America. They settled together, built their houses of worship, organized mutual-aid societies, and tried to transmit to their children, growing up without Old World memories, a sense of their own cultural heritage. But the immigrants never hoped merely to transplant in America the world they had left behind. They wanted to retain their individuality and ancestral identity, but at the same time they wanted to become Americans.

And they were, also, pressured to become Americans by those who had arrived before them. Americans did think of their country as a haven for the oppressed of the world. They welcomed immigrants. But they expected the newcomers to become Americans like them. In 1819, John Quincy Adams described America's expectation of immigrants this way: "They must cast off the European skin, never to resume it. They must look forward to their posterity rather than backward to their ancestors."

The American environment, notably its geography and landscape, transformed the immigrants. The breadth of America's land and the vastness of its space with its great plains and big sky, its lakes and rivers, its woods and mountains, the abundance of its natural resources, the rich yield of its soil—all these gave the land and its citizens an expansiveness, an openness, a freewheeling character. The new immigrants were always on the move, propelled by their restless energy to seize, to grasp, to make the most of America's natural wealth. They were inquisitive and pioneering, acquisitive and building. The bigness of the country generated independence and initiative. The society was open and fluid. Every man could make of himself what he wished, to fulfill his wildest ambitions.

Just as influential a factor in transforming the immigrant into an American was the Constitution of the United States. The Constitution guaranteed political equality, which, in turn, bred democracy. And the Constitution provided the necessary protection lest democratic rule infringe on the rights of the minority or diminish any man's liberty.

The Constitution of the United States gave the Jews what they had long been denied and what they continued to be denied in the countries of Europe—the right to hold public office. Article Six of the Constitution declared that "no religious test shall ever be required as a qualification to any office or public trust under the United States." Just as groundbreaking was the Bill of Rights, which guaranteed fundamental liberties to everyone. Its special significance to the Jews was the first part of the first article: "Congress shall make no law respecting an establishment of religion, or prohibiting the free exercise thereof. . . ."

Freedom of religion, the right of each person to worship as he chose, without the state's interference on behalf of one religion or against another, without the state's preference for one among many, was a new and revolutionary departure in eighteenth-century political thought and policy. With this clause of the Bill of Rights, the Founding Fathers set America on a new course, guaranteeing the equality of all religions before the law.

Under the Constitution, a man's religion was no obstacle to his citizenship, no bar to his right to hold public office, no hindrance to his participation in the larger community. The Constitution gave the Jews what they had everywhere been denied in Europe—equal citizenship, equal rights, and equal responsibilities in the state.

To be sure, many times in American history the political reality diverged from the Constitutional ideal. It took several decades before all the states gave to Jews the right to hold state office, even though under the Constitution they could hold federal office. The discrepancies that existed between the law and the social reality could be accounted for by the fact that though the Constitution was indifferent to religion, the American people were not. America was, in its everyday life, a Christian country. For most of the nineteenth century, evangelical Protestantism dominated what we now call America's civil religion. From colonial times on, America's culture and the social life were permeated by the symbols of Christianity.

Still the authority of the Constitution prevailed and the separation of church and state produced America's unique system of voluntarism. Without benefit of the state's financial support, or its political backing, or its moral suasion, members of each religious group—faith, denomination, or sect—voluntarily supported and maintained their own religious institutions out of their own pockets, out of their own commitments. Thus, the Constitutional wall of separation between church and state and the social system of voluntarism legitimated religious pluralism in the United States.

Both Catholicism and Judaism succeeded, thanks to the persistence of their believers and the vigor of the Constitution, in finding acceptance and respect as equal participants in America's religious life, along with evangelical Protestantism. In fact, both Catholicism and Judaism came to be considered two of the three major faiths of the American people. As for the Jews, we must recognize that in no other country had they ever attained such perfect liberty. They enjoyed full equality and all rights as citizens and at the same time they were free to maintain a great network of private institutions that would ensure the free exercise of their religion and their right to teach it to their children.

No wonder that the East European Jews began to stream to this country *en masse* late in the nineteenth century. To be sure, many thousands had come from Eastern Europe—not to mention Western Europe— even earlier. Haym Salomon, who helped to bankroll the American Revolution, emigrated from Poland around 1772. Others followed. But from 1881 the East European Jews came in the millions.

These East European Jewish immigrants were the classic greenhorns. Like Caesar's Gaul, they may be divided into three parts.

The rawest among them were the *shvitsers*, the go-getters, driven by the desire to find gold in the streets of New York. They were the hustlers and the hard workers, on the lookout to make money, to get ahead. They were indifferent to the observance of Judaism and even to the Jewish community. Early on they had abandoned whatever traditions they had grown up with. In a decade or so after they arrived, they emerged as the *allrightniks*, satisfied with their accomplishments and their accumulations.

A second type of greenhorn was the religiously observant Jew who tried to transplant his East European world and its practices in the New World. By 1888, these Orthodox Jewish immigrants had established dozens of congregational clusters in New York City. Several of them, against the advice of those who understood America better than they, imported from Vilna a learned rabbi to serve as New York's chief rabbi. They expected to finance his rabbinate through the imposition of a tax on kosher meat.

In tsarist Russia, the rabbinate was in fact subsidized by a tax on kosher meat, one of the most unpopular practices of the *kehilla*, the organized Jewish community, and it created tensions between the *kehilla* and its constituents. That system worked only because the *kehilla* operated on the borrowed authority of the tsarist government. In New

York, the kosher meat industry, rife with corruption and scandal, was always difficult to regulate and supervise. The very notion that a chief rabbi could operate authoritatively in the chaos of New York's uncontrolled freedom revealed how green these observant Jews were. It was predictable that the grandiose idea of a chief rabbi for New York would fail, and it failed ignominiously. The rabbi, who remained in New York, lived in humiliating poverty and scorn until his death in 1902.

The pious Jews attempted also to transplant the *heder* and the Talmud Torah in America, but at best these operated as supplements to the public schools. Indeed, the children of the pious Jews fled the dreariness of the Talmud Torahs and the Old World rigidity of their *melamdim,* their greenhorn teachers. The children themselves grew up on the street, reveling in American freedom, drawn to a forbidden world of games and sports, movies and adventures. Actually, most immigrant Jews looked to the public schools to teach their children to become Americans. From the start, they saw the public school and the education it offered as the vehicle which promised success in the big world outside.

The third type of greenhorn consisted of the radicals, the free thinkers, who wished to transplant their political ideologies to America. Socialists, anarchists, syndicalists, and combinations thereof, they came with ideas shaped by confrontation with the tyranny of tsarist rule and by experience with the violence of pogroms. These radicals looked at America and its political institutions through the distorting glass of East European politics. They did not understand America at all. For nearly two decades they were absorbed in theoretical questions of radical politics that had little relevance to the lives of the immigrant Jews. They also aggressively attacked the "clericalism" of traditionalist Jews, ridiculed their observances, and instituted the Yom Kippur balls, a public mockery of Judaism's most sacred holy day.

Of the three greenhorn categories, it was the *shvitser* who accommodated most rapidly to America. He seized every advantage to avail himself of America's freedom—to work at whatever he chose to do, to educate himself and his children, to live where he pleased, to become what he strove to be, emancipated from a rigid and stratified society and from a hateful persecuting government.

The radicals, and the secular Yiddishists, learned to accommodate to America, too, though it took them much longer. Eventually they became pragmatists, adapting their socialism to practical trade unionism and to a politics of democratic liberalism.

Though America legitimated religious pluralism, the irony of history is that accommodation to America proved most difficult for the Orthodox Jews. That was because their brand of Judaism was most particularistic, demanding a high degree of separation from the larger society. The early history of Jews and Judaism in the United States, a history of the neglect—even abandonment—of Judaism, of intermarriage and disappearance, of the rise and domination of Reform Judaism, confirmed the Orthodox Jews' worst fears about America: it was indeed a *treyfene medine,* a nonkosher state. Therefore those Orthodox Jews who came to America tried to erect hedges around themselves, their beliefs and their practices, hoping to preserve their old ways against the inroads of the new.

All these greenhorns, of whatever type, had become the consumers of a developing Yiddish culture which in fact became the bridge between the Old World and the New. The culture of Yiddish—its press, theater, and literature—provided the comfort of home in the alien world of the English language, but at the same time it introduced the Jews into the mainstream of modern secular society. Yiddish culture braked the headlong flight into assimilation, while its advocacy of secular values eased the adjustment of the Yiddish-speaking immigrants to American society.

Probably most East European immigrants living in the slums of the great industrial cities of America at that time combined a little of each of these three greenhorn types. Though not all of them shared the single-minded intentness of the *shvitser* to make money, they all wanted to get ahead and most of them eventually did, or saw to it that their children did.

By far not all of them shared the determination of the observant Jews to hold fast to Judaism as they had practiced it in the Old Country.

212

Yet on the High Holy Days great numbers went to services. Most immigrants bought kosher meat, even if they no longer observed the other laws of *kashrut*. They were all profoundly aware of their Jewishness, even if they were no longer clear about how to express it.

Certainly they did not all share the radical, revolutionary outlook. Yet most subscribed to the secular messianism which the radicals preached: the hope for a better world. Not all of them shared the destructive anticlericalism of the anarchists, yet many happily rejected rabbinical authority and *halacha*, Jewish religious law. The elements of Jewish tradition to which they remained attached were those that suited an ethnic identity rather than a religious one.

The first twenty-five years of the mass migration transformed the American Jewish community and also transformed the way in which American Jews regarded themselves. By 1906, the American Jewish community had become far more heterogeneous than it had ever been before. The first wave of East European Jewish immigrants had already become Americanized and was producing a native-born generation.

Meanwhile the flood of immigration continued unabated. But the immigrants coming after 1906 were different from those of the earlier generation. For by this time, the Jews in Eastern Europe had also begun themselves to undergo secularization, political radicalization, and modernization. The immigrants who arrived after 1906 were more sophisticated than their predecessors and more experienced in the struggle for political liberty and the rights of labor.

And so the process of Americanization, the rise of a new native-born generation of East European Jews, and the changed caliber of the East European immigrants turned the Jews in the United States into a highly differentiated community in the years after 1906. Not only were there the fundamental differences between native American Jews and immigrant Jews, between Jews of German origin and Jews of Russian-Polish origin. Now a wide range of class and status distinctions existed. In the openness of American society, East European immigrants and their children had already achieved status, besides financial stability. They were ready to challenge the authority of the established Jewish leaders and to take over the leadership of the Jewish community. That challenge by the upwardly rising East European Jews reflected the conflict between different concepts of Jewish identity, different political outlooks, and different Jewish agendas.

By 1906 a number of views as to the nature of Jewish identity and Jewish communal life had emerged among American Jews. These views had been shaped originally by the conditions of Jewish life in Europe and by ideas about those conditions.

The German Jews articulated a view of Jews as adherents of Judaism, bound together by the tie of religion. It was a definition of Jews that had evolved during the French Revolution, when the Jews in France sought political equality.

In 1791 the French Revolutionary National Assembly debated whether the Ashkenazi Jews in France, who enjoyed certain rights of communal autonomy, should have the same rights of citizenship as the Sephardi Jews, who did not constitute such a separatist community. The National Assembly's decision hinged on defining the nature of Judaism. Was Judaism the religion of the Jews as a people, a corporate entity desiring its own autonomy? Or was it the religion of individual Jews, the observance of which would not prevent them from fulfilling their commitments as French citizens?

The Assembly opted for the latter view, since it already held that religion was a private and individual matter. Consequently, the Assembly abolished the rights which the Jews had held as an autonomous community and voted to bestow all civic rights upon "individuals of the Jewish persuasion." The formula had been most dramatically put by Clermont-Tonnerre in the Assembly's debate on Jewish rights: "To the Jews as a nation—nothing; to the Jews as individuals — everything."

That formula then became the model for Jewish identity in Western Europe and the basis on which Jews pursued political emancipation. But it was not geared to the multinational empires of Central and Eastern Europe, whose subjects wanted, besides the individual rights of citizenship, also group rights, sometimes called minority rights—

214

the right to maintain schools in their own language, support for newspapers and journals in their own language, cultural rights. In the Hapsburg Empire, they even spoke of political autonomy. In that milieu Jews, too, wanted group rights—official Jewish schools, a subsidized Jewish press, Jewish institutions to be recognized and supported by the state. In that part of Europe, in the age of nationalism, Jews identified themselves as a national minority, regardless of whether they observed the rituals of Judaism. The Western model of Jewish identity exclusively by religion they considered inadequate. They even mocked it.

There is a wonderful story about this discrepancy of views about Jewish identity. It takes place in Warsaw during World War I. The Germans were then in occupation, but it was a benign occupation. Two German Orthodox rabbis were attached to the German civil administration, which consulted them about how to reestablish a Jewish communal organization along modern, that is, Western lines. The German rabbis proposed to organize the Jewish community as a *kehilla* with an exclusively religious character. But the Warsaw Jews, including the ultra-Orthodox Aguda, regarded themselves instead as a national-religious community, in which the linkage between people and faith was indissoluble. So whenever these two German rabbis appeared on the Warsaw streets, Jewish children would run after them, pointing their fingers, mockingly shouting: *"Nor a religye, nor a religye"*—only a religion, only a religion.

In the United States, the channel for Jewish identity had from the start been that of a religion. Unlike the practice in most European countries where rights accrued only to those of the established religion, in the United States every citizen, regardless of his religion, enjoyed full political and civic rights. All Americans had ties at one time or another to family and community in the Old Country, but they refashioned these ties into religious ones. The old European-style political linkage between church and state became, in America, joined in what has been characterized as the ethnic church, which is merely a private voluntary institution.

American Jews followed this pattern. They too defined themselves

215

by religion, even if they were not always religious. They explained their ties to Jews in other parts of the world as religious ties, though their feelings of Jewish solidarity derived from a common history and a community of fate as well as from a community of faith. Judaism thus became the vessel into which all the vague and inexpressible feelings of Jewish commonality were gathered. This form of Jewish identity served American Jews quite satisfactorily all through the nineteenth century. It also harmonized with the West European concept of Jewish identity the German Jews brought to America.

But the East European Jews brought secular and national modes of Jewish identity to America, and these came into conflict with the prevailing American mode. Take the nationalist or Zionist formula, for instance. While Zionism borrowed heavily from the imagery of Judaism and from its messianic longings, it was at bottom a secular national movement, and in fact for a long time Orthodox Jews opposed it (as some extreme groups today still do). Zionism as a Jewish political movement emerged when nationalisms of all sorts were sweeping Europe, and it provided the East European Jews with a powerfully attractive option of a secular national identity.

In the United States, however, Zionism had little impact in its early days. In 1898, the Union of American Hebrew Congregations declared itself "unalterably opposed to political Zionism." Even though Zion was "a holy memory," it was America that stood for the "new Zion." Jacob Schiff, American Jewry's most prestigious and powerful leader, feared that political Zionism would place a lien on the Jew's American citizenship and endanger the relations of American Jews to their own country.

In those early days, the Zionist movement was poor in numbers and organization, but it commanded sentiment, especially after the issuance of the Balfour Declaration in 1917. In the coming decades the Zionists aggressively argued their position, claiming to be more representative of the Jewish masses than the German Jewish elites who were still speaking as the leaders of America's Jews.

The Jewish Left, too, challenged the then-standard concept of the Jews as a religious group. The Jewish Left drew its notions of Jewish

216

identity from the experiences of Jews in the multinational Hapsburg and tsarist empires of Central and Eastern Europe before World War I. It saw the Jews as a national minority, whose culture derived primarily from the Yiddish language and its literature. Furthermore, the Left clung to the Marxist view of class division and class war, sharply differentiating the interests of the Jewish "masses" from those of the Jewish "bourgeoisie."

In the decades that followed World War I, the course of Jewish identity seemed to run downhill as Jewish commitments themselves appeared to ebb. We can track the decline through the years.

The 1920s might be considered the age of the *shvitser,* when Jews largely abandoned their religious identity. It was a time of growing intermarriage. Secularism prevailed. This was so not just among the Jews. Secularism prevailed in the whole country. In fact, it can be said that a religious depression preceded the economic depression. And when the Great Depression came, many Americans channeled their reawakened religious and ethical impulses into secular or radical protest movements. As hunger and distress spread across America, Americans focused their attention on social and economic questions, relegating religion to the irrelevancies of the time. Still, it was a time when Yiddish culture flourished, and within that milieu Jewish identity had an unmistakably national or ethnic stamp.

In the 1930s even the secular options of Jewish identity began to disintegrate. Jews strove to be either Americans or cosmopolitans. Except for pockets of observant Jews, except for pockets of immigrant Yiddishists, except for pockets of Zionists, the mass of American Jews—immigrant and native-born—looked upon Jewishness and Judaism as disabilities, liabilities, and impediments to becoming full Americans.

In those years most European immigrants relinquished the language of their old country, but few groups discarded their language as rapidly as the East European Jews abandoned Yiddish. Even more destructive of Jewish identity was the fact that at least three-fourths of Jewish parents in the 1930s neglected to give their children any Jewish education or to transmit to them any knowledge of Judaism.

But the decade of the war years and the aftermath brought a sea

217

change to the shaping of Jewish identity. First came the impact of Hitlerism on Jewish consciousness and then American participation in the war against the Third Reich. Finally the news of the murder of the European Jews dramatically transformed the way Jews regarded themselves and their world.

The war years had a transfiguring effect on the sense of identity of those tens of thousands of American Jews who went into the armed forces. Their induction launched their discovery or rediscovery of themselves as Jews. Away from the familiarity of Jewish home and neighborhood, Jews in the armed services turned increasingly for the comfort of community to Jewish chaplains and local Jewish hospitality wherever they were stationed. They suddenly had a great hunger for all sorts of Jewish information. The National Jewish Welfare Board, which served the religious needs of Jews in America's armed services, was called upon to provide enormous quantities of Bibles, prayer books, and the ABC's of Judaism and Jewish history. For many servicemen, wherever they fought, the daily confrontation with death stirred latent religious feelings. Despite the theologians' denigration of "fox-hole religion," these feelings persisted well into their later civilian life.

The news of the murder of the European Jews shook American Jews. Those officers and men in the European theater who helped to liberate the camps—Jews and non-Jews alike—were never again the same. Their encounters with the survivors of Hitler's Final Solution remained forever seared into their memory. Then followed the creation of the State of Israel, when the Zionist option finally took hold of American Jews.

For American Jews the new state became the embodiment of the life force of the Jewish people, the phoenix arising from the ashes of the Holocaust. But it was not long before a new distinction in this consciousness of Jewish identity made itself felt. American Jews were Zionists in the sense that they loved and supported Israel. Though they were lavish with their love and money for the Jewish state, most American Jews chose not to settle there. They remained convinced that America was their home, that in the final analysis Zionism was not their kind of Jewish identity.

218

*   *   *

American Jews shared very noticeably in the remarkable rise in religiosity that characterized postwar America, a development that no one in the secular 1920s and the radical 1930s foresaw. In large part the war experience had laid the groundwork for this development. Then, living in suburban communities, often where Jews had never lived before, native second- and third-generation American Jews had to confront the question of their Jewish identity for themselves and, even more, for their young children. No longer able to live off the dwindling Old World capital of traditional Judaism, no longer satisfied as to the viability of secular Jewish options, the post–World War II Jews turned to American versions of Judaism to give them a workable form of Jewish identity. Themselves unfamiliar with basic Judaism and largely ignorant of Jewish religious tradition, they turned in extraordinarily large numbers to the synagogue to provide them with the content and the forms of their Jewishness. The synagogue became in the 1950s what it had been throughout its millennial past—the prime vehicle of Jewish continuity.

In those years the Conservative movement grew most rapidly. It appealed particularly to third-generation Jews, for it catered in just the right proportion to that inarticulate longing for the emotional reinforcement which traditional observance provides without the binding commitment of Orthodoxy. Conservatism's powerful pull influenced also the course of the Reform movement, drawing it back toward the practice of a more traditional form of Judaism.

In the next generation, beginning with the watershed year of 1967, American Jews went through another crisis of identity. As Israel's fate hung in the balance during the long weeks of tension before the Six-Day War, American Jews closed ranks. They responded not only to Israel's exigent needs but to their own sense of identity. Now a new sense of Jewishness had come to the fore. It carried the conviction that being Jewish was as important as and possibly even more important than being American.

Perhaps that transformation came about because America itself was changing. The civil rights movement had turned angry and violent,

219

hostile to Jews. The New Politics had become pro–Third World and anti-Israel. Elements in the black community were giving voice, loud and clear, to a vicious anti-Semitism. Taking account of these developments, American Jews began to shift in their politics and to intensify their Jewish commitments. They began publicly to affirm an outspoken Jewishness which before they had revealed only privately.

Suddenly—so it seemed—and unpredictably, even implausibly, traditional Judaism made a comeback. Orthodoxy, which for decades belonged only to the old and the alien, now came alive in America. It emerged in the decade after the Six-Day War youthful and vigorous and began to transform the landscape of American Judaism.

Revived Orthodoxy was the product of cross-fertilization, paradoxicality, and heterodoxy. Its origins were indelibly foreign and also indigenously American. Its energy derived from the most inflexible tradition and also from alienation. It was an outgrowth of the counterculture and, at the same time, a recoil from it.

The new Orthodoxy had its origins in Eastern Europe and was brought after World War II by survivors of the Holocaust. Having outlived the gas chambers of the Third Reich and the gulag of the Soviet Union, they came to the United States with their traditions, their learning, and above all their passion for Judaism. They built *yeshivot* and day schools with sacrificial effort. They shamed the established American Orthodox and Conservative institutions by their passion. By example they vitalized them. The *baal-teshuvah,* the returner to Judaism or to a more intense observance of it, now became a familiar phenomenon.

The counterculture, meanwhile, had penetrated into traditional Jewish bastions and its effect was to radicalize Judaism. In the Conservative movement, young people alienated by the bigness of the synagogues in which they had been reared began experimenting with *havurot,* small fellowships whose practice of Judaism would provide religious intensity and communality. The Orthodox equivalent was the revival of the *shtibl,* the East European Hasidic prayer house, which offered intimacy and immediacy without the synagogue's institutional accoutrements.

220

Orthodox young people sought also to make their movement responsive to contemporary society. One need only mention the ferment that feminism has created in some modern Orthodox institutions. It is an engaging irony that the feminist movement, which began by assaulting traditional Judaism because it treated women differently from men, soon inspired women to enhance their literacy in Judaism if they wanted to attain equality. Committed Jewish women began to pursue higher Jewish learning, even to aspire to the rabbinate. The Reform movement trained women as rabbis and cantors and more and more Reform congregations engaged them. The Conservative movement extended women's rights in the synagogue and, after a struggle, approved their admission to rabbinical training.

The vigor of the new Orthodoxy was catching. The new Orthodox were not self-conscious about demonstrating their Jewishness in public. In time we became accustomed to the sight of young people on college campuses, on big-city streets, in hospitals and scientific laboratories, even in concert halls and the theater, wearing *kippot,* publicly demonstrating their Jewishness. Kosher eating houses were established at many colleges.

What is strikingly new about this contemporary generation of Orthodoxy and renewed traditionalism is that many of the young people—not all, to be sure—are ready to participate in the larger society. And not only in its economic and professional life but even in its cultural pursuits and its political activities. Like generations of American Jews before them, the new Orthodox have made their accommodations to America, even if they draw firmer lines than did their predecessors. They have chosen to be Jews on their terms, and they have asked America to accept them on those terms. This marks a new departure for American Jews in their relation to American society. It is this sense of security both in one's self as a Jew and in America as a free society that has made modern Orthodoxy work.

The history of the Jews in the United States—thus far—has been a history of good times, of expectations realized. There were times of trial and trouble, but even at their worst, these never compared in scope or in malignancy to the calamities that befell the European Jews. In the United States Jews prospered as never before in their history.

Despite justifiable Jewish fears that America's freedom would subvert Judaism and seduce Jews from their faith and their people, and despite the genuinely alarming rates of intermarriage, the historic experience so far has been that the majority of American Jews have chosen of their own volition to be Jews and to raise their children as Jews. America has demonstrated that Judaism can flourish in a free society, and the freedom of America has further demonstrated the vitality and adaptability of Judaism.

In the words of the foremost scholar of Judaism, the late Gershom Scholem, "Judaism has proved itself infinitely adaptable without losing its original impetus." American Judaism, for all its divergences from the Judaism of the past, would still be recognizable if, with the aid of a time machine, a *minyan* of Polish Jews of the nineteenth century were to arrive on the West Side of New York or attend services in a typical Orthodox or even Conservative synagogue. Even the Jews of medieval Regensburg would find our liturgy entirely familiar. For our Judaism is in the mainstream of Jewish tradition which has continued through the ages, always the same, yet always being altered.

America has demonstrated that Judaism can flourish in an open and pluralistic society. A confident and affirmative American Judaism has engaged the larger society—secular and Christian—and has emerged from that engagement intact and enriched. The interplay of living cultures stimulates growth, while a Judaism hedged in by a high protective wall will wither for lack of air and sunlight. The American Jewish experience—still in process, still vulnerable, still experimental—has so far shown that with the will to do so, Jews can preserve and sustain Judaism and Jewish culture while participating in the larger society. In this our present way of life, each Jew must figure out for himself the precise calibrations by which he can maintain the fine balance he wishes to achieve between living in the general society and living as a Jew. That is what life in a genuinely pluralist democracy entails.

──── 13 ────

EAST EUROPEAN JEWRY AND US

We are all familiar with the stereotype that the words "East European Jewry" conjure up: the *shtetl*, the small town with its cobbled main street and muddy alleys, its tiny crooked-roofed houses, crowded together in airless density. We see the Jews in this *shtetl* walking down the main street to the *shul* and we evoke the images of the men in *tallis* and *tefillin*, lost in rapturous prayer or hunched over a table absorbed in a *blat gemorre*, a page of the Talmud. And in our mind's eye we see the women in the marketplace, selling produce or dry goods, bargaining with their customers, gossiping among themselves. We see them as pious and poor, subsisting on crumbs in this world, believing that in the Days to Come, in the World to Come, the righteous will be rewarded with feasting on the Leviathan.

Every stereotype is based on some reality. Eastern Europe *was* the heartland of Jewish tradition, of normative rabbinic Judaism with its emphasis on the centrality of Talmud and Jewish law. It was the realm of the *yeshivot* and *hedarim*, of the great centers of learning. It was also the cradle of Hasidism, of charismatic rabbis, of ecstatic piety. Time was when the singsong chanting of the thousands and thousands of *yeshiva bokherim* studying Gemara was said to have resonated across the land from the Danube to the Dnieper.

Tradition, Talmud, piety—these are both the stereotype and the reality. Tradition, Talmud, piety are the heritage that East European

223

Jewry passed on to the Jews of America and in Israel. But they are only part of the reality of East European Jewish life and culture, and only part of the heritage bequeathed to us. There was also another reality and another heritage—the experience of Jewish modernity as it worked itself out in Eastern Europe and as it was transmitted to subsequent generations.

I once had an extraordinary opportunity to witness at first hand the reality of East European Jewish life. That was when, almost on the eve of World War II, I left New York to study for one year at the Yiddish Scientific Institute—YIVO, then headquartered in Vilna, a city known for generations as the Jerusalem of Lithuania. Some twenty years later, following the gentle suggestion of the late Professor Abraham Joshua Heschel, I put together a book about East European Jewry, *The Golden Tradition.*

While working on that book, I realized that we American Jews are not only the descendants of East European Jews but indeed their inheritors, even if we do not fit the stereotype of tradition, Talmud, and piety. We may be Americanized, Anglicized, acculturated, secularized, modernized, yet we are their children and grandchildren, flesh of their flesh. And we are in fact truer than one might think to the wisdom they transmitted to us on how to cope with modernity.

The East European Jews became virtuosi in inventing theories and formulae for accommodating their Jewish heritage to the modern world. To be sure, they were preceded by the German Jews in the assault against an encrusted religious tradition that refused to come to terms with the modern world. But the East European Jews provided more models and showed a greater diversity of response, if only because of their greater numbers and the more varied national subcultures among which they lived.

The world which broke in upon Jewish traditional society in the wake of the Enlightenment, the Industrial Revolution, and the French Revolution offered the Jews new opportunities, opened up new channels for private and public fulfillment—the pursuit of higher education, advancement in an industrially expanding economy, the study of science, new horizons of secularism. It was a time when faith in man had begun to supersede faith in God, when belief in progress exceeded belief in the World to Come. It was also a time when the rise of the nation-state introduced ideas about the rights of man, the rights of citizenship, liberty, equality, and fraternity. With the nation-state came also the idea of the rights of nations and cultures; soon nationalism would become the major revolutionary idea. People everywhere dreamed of the sovereignty of their own nation, of the day when they could live under a government of their own, using their own language, free to develop their own culture, acting out their own history in accordance with their own traditions and true to their own destiny.

The Jews in Eastern Europe, as in Central Europe, were stirred by these new ideas and new movements. Indeed, all over Europe from West to East, Jews were often in the forefront of these movements, as propagandists and disseminators of ideas and as organizers of action. That fact alone should help to dispel the sentimental conception which has fixed the East European Jews, as if they were illustrations in a medieval Haggada, in attitudes of utter piety and conditions of utter poverty. The fact is that East European Jewry was a dynamic and diverse society, alive to contemporary currents and ideas, sensitive to the great changes taking place all over Europe.

The East European Jews innovated theories and experiments in a variety of Jewish nationalisms—Zionism, cultural autonomy, territorialism. They created Zionism as we know it today. They shaped our liberal and radical political traditions. They created a modern literature in Yiddish and in Hebrew. They developed our sense of peoplehood. All of these are part of our heritage.

Modern Jewish politics was forged in the crucible of nineteenth-century Europe, in that universal striving for liberty and political equality that swept the continent. In that struggle for emancipation, for the right to share in the privileges and obligations of citizenship, the modern Jewish agenda fit perfectly. In Western and Central Europe, Jews joined the liberals, who upheld a political order which offered the Jews rights as citizens, security as a religious and communal group, and economic opportunity as individuals. In contrast, the illiberals who opposed extending rights even to their own ethnic and religious groups especially opposed giving rights to Jews. The illiberals comprised the old order—the aristocracy, the military, the nationalists, the Christian churches—all the elements that came to constitute the political Right and that after 1848, during the long years of the counterrevolution, seemed once again to have gained ascendancy.

In Eastern Europe, liberal politics, which had blossomed in the tsarist empire in the 1860s and 1870s, was all but extinguished after 1881 when terrorist revolutionaries assassinated Alexander II. Thereafter, reaction and repression became the hallmarks of tsarist rule and eventually the liberals, the constitutionalists, the centrists were crushed between the millstones of the Right and the Left. Politics in the tsarist empire became radicalized. It ceased to be the art of compromise and became instead a new religion. Revolutionary politics in particular promised a messianic age that would bring upon the earth a utopia, a social order that would eliminate evil, injustice, and inequality. The terms and tactics of this politics were secular, yet its zeal, and the commitment which the revolutionary movement demanded of its followers, were the equal of any religious movement. This was especially true for the Jewish radicals, who had abandoned their own religious traditions and were in need of new ones.

There is no need to spell out how much this liberal and radical political heritage has become a given in our contemporary Jewish culture all over the world. To take but one example, it has even influenced the way we think about trade and commerce, about business.

Jews were historically the middlemen, the people who bought and sold. But their economic usefulness did not win them much credit. With the rise of the Enlightenment and the new national ideologies, the middleman came to be regarded as the villain in the unfolding new scenario of economic life. The French Enlighteners, from Rousseau on, idolized the peasants as pure and unspoiled creatures. Then, with the coming of the industrial age, the proletariat became the new ideal. The businessman was looked upon as a parasite, making his livelihood off the primary labor of peasant and worker. Those nineteenth-century ideas, now tattered and clearly irrelevant in our world-wide hi-tech society, long blinded us to the fact that Jews were for generations the sinews of European trade and commerce and indispensable partners in creating a civilized world. Even today, those ideas still infect many an attitude toward business and toward Jews who engage in business—not least among Jews themselves.

When we consider the movements for Jewish nationalism and national renewal that arose in the nineteenth century, once again we can see the continuities between the Jews of Eastern Europe and us. The ideas of Jewish nationalism sprouted, so to speak, from the cracks in the foundations of traditional Jewish society. Nearly all the innovators, initiators, and founders of movements of Jewish nationalism were men who had been alienated from Judaism, who hated the walls which the rabbis tried to build to prevent the modern world from seducing the Jews away from their commitment to Torah. Still, those new ideas and their originators were authentic products of the very Jewish world which they were rejecting.

"Zionism," Theodor Herzl once said, "is a return to the Jewish people even before it is a return to the Jewish homeland." It was true for him and true for his intellectual precursors. Consider the case of Leo Pinsker. Born in 1821, raised in Odessa, he studied medicine at the University of Moscow, and returned to Odessa in 1849 to practice his profession. Odessa, the newest city of Russia, was a conglomeration of Russians, Ukrainians, Jews, Poles, Greeks, and Levantines, and consequently the most liberal of Russian cities in its openness to ethnic and religious diversity.

Odessa was also the most secularized and assimilated of cities where Jews lived. Many of its leading Jews were also assimilationists, that is, they perceived assimilation to be a desirable goal to which all Jews should aspire. Pinsker shared that view and soon became active in the Odessa branch of the Society to Promote Culture Among Jews, the institution which embodied the goals of those who were in a hurry to make it in the larger society.

In 1871, at Easter time, a pogrom broke out in Odessa, to the chagrin and horror of those who believed that Odessa had already accepted Jews as equals among all the various nationalities in the city. The pogrom had the effect of paralyzing the work of the Society to Promote Culture Among Jews; how could one continue to foster assimilation in a society which wreaked violence upon its Jews?

Ten years later, in 1881, when riots were the order of the day all over tsarist Russia, following the assassination of Tsar Alexander II, Odessa once again witnessed a pogrom. It was then that Pinsker, now twice traumatized, abandoned his assimilationism for Jewish nationalism. In his pamphlet *Auto-Emancipation*, he appealed to the Jews to reclaim their self-respect and dignity, and he called on non-Jews to recognize that the Jews were a nation, no different in their aspirations from the Serbs and the Rumanians. Pinsker exhorted his fellow Jews to dedicate themselves to a movement for national reawakening and a national homeland. The effect of his pamphlet was to give new life in Russia to the struggling Hovevei Zion, the Lovers of Zion, the forerunners of the Zionist movement.

In the next decade, in 1894, the Dreyfus affair was to affect Theodor Herzl the same way the Russian pogroms had affected Pinsker. Thereafter, the proto-Zionist movement, which had been sentimental and philanthropic, turned political and economically hard-nosed. East European Jews became the mainstays of the Zionist movement; they became Herzl's battalions. The pogroms, and the Dreyfus affair, brought estranged Jews back to the Jewish community. Few became religiously observant, but all became nationalists.

In those days, two kinds of Jewish nationalism began to flourish in Eastern Europe. The primary movement was, of course, Zionism, which tapped deep religious longings for a return to Zion and responded to Jewish messianic expectations. Zionism combined ancient traditionalist aspirations with those of modern politics.

The second variety came out of the Left. It was fueled by a revolutionary impulse—not only by the desire for political freedom and civic equality, but also by utopianism, the longing for an ideal order in an ideal world of perfect justice and brotherhood. We may call it secular messianism. In time, the Jews in the Russian radical movement

228

developed a specific Jewish component which the political and social realities of the time forced upon them. The Jewish Socialist Labor Bund—*der algemeyner yidisher arbeter-bund*—evolved its own form of Jewish nationalism.

The Bundists had national cultural aspirations. They formulated their goal as cultural or national autonomy within a multinational socialist state. They wanted to be like other national minorities, to have their own self-governing institutions, to publish newspapers and operate schools in their own language. They championed Yiddish as the Jewish national language, to distinguish themselves from the Zionists, who had reclaimed Hebrew and were to fashion it into a living language.

Now, in the perspective of a century, we recognize that Zionism and Jewish socialism were siblings competing for the love and loyalty of the East European Jews. Both movements, however antagonistic to each other, grew out of the same roots and were shaped by the same forces of modernity. Both were antitraditionalist, though both drew upon traditionalist myths and symbols. A lovely anecdote illustrates this tension. Chaim Weizmann, in his memoirs, describes the hospitality his mother extended to her sons' friends. She was a pious woman who maintained a traditional Jewish household. Her son Chaim became an active Zionist. Her other son, Shemuel, became a revolutionary. She used to say: "Whatever happens, I shall be well off. If Shemuel is right, we shall all be happy in Russia; and if Chaim is right, then I shall go to live in Palestine."

To be sure, not all Jewish radicals were motivated by Jewish impulses. There were those who enlisted in the Russian revolutionary movement to escape Jewish pariah status, to forge a new identity that would make them part of the Russian peasantry. Some became active in the Narodnaya Volya, "The People's Will," a revolutionary populist group that turned to terrorism because its ideas were not effective or convincing enough to muster popular support. It was the Narodnaya Volya which planned and carried out the assassination of Alexander II in 1881.

Six weeks after that event, a tidal wave of pogroms spread across

Russia, engulfing over two hundred Jewish communities, making 20,000 Jews homeless, economically desolating some 100,000 others, causing untold property losses. Men, women, and children were beaten, raped, murdered. The government had instigated the pogroms to cast blame on the Jews for the tsar's assassination. Nevertheless, the Narodnaya Volya applauded and justified the pogroms as a "truly popular movement," reasoning that if the peasants turned their revolutionary energy to killing Jews, they might soon do the same to the tsar and his government.

The Jewish radicals were stunned by the Narodnaya Volya's turnaround. It had been the one group in Russia from whom they had expected moral support. Instead the terrorists had abandoned them, betrayed them.

What could be more contemporary? Is this not what happened again to the Western Jewish enthusiasts of Stalinist Russia in the 1930s, when the Soviet regime destroyed even the remnants of secular and pro-Communist Jewish organizations? And again in the late 1940s and early 1950s, when the enthusiasm of the Soviet Jews for Israel was branded as bourgeois nationalism, inimical to the Soviet Union? Or in 1952, when Soviet Yiddish writers were murdered as a first step in a general roundup of the Jews? Only Stalin's providential death at the time prevented this. Those years witnessed the massive defections of Jews in the West from Communist and Communist-front institutions.

And did not something similar happen to many American Jews who were active in the civil rights movement in the 1960s? In 1967, when Israel's existence hung in the balance and the New Left as well as the Old Left supported the Arabs, and then after the Six-Day War joined in attacking Israel for winning, the many Jews in those movements felt just like Russian Jews nearly a century earlier—ashamed and betrayed.

The trauma of betrayal by the Left has, indeed, brought many radical Jews back to the Jewish community. This too is an old story. After the pogroms and the repressive anti-Semitic legislation which the tsarist government enacted in the 1880s, the radical Jewish students

held a meeting to consider their response to the situation. They decided to go to the synagogue—not to pray, but to show their solidarity
with the Jewish people. In St. Petersburg they went as "silent witnesses"—their expression. In Kiev they prepared speeches to deliver.
Thousands came; there was not enough room inside the synagogues,
so they just stood outside. Is this not just what happened again in the
late 1960s in the Soviet Union, when young Russian Jews began
congregating on Simhat Torah outside the synagogue in Moscow and
Kiev and elsewhere, singing Hebrew songs, dancing? And was not the
intent and effect the same—to demonstrate publicly their newfound
sense of Jewish identity and solidarity? Today, as then, they choose
to do so in or near the only unambiguously Jewish institution—the
synagogue.

They were no different from us. We have seen in our time the
powerful impact of the Holocaust, the Six-Day War, the Yom Kippur
War on alienated young Jews. We have seen in our time how hundreds
and even thousands of Jewish dropouts to the counterculture in the
1960s were returned to Judaism by these events. A whole network of
yeshivot for *ba'alei teshuvah* came into being in Jerusalem, in New York,
in London, offering spirituality, fellowship, an introduction to Jewish
learning.

Back in Eastern Europe, too, the return of alienated Jews was often
the first step in a return to tradition, even to faith. One such story is
that of Nathan Birnbaum, a seminal figure in his time. Although he
was never really alienated from his Jewish identity, his transformations
describe an extraordinary Jewish odyssey. Born in Vienna in 1864 of
observant East European parents, he attended German schools and
the University of Vienna. Soon he was deeply involved in the Zionist
movement, and gave a paper at the first Zionist Congress in Basel in
1897. But then he became dissatisfied with Zionism as an answer to
the fundamental problems of Jewish existence. He turned his attention
toward East European Jewry, whom he considered to be the real and
living body of the people. He developed a theory of *galut*-nationalism,
which turned him into an advocate for Yiddish, the *galut*-language
par excellence. In 1911 he lectured in all the major Jewish centers in

231

Russia and Poland. While there he underwent one of those oceanic mystical experiences:

> I myself did not know what was happening to me. Later, I looked upon it as a dream. . . . I was already close to the recognition of the eternal and living substance of religion, but I still somehow resisted, until the blessed moment arrived and He showed Himself to me in His whole creative splendor. . . . It was when in Russia, at a discussion in St. Petersburg, after a lecture given by someone else, that suddenly it became clear to me that I must rise and bear witness to the Lord God. And I rose and in a passionate speech poured out my whole heart. Then I first realized that a great new obligation awaited me.

Birnbaum devoted the rest of his life to writing about messianic Judaism and to furthering Jewish religious faith.

Not everyone came back, however, either to the Jewish people or to the Jewish God. There were those who found the burden too oppressive, who collapsed under the pressure of persecution. They ran away from Jews and Judaism. They become apostates, renegades. One such story out of the East European past is that of Pauline Wengeroff, who was born in 1833 in Bobruisk, White Russia, into an observant home. Like most girls of middle-class Jewish families, she received a general education and became an avid reader of German, Polish, and Russian newspapers and novels. She married a Lubavitcher Hasid, who became a successful businessman. The more he prospered, the less observant he became. And he prospered greatly. All this happened in the 1860s and 1870s, under the beneficent rule of Alexander II, when educational and commercial opportunities began to open up to Jews.

The Wengeroffs moved to St. Petersburg. Here is Pauline Wengeroff's description of Jewish life there:

> The society we became part of consisted of distinguished and cultivated people, most of whom lived a carefree existence in

wealth and luxury. The St. Petersburg Jewish community had a magnificent synagogue and even two rabbis—one modern and seminary-trained, the other Orthodox. But the Jewish community had abandoned many Jewish customs and traditions. The more fashionable even celebrated Christmas. Only Yom Kippur and Passover were observed, but in an up-to-date way. Some Jews drove to the synagogue in their carriages and ate in the intervals between the Yom Kippur service. Passover was kept, even among the most progressive. It remained a festival of remembrance, joyful because it recalled not the Exodus from Egypt, but one's own childhood in the *shtetl*. The *seder* was observed in a highly abbreviated form. Even baptized Jews kept the *seder*. Though they did not themselves make the holiday feast, they welcomed invitations from their not-yet-baptized friends.

That was a portrait of Jews in St. Petersburg a hundred years ago. How different is it from people we all know? Pampered and self-centered, children raised in these circumstances grew up without tradition or knowledge of tradition, without the rich memories of a Jewish childhood. Not surprisingly, then, Wengeroff's children, and others like them, abandoned Judaism when the chips were down. The pogroms of 1881 and 1882 were followed by the systematic persecution of Jews through legislation. Jews were restricted as to where they could live and where they could work. Their access to higher education was severely limited by quotas. Jews now faced insurmountable obstacles to success in the larger society, to professional achievement, business careers, to the acquisition of money and status. Wengeroff tells her story:

In the eighties, with anti-Semitism raging all over Russia, a Jew had two choices. He could, in the name of Judaism, renounce everything that had become indispensable to him, or he could choose freedom with its offers of education and career—through baptism. Hundreds of enlightened Jews chose the latter. These apostates disbelieved in all religions; they were nihilists. My children went the way of so many others.

Pauline Wengeroff's memoirs read like the stuff of Jewish soap opera. But this was a real tragedy, not invented, not sentimentalized. She understood what had happened. "The baptism of my children," she wrote, "was the hardest blow of my life. But the loving heart of a mother can bear a great deal. I forgave them; the blame was on us parents."

The classic case of apostasy in those days was that of Daniel Chwolson, a Jewish careerist *par excellence*. This outstanding Orientalist scholar converted to the Russian Orthodox faith in order to become a professor of Hebrew and Syriac at the University of St. Petersburg. Yet though no longer a Jew, he remained close to Jews and helpful to them in times of trouble. Many years after his apostasy, he was asked if he had converted out of conviction. He is said to have replied, in Yiddish: "Yes, I was convinced that it was better to be a professor in St. Petersburg than a *melamed* in some God-forsaken mudhole."

That ultimate choice has not confronted us here in America, but we should not fool ourselves. There may not be as much flight from Jewishness as there once was, but there is flight. Many American Jewish mothers, when their children come to marry, have sorrows nearly as poignant as Pauline Wengeroff's.

I have discussed East European Jews and us in terms of politics, concepts of personal and national identity, attitudes toward Jewish tradition, anti-Semitism, and apostasy. My final theme has to do with language and culture, specifically, the language and culture of Yiddish.

The Jews, throughout their history, have had more languages of their own than any other people. Yet nowadays, we Diaspora Jews are largely without any Jewish language. For most of us, our Hebrew barely suffices for the prayer book. As for Yiddish, it had been for generations the stepchild of the Jewish languages among educated Jews. As a vernacular, it was associated with the lower classes, with people un-

234

educated in the language of the land and often ignorant of Hebrew, the language of Judaism. Yiddish was offensive to the emerging Jewish middle classes in Eastern Europe, for they thought its use impeded their integration into Gentile society and even accused it of generating anti-Semitism. This social snobbery toward Yiddish is reflected in an anecdote about the great Franz Kafka, a Jew from Prague who wrote in the German language. The Jews of Prague were located, sociologically and culturally as well as geographically, between Warsaw and Berlin. Their attitude toward Yiddish was determined by their social and economic ambitions. Many forgot, or claimed to have forgotten, their Yiddish, so intent were they on becoming German speakers. It is a bitter irony that this ambition to partake of German high culture had the effect of alienating the Czechs, who had their own national agenda with regard to the Czech language.

Kafka, in any case, had fallen in love with a troupe of Yiddish actors from Warsaw who had come to play in Prague in 1913. He became great friends with Yizkhok Levy, also known as Jacques Levy, a leading actor in the troupe, and undertook to arrange an evening at which Levy would do readings from Yiddish. Kafka did everything in preparation for the event—mailings, hiring the hall, publicity— and he also served as host. This is the way he introduced the players: "Before the Polish Jews begin their lines, I want to tell you, ladies and gentlemen, how very much more Yiddish you understand than you think you do." He was saying that the assimilated Jews of Prague were part of the culture of the East European Jews, that beneath the skin-deep veneer of German speech and culture was the solid flesh of their Yiddish background.

The contempt for Yiddish was also a common phenomenon in this country. It was not so long ago that many American Jews, children of East European Jewish immigrants, or themselves immigrants who had come as young children, denied that they knew Yiddish, derided Yiddish as a "jargon," as they tried to escape their own Yiddish-speaking origins.

But the status of Yiddish has changed in recent years. There are two reasons. First is the normal passage of time and the progress of

235

the generations. In the United States, as in other places where Yiddish was once spoken—England, Argentina, Mexico, Australia—the integration of the Jews has been so thoroughgoing that the use of Yiddish as a primary language of communication declined precipitously. Yiddish lost its social function as a living language in which one pursued one's livelihood and conducted one's personal life. Paradoxically, that allowed it to gain appeal as a literary language, as a vehicle of a now-lost culture.

The second reason for the change in the status of Yiddish, the most terrible of reasons, is the Holocaust. With the murder of the six million European Jews, the whole foundation of Ashkenazi Jewish culture crumbled. Our realization that Ashkenazi Jewish civilization came to an end has prompted a renewed interest in Yiddish these days. We have witnessed the rise of a mini-establishment of Yiddish studies across the country, in colleges and universities and in adult-study groups. My own involvement these days with the promotion of Yiddish is through the Library of Yiddish Classics,* a publishing program of the Fund for the Translation of Jewish Literature, which aims to bring to non-Yiddish-speaking readers the great works of a vanished civilization.

Some of the interest in Yiddish arises out of a sentimentality for the past; some is fueled by a search for roots. But one thing should now be clear—that Yiddish, no less than Hebrew, ought to be studied as a matter of national duty. Without it, we cannot understand the history, the culture, and the achievements of the East European Jews.

We are the heirs of those Jews. We have inherited their traditions and their inventions. But we are not identical with them and we cannot, nor should we, imitate them. Nevertheless, if we are to continue the living Jewish traditions from which *they* were so swiftly and cruelly cut off, if we are to cherish the heritage they transmitted to us, we must know and understand them and their culture, without sentimentality and without disdain.

*This series is published by Schocken Books.—ED.

THE BUSINESS OF AMERICAN JEWS

(NOTES ON WORK IN PROGRESS)

In 1928 the Russian Jewish historian Simon Dubnow published an article, "Vos felt in undzer ekonomisher geshikhte" (What Is Missing in Our Economic History), in the first volume of YIVO's *Ekonomishe Shriftn.* The title signals the gist of Dubnow's complaint concerning the undeveloped status of Jewish economic history. Three years later, Julius Brutzkus, another chronicler of Russian Jewry, characterized economic history as the stepchild of Jewish historiography. Nearly three decades later, Cecil Roth, in a bibliographical essay on the economic history of the Jews, described the field as "largely a matter of hit-and-miss." More recently, Lawrence Schofer, in the 1979 *Leo Baeck Yearbook,* characterized it as "something episodic, anecdotal, and ill-organized."

All these historians were lamenting the backward state of Jewish economic history in Europe. What shall we say, then, of the economic history of American Jewry?

For some years now I have been engaged in research in preparation for writing a broad-gauged history of American Jews. What I have learned has led me to conclude that economic history is an essential and indispensable element in American Jewish historiography—more so than in the history of the Jews in other places. Indeed, in the United States the history of Jews, as I see it, has been for the most part a history of their social and economic evolution.

This is not to dismiss the many other strands—political, communal, religious, institutional, intellectual—all of which need to be interwoven. What it comes down to is a matter of proportion, of highlighting the most significant elements and developments. And here I think I could convincingly make a case that economic history occupies or should occupy a larger place in the story of American Jews than in that of the European Jews. For instance, in stark contrast to the European Jewish experience, there is only the slimmest account to be written of the Jewish struggle for emancipation in this country. The struggle for civic rights, a fundamental element of Jewish existence in the countries of Europe, turned out here to be a relatively minor matter which affected small numbers of Jews in a mere handful of states. Similarly, there is only the slimmest account to be written of pogroms and anti-Jewish violence in America, of discrimination against Jews as conceived and practiced by government, federal, state, or local.

This is not to say that there is *no* history to be written of anti-Semitism in the United States. Indeed, there is much still to be unearthed, analyzed, and explained about America's unique variant of this universal phenomenon. Happily for us, however, the history of anti-Semitism occupies a much smaller space in the span of Jewish history in the United States than it has in Europe or in the Muslim world.

By "economic history" I do not mean an economic *interpretation* of Jewish history. It would hardly be my intention to analyze Jewish history from a Marxist point of view, or from any other viewpoint which tries to explain all historical phenomena from an economic or materialist perspective. Nor do I mean economic theory. Nor do I refer to conventional economic subjects—labor and capital; wages, profits, and prices; monetary policies; tariffs and taxes—in their possible application to Jewish history.

I see economic history as a variant or subcategory of social history. A Dutch historian, P. J. Blok, defines social history as dealing with "the thought and the work, the daily life, the belief, the needs, the habits, of our ancestors." It is that aspect of "the work . . . of our ancestors" which I regard as the basic component of any economic

238

history of the Jews. I want to know how the Jews in America made a living from 1789 until 1967, the *terminus ad quem* which I have set for my history. That is, I would like to have at least a rough sketch of the history of Jewish occupations in America in that period. I would also like to know about regional differences: Did Jews in the West engage in the same kinds of occupations and in the same proportion as Jews in the East or the South or the Midwest? What were the major shifts in occupational patterns with the geographical expansion of the country and its evolving industrialization?

To find some answers—if only suggestive ones—to these fundamental questions, it is necessary to begin almost from scratch. The difficulty is that we have few reliable data bases. With rare exceptions, Jews are not recorded as such in official statistics and censuses, so we do not always know where or how to locate and identify them.

Take trade. Everyone knows that an extremely high proportion of Jews at almost any time in their history have been engaged in trade and commerce. But we have no dependable figures on either the numbers or the percentage that Jews have constituted in any particular field, or their proportion in relation to all gainfully occupied Jews in any field. Nor do we have solid information about whether Jews perform specific functions that differ from those of other ethnic groups in the same occupations. Or whether they perform the same economic functions, but operate in different ways. Nor do we have reliable data that tell us something about the scope and variety, the character and the dimensions of the trade in which they have engaged.

Take business enterprise. Everyone knows that Jews have played a notable role as entrepreneurs in certain fields such as merchandising, the clothing industry, the entertainment industry, the development of technology. Yet even though the study of business and entrepreneurial history has been a thriving endeavor at Harvard, Chicago, and Columbia, the field has never attracted the interest of Jewish historians. As far as Jewish entrepreneurial history is concerned, the available materials are largely anecdotal. Even biographies are in short supply.

Getting the basic data about Jewish occupational history is just the

beginning of a quest to understand how the Jews got into those occupations in the first place. We have insufficient knowledge of how
Jews made occupational choices in different times and at different
stages in America's economic development. What determined their
entrance into certain occupations? Was it family or community tradition? Was it prior familiarity? Was it the presence of relatives and
friends? Was it perhaps a matter of personal inclination—or that old
bugbear, group proclivity? Was it the opportunity at hand? Or was it
the fact that other avenues were closed? How significant was capital,
or the lack of it?

Knowing more about the occupational character of the Jewish community would help us better to understand the socioeconomic and
financial status of the Jews in America. And much more: occupation
and income can tell us about other kinds of social processes, such as
acculturation and assimilation. Some occupations proved to be bridges
to involvement in politics and to political positions. Others brought
wealth or prestige and thus gave access to non-Jewish circles which
otherwise would have remained closed. In such situations many Jews
found themselves tested with regard to their continued loyalty to
Judaism and the Jewish community. Thus, the relationship between
economic life and acculturation becomes a fundamental factor in ex-
amining the social and communal character of the American Jews.

These are some of the questions for which I have sought answers.
When in the course of my researches I found that the kinds of data
I was looking for did not exist, I concluded that the only thing to do
was to create them, to make my own building blocks. I decided to
collect biographical material about an amorphous body of Jews whom
I designated "achievers." These were, according to my specifications,
Jews who had "made it" in their time, so that during their lives or in
obituaries at the time of their death they were eulogized as distinguished citizens whose local community took pride in them.

My plan was to create a socioeconomic profile. Achievers—a rather
wide-ranging category that would include many middle-middle-class
Jews as well as upper-middle-class and upper-class—were to be a major

segment of this profile. I had some notions about how to get data for the nonachievers, that is, the poor, the working class, and the lower middle class. As for the achievers, I cast a wide net to find individuals who exemplified the range of occupations in which Jews were engaged, who represented the geographical distribution of the Jewish population, who reflected the successive waves of Jewish immigration, and who illustrated a sequence of generational cohorts, thus providing some opportunity to study social mobility over time. I hoped that the accumulation of such data would make it possible to go beyond the descriptive level—a necessary first stage of historical writing—in order to analyze and then explain how Jews functioned economically and how they fit into the economic life of the larger society.

I managed to accumulate a file of about 1,500 or more such achievers. About some I had only a bare statement: election to public office, for instance, or an award for an invention; about others, more. I developed a questionnaire on which to enter the information I was looking for, and at some point a friend of mine who ran a survey-research firm coded the questionnaire so that the data could be put through a processing machine. But I came to realize that the full accumulation of such data was quite beyond my means. The project required the resources of a research center, and more time, personnel, and funds than I could possibly muster.

Still, I have my files and they have given me insight into some of the dynamic social processes that flow from the interaction of occupational position, personality, and culture. These files can serve as building blocks even if the structure to be erected with their help cannot be much more than skeletal.

In addition to my achievers' file, there is another set of building blocks I have put together. I have accumulated a few hundred credit histories of Jewish business people in the United States for the period from the 1840s to the 1890s. These come from the records of the earliest credit agency in the United States, called the Mercantile Agency, which was the forerunner of Dun and Bradstreet. To understand the character of these early credit histories, it is necessary to know something of

241

the origins of the Mercantile Agency. The story is not only enter-
taining but also extremely informative about the early relations of Jews
and Christians in the business community.

The Mercantile Agency was founded in 1841 by Lewis Tappan, a
silk merchant whose business had failed in the Panic of 1837. Tappan
was an evangelical Protestant and an abolitionist, who believed that
panics and depressions were God's chastisement for moral waywardness
rather than the consequence of economic and financial operations.
His older brother Arthur, who was his partner in the silk business and
then in the Mercantile Agency, was one of the Protestant evangelicals
involved in the Maria Monk scandal—the publication of a lurid account of life in a Catholic convent in Montreal where fornication and
murder were supposedly everyday occurrences. The whole story was,
of course, fraudulent and constitutes one of the uglier chapters in the
history of American Protestant bigotry.

There is no record that Lewis Tappan participated with his brother
in this anti-Catholic conspiracy, but he certainly shared his cultural
outlook. We know that Lewis thought a good businessman should
work hard, dedicate heart and soul to business, abjure drinking, swear-
ing, smoking, whoring, and going to the theater. Above all, he
thought it a sign of high morality for all good and God-fearing men
to pay cash. There is a delightful irony in the fact that this hard-
money man who disliked the very notion of paper credit should have
founded a credit agency.

Until then, credit had largely been established on the basis of
personal ties (as in part it still is). A buyer, ordering merchandise,
would enclose letters of reference from his minister and other locally
known and well-established persons. But as new streams of immigrants
were constantly arriving in the United States and as the frontiers of
the country kept moving westward, the old personal ways of doing
business became anachronistic. The rapid increase in the population
and the enormous distances between commercial centers conspired
against a system of credit based entirely on personal contact.

To set up his Mercantile Agency, which he first began to operate
in the Northern states, Tappan needed a network of reliable corre-

spondents. They would have to inquire about the financial and moral standing of business people who were applying for credit from manufacturers, merchants, and banks. Tappan preferred to get local lawyers in those far-flung places because they often handled collection cases and dealt with business people. But above all he wanted correspondents who shared his value system. In a note to himself, he wrote: "Want some one every where we can write for inf[ormation]—ministers, abo[litionists], or someone." In the early days of the Mercantile Agency, many of Tappan's correspondents were indeed evangelical abolitionists—which caused difficulties for him when he began to recruit correspondents in the South.

Having established his network of correspondents, Tappan began to advertise for subscribers. By mid-August 1841 he had already signed up 133. In time, the business grew and spread all over the country. In 1846 Tappan took on a partner, one Benjamin Douglass, of a family of Scottish Presbyterian settlers in Maryland. Douglass was a New York merchant who shared his Maryland family's proslavery convictions. While Tappan surely abhorred those views, he must nevertheless have been pleased with Douglass's religious orientation. R. G. Dun, who later took over the agency, characterized Douglass and his family as "religious fanatics."

Against this background it is easy to understand how the credit reports which we find in the early records of the Mercantile Agency must have given Tappan and Douglass deep satisfaction. For the reports do not limit themselves to information only about the subject's credit and credibility. They are studded with tidbits of social facts and prejudicial statements that reflect their writers' moral and religious standards.

The reports which the correspondents sent to the New York main office were entered in enormous ledgers that remind one of Dickens. Here, to give just a single example, is one of them:

> James Samson is a peddler, aged 30; he comes to Albany to buy his goods, and then peddles them out along the canal from Albany to Buffalo. He is worth $2,000; has a wife and three

children . . . drinks two glasses cider brandy, plain, morning and evening—never more; drinks water after each; chews fine cut; never smokes.

The ledgers, filled with handwritten entries, with code numbers for the correspondents and the clients, were kept for almost fifty years. By the end of the 1880s, the typewriter began to take over. In the course of that half-century, the Mercantile Agency, by then the R. G. Dun company, had accumulated 2,580 volumes. In 1962, the successor agency, Dun and Bradstreet, deposited these volumes in the Baker Library of Harvard's Graduate School of Business.

In its earlier decades, the Mercantile Agency's correspondents usually noted the religious and ethnic background of the businessmen whose credit they were investigating, and their language was often pejorative. A report might note that an Irish merchant drank too much whiskey or that a German manufacturer drank too much beer. Remarks about Jews were often unfriendly, yet prejudice would usually give way to a grudging admiration for their thrift, sobriety, industriousness, and especially their attentiveness to business.

Here is an abbreviated extract from a running credit history of one Saul Aronson, a New York City shirt manufacturer. The first entry is dated June 1854; the last is March 1859:

Is a German Israelite. Age 52. Married. Began here May 1853. Was many years in the jewelry business and shirt manufacturing and is said to have had, as he now has, some connexion with his brother. . . . Has been lately in the wholesale manufacture of shirts chiefly for the California market. . . . Is industrious and energetic and his wife is commended as still more so. . . . His trade is quite large. He is correct in his habits, punctual in engagements, and has the confidence of the trade. . . . Has made money, is a close, screwing Israelite; has several sewing machines in operation; gets his goods made up by poor women. . . .

244

Abraham Kohn, who had a store of furnishing goods and cloth in 1865 in McGregor, Iowa, is described this way: "Capital unknown, fair stock and does a fair business, a good kind of Jew." Six months later, he is characterized as "a sharp enterprising Jew with good trade." Three years later, the correspondent says of him: "He is a Jew, but seems honest."

In 1863, a correspondent writes of one Julius Houseman, an immigrant from Bavaria who was in the clothing business in Grand Rapids, Michigan:

A Jew of the better class, about 40 years old and married. Good businessman. By our county records owns real estate in this city and worth $15,000. Is represented to be prompt. The worst thing we know of him is that he is a Jew.

Houseman seems to have maintained his good reputation through the years. In 1871 the reporter notes that Houseman "was the most reliable and responsible Jew" in his firm, that he was a member of the state legislature, was "highly esteemed" and "probably worth $25,000." Actually, by this time Houseman had already had a good start on his career in Michigan Democratic politics, having earlier served eight years as alderman in Grand Rapids. In 1872, after a term in the state legislature, he was elected mayor of Grand Rapids, and then reelected for another term. A few years later, by now quite wealthy from other financial activities, Houseman retired from his business, turning it over to a cousin who had been his partner years earlier. In 1883 he would become the first Jew to be elected to Congress from Michigan.

Houseman's case illustrated for me the possibilities of collating data in a credit history with biographical data which I had accumulated in my achievers' file. I am quite sure that Houseman's political eminence in Michigan's fifth district developed out of his role as a most reputable merchant and businessman in Grand Rapids, that there was a dynamic connection between his occupation and his political career. And Houseman was also associated with the Jewish community as a founder and first president of the Grand Rapids Reform congregation. He was

245

also a founder of the local B'nai B'rith society, and its first president. It would be important to know whether his connections to the Jewish community antedated his political career or whether his political career demanded an ethnic or communal base. The dynamic interaction at work here between the individual, the business community, the Jewish community, and the political world is what the historian needs to elucidate.

The credit histories can enlighten us in many ways. For one thing, they provide an unprecedented wealth of detail to document the central and supportive role of the family in achieving success in the high-risk undertaking of business. Most businesses require a system of mutual trust if they are to succeed. In the old days, merchants risked their very lives, traveling through unsettled country in peril of nature or bandits, or sailing the high seas in craft too fragile to weather winter storms. Business people risked their capital in extending credit, in buying and selling. The commodities they held in stock could be stolen, could spoil in heat or go up in flames. Even the most astute businessman could not know for sure which goods would sell and which would not, or why. To shore up these uncertainties, risks, and possible losses, businessmen counted on people they could rely on. The family obviously constituted the nucleus of such a network.

The historian Bernard Bailyn has described the role of kinship in the rise and development of trade in seventeenth-century New England. He did so on the basis of family letters and chronicles. The nineteenth-century credit histories make it possible to document the role of the family with even more abundant sources than Bailyn could command.

The whole system of credit, in which both lender and borrower took risks, depended upon trust. Lewis Tappan's Mercantile Agency was itself organized around an extended family of sorts—the network of Protestant evangelicals, a group of like-minded people with shared values and commitments. Jews, for their part, had their own network of trust. Its inner circle consisted of family members. But there was always also a wider network consisting of Jews who came from one's own Old Country town, of Jews whom one knew from the synagogue or from a fraternal organization, of Jews who spoke Yiddish—a network which rested on the pervasive sense that all Jews were brothers.

Let me cite just one abbreviated credit history to show how the family connection is presented. This is the report on the Schloss Brothers, a cloth and clothing firm in New York City. It begins in July 1852:

> German Israelites 13 years in the country. There are 4 brothers in the firm, 1 here, 2 in San Francisco, and 1 in Germany. Moses who resides here purchases for the firm; he used to keep 2 stores in Albany, removed thence to St. Louis and while there formed the above partnership, say 2 years ago. They are one of the most respected concerns of their class in the City, sagacious and re- liable businessmen and have been very successful. . . . They state they are worth $100,000. . . . They do an extensive and safe business with the West and Northwest; have stood the test of the hard times very well. . . . They do a heavy California trade, but mostly among their own friends.

That last phrase, "mostly among their own friends," probably refers to fellow Jews. This Jewish network—much more extensive than the primary network of fathers and sons, brothers, sons-in-law, and broth- ers-in-law—served to strengthen the position of Jews in business. The Schloss credit history also illustrates how the Jews tracked the geo- graphic expansion of the country and how family connections enabled them to synchronize their business expansion with the moving frontier and with the country's industrial growth.

Besides the role of networks, the credit histories illuminate other themes as well. One of them is occupational and financial upward mobility. Marx Schutz owned a dry-goods store in New York City in 1851. Here are a few extracts from the report on him:

> Jew, married, formerly a peddler; commenced business in his present store about 1842 or 3; he now owns it, is esteemed and

well off. His sales are mostly to peddlers and seems to control a large trade of this class. He purchases very much for cash, employs one clerk and is assisted by his wife, has a stock of $4–5,000 suited to peddlers. . . . He has two brother [each with his own store]; were all peddlers and commenced business about the same time. . . . [In 1856] his partner is his brother-in-law, a very clever businessman. . . . The firm, together, is worth $30,000, is firm and solid and A No. 1 in every respect.

The credit histories also tell us about the numerous instances of bankruptcies and failures in the panics of 1857 and 1873, and give interesting insights into business problems during the Civil War. We can learn from the credit histories something about the courage and persistence of Jews in trying to make a living. When things failed to work out in one place, they picked themselves up, moved west or south or north, and started over again. From time to time we get brief and bare insights into the social circumstances of the Jews, details about how they lived and comments about their reputation in their own community.

Thus, Abram Jesse Dittenhoefer, one of my achievers, was born in Charleston, South Carolina, in 1836 to German Jewish immigrants. His father Isaac was a merchant. In 1840, the family moved to New York. Abram went to Columbia College, got his B.A. in 1856, practiced law, and immediately went into politics and played an active role in the Republican party. Though his father had warned him that the Republicans were less hospitable to Jews than the Democrats, he chose to go with the Republicans because of his antislavery views. In fact, he was a presidential elector, nominating Lincoln in 1864.

Yet if one relies only on the Jewish press, one would never know that Dittenhoefer was somehow also implicated in the corrupt dealings of the Whiskey Ring, a scheme whereby top Internal Revenue commissioners channeled the income from excise taxes on liquor into the coffers of the Republican party instead of into the U.S. Treasury.

According to the R. G. Dun report at the end of 1871, Dittenhoefer was the defending lawyer for the Whiskey Ring. In 1875, the credit report states:

> We learn from respectable people he has been in the profession several years. . . . Regarded as a man of considerable ability, a shrewd buyer and during the whisky frauds is thought to have made considerable money. Is very popular with his Jewish friends.

My favorite credit history is the one on Judah Touro (1776–1854), the great merchant and philanthropist who was born in Newport, made his fortune in New Orleans, and gave away most of his wealth in charity. It is very brief, and starts off in 1849:

> Israelite, owns real estate, bank stock, etc. There is no telling how much the old rat is worth. He allows Parson Clapp to preach in his church. Has lately presented a church to the Jews. I give you my word, I should like to have his note for a *million.*

The credit histories are to history something like X-rays are to portraiture. By themselves they will not shape a biography of any subject, but they show the forms and structures—healthy and un-healthy—beneath the surface. It is also the case that the data in these credit reports are not always reliable, since much information—certainly in earlier times—was based on gossip, hearsay, and even malicious rumor. The Mercantile Agency was, in fact, many times sued by businessmen for defamation. I myself stumbled upon the existence of the agency from references in the *Asmonean,* the New York Jewish weekly published during the 1850s to serve the interests primarily of the Jewish business community. The paper ran several editorials sharply criticizing the agency for its prejudicial comments and judgments about Jewish businessmen.

But whatever their shortcomings and flaws, these data are extremely valuable. From them we can see literally before our eyes the dynamics of business change. As you follow one man's credit history through the years, you can see him go from peddler to retailer; from retailer to jobber to wholesaler; from general store to specialized store; from selling to manufacturing; from retailing to banking; from retailing to politics. All these progressions reflect a variety of patterns, and in this way the individual case histories make it possible for us not only to trace the developments themselves but to fit them into the larger framework of the American economy as a whole.

This brings me to the last item on my agenda of building blocks— mercantile occupations. The credit histories and also my achievers' file make it possible to see the enormous range of these occupations, from the lowliest peddler to the merchant prince and merchant banker. I have made a list, in alphabetical order, of nineteen distinct mercantile occupations, excluding banking, shipping, and transportation:

Agents—buying and selling for a principal
Auctioneers
Brokers
Commercial travelers, that is, traveling salesmen
Commission merchants
Contractors
Cotton factors
Department-store proprietors
Exporters/importers
Jobbers
Junk dealers
Pawnbrokers
Peddlers
Pushcart dealers
Rag dealers
Real-estate agents
Retailers/proprietors
Secondhand dealers
Wholesalers/proprietors

It would be an endless task to itemize the variety of goods which were bought and sold, locally, regionally, nationally, and internationally, but these are some basic categories:

Food and drink: produce, grain, feed, flour; meat and meat products; dairy products; bakery products; liquor; tobacco

Clothing: apparel—dresses, coats, suits, shoes, hats, and caps; underwear—shirts, socks, stockings; accessories—gloves, handbags, umbrellas, scarves

Dry goods: fancy goods—yard goods and trimmings; notions—buttons, needles, thread

Jewelry: gold, diamonds, gems; watches, clocks

Furniture

House furnishings: tableware, oilcloth, lamps, shades

Textiles, carpets, leather and skins

Metals

Machinery and hardware: nails, nuts and bolts; cutlery, scissors, chains, pipes, tools

Wood: lumber, boxes, barrels

Fuel: gas, oil, coal, mining

Chemicals, paints and varnish; drugs

Glass and glass products

Papers and paper products

Books: printing and publishing

Not on this list are stocks and bonds and real estate, which are not—at least to my mind—quite the same kind of commodities.

What is the purpose of all this? To begin with, the purpose is simply

251

documentation, to identify and describe the ways in which Jews made a living in America. Secondly, the purpose is to show how their occupations not only served them in providing a source of livelihood, but how they served the American economy. And there is a third purpose, or perhaps a bias. I would like to restore to the merchant and the businessman the recognition of their social usefulness and the moral dignity of which they were stripped first by the French Enlightenment, then by the German Marxists, and finally by the East European revolutionaries.

All of us are, by the force of tradition, heirs to those ideas which for generations have denigrated trade and commerce, and which have romanticized the peasant and idealized the proletariat. It is strange that although we now live in a society where the largest proportion of the labor force is engaged in service industries, and where a tiny proportion of the labor force is engaged in agriculture and mining, we are still captive to Marxist notions about the unproductivity of the middleman. I wonder whether that idea did not originate and take hold in a fundamentally agricultural society—as France was in the eighteenth century, Germany in the nineteenth, and Eastern Europe still in the twentieth. In England, by contrast, whose mercantile history is venerable, ideas about commerce have been quite different. Joseph Addison, in a wonderful essay which appeared in *The Spectator* on September 27, 1712, wrote about the Jews and their commercial role:

> They are, indeed, so disseminated through all the trading parts of the world, that they are become the instruments by which the most distant nations converse with one another, and by which mankind are knit together in a general correspondence: They are like the pegs and nails in a great building, which, though they are but little valued in themselves, are absolutely necessary to keep the whole frame together.

That English tradition remained with the American Thomas Paine, who in *The Rights of Man* described himself as "an advocate of commerce." For, he wrote, "it is a pacific system, operating to cordialise mankind, by rendering nations, as well as individuals, useful to each other."

I will close with another celebration of the merchant, and particularly of the Jewish merchant. The author is Vladimir Jabotinsky and the passage (which appears in my book *The Golden Tradition*) is from his memoirs about his native Odessa, a great port city and a commercial center.

> Who built all this? Who was the true creator of these enormously beautiful cities, harbors, railroads, highways, the grain elevators and ships, the theaters and the hospitals and the universities? The merchant. . . . Without the merchant—no harbors and no ships, and no cities (villages would have sufficed), not even the wagoners. Why the piles of wheat? Those grain merchants, on a small steamer or even on a common wagon, travelling from place to place, discovering a wheat field here and a market there, a producer here and a purchaser there—they tied the earth together with thousands of threads and wove a net of arteries for the blood traffic of the economy, laid the foundations for everything which is called culture.

Jabotinsky then sums up Jewish economic history:

> If you are a doctor or a tailor's apprentice or a rabbi, trade is not your calling, but it was my father's calling and my grandfather's and probably yours too; in the historical sense, the collective chief calling of our people in the course of seventy generations. They began when the world was a wilderness with wild beasts, and through their connective labor they transformed the wilderness into a chessboard of cities and roads.

— 15 —

THE POLITICS OF AMERICAN JEWS

P olitics has been an avocation of the Jews for a mere two hundred years, and as Mark Twain once noted, despite their splendid capacities in other fields, they have not excelled at it. Twain wrote, of course, before the development of political Zionism, but so far as the American Jewish community is concerned, the 1984 political season offered little that might have persuaded him to change his mind.

Modern Jewish politics was forged in the crucible of nineteenth-century Europe, in the striving for liberty and political equality that swept the European continent from West to East. Heinrich Heine described the great task of his time as "the emancipation of the whole world—in particular of Europe." In that struggle for emancipation, for the right to share in the privileges and obligations of citizenship, the particularist Jewish agenda fit perfectly into the universalist political agenda as Heine defined it.

The Jews found that, with few exceptions, those who would deny them political rights represented the old order—the aristocracy, the military, the nationalists, the political Right, and above all the Church. This was, on the whole, a true perception. Alexis de Tocqueville had noted that in France just before the Revolution, he "had

254

almost always seen the spirit of religion and the spirit of freedom marching in opposite directions." Therefore, in pursuing the politics of emancipation in Western and Central Europe, Jews joined the liberals and the liberal parties. Liberals advocated the rights of man, the liberty of the individual, freedom of conscience and of worship. Liberals upheld a political order which offered the Jews rights as citizens, security as a religious and communal group, and economic opportunity as individuals.

Thus, what has come to be known as the Jewish liberal "tradition" was shaped originally by the politics of emancipation in Western and Central Europe. One classic anecdote will suffice as illustration. In the Hapsburg Empire, Jews won the right to vote and hold office during the revolution of 1848. One of the five Jews elected to the revolutionary Austrian parliament was Rabbi Dov Berish Meisels. He took his seat on the Left, joining the Radicals. When the speaker of parliament asked for an explanation of this apparently anomalous political gesture on the part of a clergyman, Rabbi Meisels, playing on the words for "right" and "rights," said; "Jews are rightless"— "*Juden haben keine Rechte.*"

In Eastern Europe, liberal politics blossomed in the tsarist empire in the 1860s and 1870s under Alexander II, to be all but extinguished after 1881 when Alexander was assassinated by terrorist revolutionaries. Thereafter, reaction and repression became the hallmarks of tsarist rule, and eventually the liberals, the constitutionalists, and the centrists were crushed between the millstones of Right and Left; politics in the tsarist empire became radicalized. Many Jews, understandably, found themselves attracted to the politics of the Left, the politics of revolution.

The revolutionary Left promised a social order from which evil, injustice, and inequality would be eliminated—in short, a utopia. The terms and tactics of this politics were secular, yet the commitment which the revolutionary movement demanded of its followers was the equal of that demanded by any religious movement. This attitude of political messianism characterized especially the Jewish radicals, who had abandoned their old religious traditions and were in need of new

255

ones. But after the Bolshevik Revolution, after the political purges and murderous excesses of the Stalinist period, the messianic fever cooled, including among Jews outside the Soviet Union who had once lent it their support. Besides, Jewish nationalist politics—Zionism— now absorbed messianic energies aplenty, and rewarded them more fully and more concretely.

The European Jews who migrated to the United States brought with them their Old World political traditions. In the mid-nineteenth century, those who came from Central Europe, where they had fought alongside the liberals for emancipation and equality, were attracted to the then newly formed Republican party. This was the party of Abraham Lincoln, the party which opposed the extension of slavery into the new territories, which condemned attempts to reopen the African slave trade, and which favored a liberal immigration policy.

Those who came later, in the mass migration from Eastern Europe, followed other political paths. The Orthodox among them practiced the politics of *shtadlones*, of intercession with those in power—at that time, the Republicans. The radicals enlisted in the Socialist party, which had its brief heyday just before World War I, or in the Communist party, whose time came in the 1930s. But most Jewish immigrants from Eastern Europe, with their fervor for liberty, equality, and justice, turned to the Democratic party. In the big-city slums, the local Democratic club became the mediator between the green immigrants and the outside world, the defender of the poor and the advocate of the working people.

It was Alfred E. Smith, New York's governor, the party's presidential candidate in 1928, who first solidified the Jewish attachment to the Democratic party, but it was Franklin Delano Roosevelt who turned the Jews into Democratic fanatics. A Jewish Republican judge once described the fierce devotion of the Jews to Roosevelt with a pun on the Yiddish world *velt*, world. The Jews, he said, have three worlds: *Yidn hobn drei velten—di velt* [this world], *yene velt* [the World to Come], *un Roose-velt*.

*   *   *

256

Under Roosevelt, the Democratic party emerged as the national party of the big-city poor and the unemployed, the new immigrants, the Catholics, the Jews, the blacks who had come North to look for work, the exploited workers of the sweatshops and the mines, the infant labor unions struggling against the unbridled power of corporate capitalism. Within a decade, all these groups forged a coalition that would keep the Democrats in power for a long time. As for the Jews, they saw the Democratic party as embodying both the political agenda of the emancipation and the social agenda of secular messianism. And they also saw it as a bulwark against anti-Semitism. In those days, in the United States as in Europe, anti-Semitism was part and parcel of right-wing politics. Father Charles Coughlin, the rabble-rousing radio priest who used his Catholic pulpit to vilify the Jews, seemed to many a living confirmation of the Church's role in fomenting hatred. Coughlin's attacks on President Roosevelt and the New Deal further convinced Jews that liberal politics was the best means of ensuring their security and serving their interests.

Actually, public-opinion polls of the thirties showed that anti-Semitic attitudes pervaded American society as a whole. Those attitudes would persist until World War II came to an end in 1945. Only then, when the Allied armies came upon the terrible camps with the dead piled high and the living barely alive, when the horrors were there for all the world to see, did anti-Semitism start to decline, and not just in America but in the West at large. For the next twenty-two years anti-Semitism in the Western world was little more than a ghostly presence, the six million murdered European Jews a ghastly reminder of its consequences.

But only in the Western world. Beyond the West, anti-Semitism continued to thrive, requiring a new kind of political response. Among Arabs the time-dishonored propaganda of the *Protocols of the Elders of Zion* circulated in new guises and disguises, one weapon among many in their ongoing war to destroy the Jewish state. In the Soviet Union, a country with a venerable history of anti-Semitism, Stalin and his successors turned the anti-Semitic gospel into a tool of domestic policy. Leonid Brezhnev, who succeeded Khrushchev in 1964, went Stalin one farther by making anti-Semitism an adjunct of Soviet foreign policy, and turning it, now labeled anti-Zionism, into another of the Soviet Union's exports of lethal commodities. The scale of this anti-Semitic enterprise in the last two decades would have stirred envy in Adolf Hitler.

In 1965 a hint of what Jews would be faced with in the coming years emerged at the United Nations. A resolution had been introduced in a committee of the General Assembly which specifically condemned anti-Semitism. The Soviet delegate, believing that his country was the intended target of the resolution, substituted another in its place. The Soviet version moved to condemn "anti-Semitism, Zionism, Nazism, and all other forms . . . of colonialism, national and race hatred, and exclusiveness." That motion never came to a vote—nor did the United Nations ever adopt a resolution against anti-Semitism—but it opened the door for the UN's ugly condemnation, ten years later, of "zionism," with a lower-case "z" as an added insult, as "a form of racism and racial discrimination." One did not have to wait for Orwell's 1984 to see Doublethink and Newspeak triumph in the precincts of the United Nations.

It was 1967 that proved the watershed year in contemporary Jewish history, marking the advent of a new set of political circumstances. This was of course the year of the Six-Day War, when Israel's life hung in the balance and when Jews everywhere became fearful of a new Holocaust. The miracle of Israel's victory gave rise in turn to a universal feeling among Jews of religious redemption. It seemed that the Divine Presence was once again manifest in Jewish history, and that the God Who had abandoned His people during World War II had at last returned to them. And if God had returned to the Jews, so the Jews began to return to Him and to their people—perhaps most dramatically of all in the Soviet Union, where Israel's miraculous victory invigorated dissident Jews and gave them renewed conviction for their struggle.

There was, however, also a dark response to Israel's swift victory. The Soviet Union intensified its anti-Semitic campaign abroad, its

258

vast propaganda machine depicting the Jewish state as an aggressor nation, the tool and accomplice of the "imperialist West," the "outpost of U.S. colonialism in the Middle East," the "lackey of capitalist America." And in the West as well, 1967 conjured up the seemingly banished ghost of anti-Semitism.

This was no resurrection of the old anti-Semitism of the fascists, reactionaries, and Christian Right. The new anti-Semitism emanated from the Left, from those whose political forebears a century ago had been the staunchest allies of the Jews in their struggle for emancipation. It infected the New Left, which split apart over the issue of Israel. Perhaps most shockingly, it infected a number of black intellectuals, professionals, and political leaders. And inevitably it made inroads into the Democratic party, then beginning its own process of internal disintegration and collapse. (In 1968, though the Democrats did finally succeed in nominating Hubert Humphrey as their presidential candidate, the party of the New Deal, as it had been constituted since 1928, came asunder. The South defected; labor began to defect; and the party's political machine ceased to operate.)

This was not the first time that Jews, including especially Jews on the Left, had been betrayed by the Left. It had happened in tsarist Russia in the 1880s. It had happened in 1939 when the Soviet Union signed a pact with Nazi Germany. For Jews who still retained an element of Jewish pride, these successive betrayals were traumatic. So, in 1967, as in earlier times, some Jews abandoned the Left for good, while others retreated into wounded privacy. Still others, of course, stayed.

Today, the worldwide anti-Semitism of the Left has become if anything more open and unmistakable. In the late sixties, at least, when anti-Semitic attitudes were still in bad repute in the West, sophistical distinctions were maintained between anti-Semitism and anti-Zionism. By 1982, during the war in Lebanon, few bothered with such distinctions any longer. And by the 1984 Democratic primary campaign it all came spilling out into mainstream politics.

Precisely because of the direction from which the new anti-Semitism flows, it is important to underscore the fact that the anti-Semitism

with which Jews were familiar in the past is at a low ebb in this country
(and elsewhere in the West). A recent Gallup poll showed that only
2 percent of Americans held unfavorable opinions about Jews. Overt
anti-Semitism of the Right, too, has decreased. The Anti-Defamation
League, which tracks incidents of anti-Semitic vandalism and violence
and monitors the activities of anti-Semitic and neo-Nazi organizations,
has found that of the eight hundred anti-Semitic incidents which were
reported for the whole of the United States in 1982, none was perpetrated by organized hate groups. The ADL estimates current KKK
membership at about 6,500 and the number of neo-Nazis at some 500.
Although one organization specializes in denying that six million European Jews were ever murdered during World War II, that is an
offense against historical truth which, however obscene, does not
threaten Jewish security as did, for instance, Henry Ford's promotion
of the *Protocols of the Elders of Zion* in the 1920s.

The anti-Semitism of the Christian churches has similarly dwindled
to a shadow of its past. Fascist governments used to invoke Christian
anti-Semitism to reinforce their ideology, while the churches' anti-
Semitic preachments sustained in turn the policies of the reactionary
and fascist states. But fascism passed away in the wreckage of Hitler's
Germany and Mussolini's Italy; it died with Rumania's Iron Guard
and Hungary's Arrow Cross. As for the anti-Judaism of the Christian
churches, it never recovered from the encounter with Auschwitz. One
by one, the Protestant denominations came to address the question
of Christian responsibility for the murder of the European Jews. The
Second Vatican Council of the 1960s, whatever its shortcomings, set
the Catholic church on a new course in its relations with Jews. Christian writings and textbooks have been revised to eliminate the "teaching of contempt." Christians are now instructed to recognize the bonds
between Judaism and Christianity and to respect Judaism not just as
the forebear of Christianity but in its own right.

This Christian education was accomplished, it is true, at a terrible
cost. But now that most churches acknowledge anti-Semitism as a sin
against God and man, even if they needed encouragement to do so,
they no longer dispense it. Even at Oberammergau, where the Passion

260

Play acts out the ancient charge of deicide, the program now contains a disclaimer that the production does not intend to blame the Jews for the crucifixion of Jesus. Just this year, the Lutheran World Federation, marking Martin Luther's five-hundredth birthday, adopted a declaration repudiating "the sins of Luther's anti-Jewish remarks" and confessing "with deep regret" that Luther's teachings had been used to justify anti-Semitism and Nazism.

None of this is intended to deny the presence of lingering anti-Semitic attitudes on the Right (or in the churches), only to stress that they seem, today, trivial when compared to the steady drumbeats emanating from the Soviet Union, the worldwide Left—including, incidentally, the Left-leaning Christian denominations—and the United Nations. The question is, How have Jews responded, politically, to this changed circumstance? And the answer is, not well.

Many American Jews, among them some leading rabbis and other official spokesmen, seem curiously reluctant to concede the decline of anti-Semitism in old places, or refuse to admit the rise of anti-Semitism in new places. Convinced that old-style Christian anti-Semitism is an inevitable feature of our society, they have located its current home in the heart of Protestant evangelical territory. Right after the election of 1980, for example, the head of a major Jewish organization claimed that the most serious growth of anti-Semitism in American since the outbreak of World War II has accompanied the rise of right-wing fundamentalism. That unfounded charge was repudiated by other Jewish agencies, but in 1984, once again, a battery of similar accusations was leveled against the evangelicals in the midst of the presidential campaign.

There is no need to question the sincerity of Jews who say they fear the threat posed by the evangelicals, but there is a need to ask whether that fear is founded on anything real. Evangelicals differ from other Protestants in their belief that they are commanded to spread the good news about Jesus and the centrality of Scripture. The first thing to know about them, however, is that they are not monolithic. Some are fundamentalists, that is, theologically conservative. But, according to a Gallup poll, more than half of all evangelicals consider themselves to be "Left of Center" or "middle of the road." They ought not, then, to be stereotyped.

Since the early decades of this century, evangelicals have regarded the Jews and the Zionist movement with sympathy. In our time, their friendship and political support for Israel have been genuine and substantial. Rationalist liberals ridicule this support because they think it is premised entirely on Christian millennial expectations. But evangelical support for Israel is derived from the Bible, from God's promise to Abraham to bless those who bless Israel and curse those who curse it. And even if the evangelicals did support Israel only for ulterior and religious ends, better such support now than the hostility which distinguishes their politicized brethren in the National Council of Churches.

The evangelicals number nearly fifty million Americans. Given such figures, it is to be expected that there are anti-Semites among them; how could it be otherwise? Yet just three years ago, *Christianity Today*, the largest and most influential of evangelical journals, published a lengthy editorial calling for "repentance, restitution, and action which will ferret out, expose, and actively oppose incipient and overt anti-Semitism." The editor also declared, "to attack Jews is to attack evangelicals and such attacks will be resisted by evangelicals as attacks against themselves."

Nor does the religious exclusiveness of the evangelicals in itself necessarily spell anti-Semitism. In 1984 many Jews recalled publicly the remark made four years earlier by the Reverend Bailey Smith, then president of the Southern Baptist Convention. He said that "God Almighty does not hear the prayer of a Jew." Smith denied the remark was anti-Semitic, and I for one believe him. After all, Jews have their own fundamentalists, who also practice religious exclusiveness, and some of whom say that God Almighty does not hear the shofar when it is blown on the High Holy Days in a Conservative synagogue. (Fundamentalists of all persuasions are privy to knowledge of God's hearing ability not vouchsafed to the rest of us.)

*   *   *

262

As for the Reverend Jerry Falwell's Moral Majority, it represents the response of antimodernist Christians to the cultural dislocation of our time. Every time America experiences a cycle of extreme social tension, in which the legitimacy of traditional moral values is questioned, Protestant America attempts to restore those moral and religious values which derive from the Bible, or, to use Jerry Falwell's favored phrase, from "the Judeo-Christian heritage." Such movements have recurred with predictable regularity in American history since the Puritans first arrived on these shores. The Moral Majority is such a movement. It speaks for religious Christians in their battle against secularization and the debasement of moral values in contemporary life; it does not speak against Jews.

Nor does it pose a serious threat to the separation of church and state. To be sure, Christian revivalists, especially when they feel beleaguered, have always tried to use the law to impose their religious views on a recalcitrant society. The archives of Congress and of state legislatures bulge with such failed bills. Over 140 bills on Sunday observance alone were proposed in Congress between 1888 and 1945. In the twenty-one years since the Supreme Court outlawed Bible reading and the recitation of the Lord's Prayer in the public schools, some two hundred bills to overturn those decisions have been introduced in Congress. But the wall of separation between church and state still stands, and stands firm.

Separation of church and state, however, does not entail the elimination of religion from society. Nor does it entail the utter privatization of religion; that was the goal of the French Revolution, not of the American. What agitates many Jews about the Moral Majority, though they might be reluctant to own up to it, is that it confronts them with the need to acknowledge that the goal of the French Revolution is also their goal. From the dawn of modernity, secular emancipated Jews have yearned not only for political equality but even more for a society in which all men would be joined in a mythic brotherhood transcending the barriers of religious difference. Since that maximum program is beyond realization, universalist Jews have been willing to settle for a minimum program, that is, for a society

263

in which religion is thoroughly privatized. The infusion of a religious element into political discussion threatens this dream of universalist Jews; that is why they oppose the Moral Majority's advocacy of Christian values even when those values coincide with Jewish ones.

This brings us to the Jewish vote in the election of 1984. Some 35 percent of the Jewish electorate voted for Ronald Reagan—about the same proportion that voted for him in 1980. That statistic does not qualify as epoch-making: the majority of Jews still remained loyal to the Democratic party. But it was not so long ago that only 10 percent of Jews, 20 at most, voted for a Republican presidential candidate; even 35 percent indicates a trend.

But if, as I believe, a political realignment is beginning to take place among American Jews, the process is occurring at a markedly slower pace than among the electorate at large. In this election, indeed, the Jewish vote was almost exactly the reverse of the national trend. That is, while almost 60 percent of Americans voted for President Reagan, more than 60 percent of Jews voted for Walter Mondale. The lopsided Jewish voting pattern resembled that of the blacks, the unemployed, and persons in households earning under $10,000 a year, even though Jews in no way resemble those groups or share their social and political interests.

Why? The answer, it seems to me, has to do with the powerful residual hold of the universalist mind-set, a hold so encompassing that it has led to an alienation of the Jews *as a political group* from their rightful place in the American consensus. At times this alienation is even acknowledged explicitly. During the 1980 election, for example, one Jewish intellectual expressed his attitude toward the United States with singular frankness: "No country on earth has been better to the Jews than the United States; but it is not our country." What I am suggesting is that this attitude of alienation may be more widespread than is generally thought; if so, it is a danger to the political health of the Jewish community.

One wonders, at any rate, whether an attitude of alienation, born out of and justified by the politics of universalism, may not have had

264

something to do with the failure of the Jewish community to address
the range of its concerns in this election. To be sure, Jewish organizations lobbied to have the correct views on Israel inserted in the
platforms of both parties, but for the most part those in Jewish institutional life seem to have been so obsessed with the Moral Majority
and the marginal issue of prayer in school or after school as to have
neglected to attend properly to the Jewish interest, even in connection
with Israel.

A case in point concerns UNESCO, the UN's cultural organization,
which has in recent years become a forum not only for anti-American
but even more for anti-Israel activities. But when the U.S. government
solicited testimony from nongovernmental agencies at a hearing on
our possible withdrawal from UNESCO—surely an outcome devoutly
to be wished by Jews—only one Jewish organization recognized that
American interests and Jewish interests coincided in this regard, and
responded positively.

What should have been on the Jewish political agenda in 1984? The
indispensable requirement for Jewish security anywhere, happily taken
for granted in the United States, is that Jews live under a government
that will protect their liberties, ensure their safety, and deal justly
with them. In this respect, American Jews, being the largest, most
secure, and most affluent Jewish community in the world, have obligations to less fortunate Jewish communities, be they in Chile, in
Nicaragua, in Ethiopia, or in the Soviet Union. In voting, and just
as importantly in their approach to the two major parties, Jews have
an obligation, as Jews, to consider how these particular interests of
theirs can best be advanced.

The Jewish agenda requires a strong government in the United
States to ensure Israel's security. Jews who care about Israel are obliged
to use their vote to that end. They did so four years ago, when for
the first time in over fifty years the Democratic candidate for the
presidency, Jimmy Carter, failed to win a majority of the Jewish vote.
In 1984, by contrast, a great many Jews seemed willing to ignore the
drift of the Democratic party into isolationism and defeatism, not to

265

mention the party's embrace of Jesse Jackson, a man overtly hostile to a strong America and a strong Israel.

On the domestic agenda, one issue Jews needed to address in 1984 was black anti-Semitism. And this was, indeed, much talked about during Jesse Jackson's primary campaign and during the Democratic convention, after which it became a nonsubject. It should not have been allowed to, since its existence is undeniable and has been documented in every public-opinion poll taken in the last twenty years. These polls have charted the decline of anti-Semitic attitudes among whites, on the one hand, and the consistent rise, on the other hand, of anti-Semitic attitudes among blacks, especially younger and better-educated blacks. Did Jews exercise any pressure, moral or financial, on the Democratic party on account of the scandal of Jesse Jackson's anti-Semitism? Did they punish the party at the polls for sheltering it, and for pointedly declining to adopt a resolution condemning anti-Semitism in the party platform?

No doubt most Jews who voted Democratic believed they were voting for the age-old liberal agenda, for the extension of rights to those still deprived of them. But the current agenda of those who call themselves liberals is less a matter of rights and more a matter of social and economic redistribution. The Democratic program to achieve that end is quotas, a policy which (since the word is still apparently taboo) now goes under the name of "affirmative-action goals, timetables, and other verifiable measurements." And what the Democrats would impose on the country they also mean to impose on their party. A resolution setting up a Fairness Commission to plan the next Democratic convention provided that members of the commission were to be chosen according to gender, race, and sexual preference: "equally divided between men and women, and . . . fair and equitable participation of blacks, Hispanics, native Americans, Asian/Pacifics, women, and persons of all sexual preferences [sic!] consistent with their proportional representation in the party." Under that system of "fairness," Jews would never have a chance.

Quotas threaten America with the fate of the Hapsburg Empire. There, the demands of diverse groups competed with the common interest, and the clamor of large groups drowned out the murmur of small ones; the system could not survive. Whether the democratic United States could survive institutional quotas we do not know, but it is certain that, politically, Jews could not.

This, at least, most Jews understand, and so have opposed quotas. Yet in continuing to give so much ungrudging support to the party that now stands for quotas, are they not, in the name of a misguided and ossified universalism, failing once again to address their political agenda with the requisite degree of responsibility?

Jews cannot live by universalism alone. Can they, then, live by particularism? Whereas religiously liberal Jews voted disproportionately Democratic in the November 1984 election, Orthodox Jews tended to vote Republican. But many of these Orthodox—not all—suffer from their own brand of alienation. To protect themselves from the seductions of secular society, they persist in trying to erect high walls around their communities, to separate themselves, if not necessarily from other Jews, then certainly from the Gentile world. While many Jewish universalists are in thrall to a nineteenth-century political tradition, many Jewish particularists are still committed to a view of Jewish life in nineteenth-century Eastern Europe.

The pitfalls of this can be illustrated with a story. In 1812 the Hasidic rabbis in the tsarist empire believed that the war between Napoleon and Tsar Alexander I was the war of Gog and Magog, which presaged the coming of the Messiah. Menahem Mendel the Seer of Lublin, the Maggid of Mezeritch, and Menahem Mendel of Rymanow all prayed for Napoleon to triumph over the tsar. They believed that by his victory the Jews would be delivered from their sufferings and persecutions. But Rabbi Schneur Zalman of Lyady, the founder of the Lubavitch dynasty, prayed for the tsar to defeat Napoleon. He explained his position in a letter to one of his followers: "If France should win, riches will increase among Jews and they will prosper. But they will become estranged from God. If Alexander wins the war, the Jews will become impoverished, but their hearts will be joined with God."

The Lubavitcher *rebbe* was correct in his prediction of what would happen to European Jews in the next hundred years. For in those days, when Jews were given political freedom they prospered, and they assimilated. As for those Jews who remained restricted to a life of poverty and persecution in the Pale of Settlement, they also remained true to their religious traditions (though changes were in the making there too that the rabbi did not foresee).

There was no way, however, that Schneur Zalman could have predicted what would happen to Judaism in a free society. We are now in the midst of an extraordinary religious renewal among Jews that is a response to the murder of the six million European Jews and a rebuke to those today who continue to wish the Jews dead. By means of this revival Jews have demonstrated their confidence in themselves and in their ability to remain true to their traditions, even in the modern world. But America for its part has also demonstrated that Judaism can flourish in an open and pluralist society. Does this not justify a greater confidence, on the part of religious Jews, in America?

If Jews need to know their own interests as well as the interests of others, they also need to know the art of politics as well as the books of the Torah. They need, in short, to live in this world, not in the world of the politically utopian or the religiously messianic. Among other things, this means staking out an independent position and resisting an automatic commitment either to the Democrats or to the Republicans. Many Jews might be surprised to learn that—Mark Twain to the contrary notwithstanding—practicing the art of politics in this sense is a task to which their traditions, and their history, have admirably suited them, and can yet serve them well.

INDEX

269